Global Risk Governance in Health

Global Risk Governance in Health

Nathalie Brender
Professor of Risk Management and Corporate Finance
Haute école de gestion de Genève, University of Applied Sciences
Western Switzerland

First published 2014 by
PALGRAVE MACMILLAN

Palgrave Macmillan in the UK is an imprint of Macmillan Publishers Limited,
registered in England, company number 785998, of Houndmills, Basingstoke,
Hampshire RG21 6XS.

Palgrave Macmillan in the US is a division of St Martin's Press LLC,
175 Fifth Avenue, New York, NY 10010.

Palgrave Macmillan is the global academic imprint of the above companies
and has companies and representatives throughout the world.

Palgrave® and Macmillan® are registered trademarks in the United States,
the United Kingdom, Europe and other countries

ISBN: 978–1–137–27356–7

This book is printed on paper suitable for recycling and made from fully
managed and sustained forest sources. Logging, pulping and manufacturing
processes are expected to conform to the environmental regulations of the
country of origin.

A catalogue record for this book is available from the British Library.

A catalog record for this book is available from the Library of Congress.

Transferred to Digital Printing in 2015

Contents

List of Figures

List of Tables

Acknowledgments

Completing this book would not have been possible without the sustained support of family, friends, and colleagues. In particular, I wish to thank Professor Claude Gilbert (The National Center for Scientific Research, CNRS), who acted as a mentor to me and gave me the opportunity to work with him on the World Health Organization's governance of the 2009 H1N1 influenza pandemic within the frame of the funded project "Emergence et Risques sanitaires" 2010–2013, coordinated by CIRAD (Agricultural Research for Development). I am grateful for his challenging questions, constructive comments, and the trust he placed in my work.

I also would like to thank Professor Claudine Burton-Jeangros for her friendship and professional collaboration that meant a great deal to me. I thank Doctor Sophie Huber-Kodbaye who accompanied me during the whole process with her friendship and thoughtful comments, as well as Professor Catherine Equey for her support.

I would also like to thank the interviewees involved in the project for their patient assistance.

This book would not have come to pass without the Palgrave Macmillan editing team. A special thanks to my editor Christina Brian for her guidance and patience.

I am also grateful to my mother and my brother for their faith, continuous encouragement, and support throughout all stages of this project. Marc provided me with infallible technical and logistical support, endless patience, and unconditional care, while our daughters, Agathe and Jeanne, always managed to cheer me up at the most critical times.

Finally, I wish to dedicate this book to my late father.

List of Abbreviations and Acronyms

AFRO   Regional Office for Africa (World Health Organization)
AIDS   Acquired Immunodeficiency Syndrome
AMRO   Regional Office for the Americas (World Health Organization)
ASEAN   Association of Southeast Asian Nations
BSE   Bovine Spongiform Encephalopathy
CAP   Community-Acquired Pneumonia
CCs   Collaborating Centers
CDC   Centers for Disease Control
CEA   Cost-Effectiveness Analysis
CHOICE   Choosing Interventions that are Cost Effective
EIS   Event Information Site
EMRO   Regional Office for the Eastern Mediterranean (World Health Organization)
EPR   Epidemic and Pandemic Alert and Response
ERL   Essential Regulatory Laboratories
EU   European Union
EURO   Regional Office for Europe (World Health Organization)
FAO   Food and Agriculture Organization
FETP   Field Epidemiology Training Programs
GAR   Global Alert and Response
GDP   Gross domestic product
GIP   Global Influenza Programme
GISN   Global Influenza Surveillance Network
GISRS   Global Influenza Surveillance and Response System
GLEWS   Global Early Warning System
GOARN   Global Outbreak Alert and Response Network
GPHIN   Global Public Health Intelligence Network
HIV   Human Immunodeficiency Virus
HK   Hong Kong
IFRC   International Federation of Red Cross and Red Crescent Societies
IHR   International Health Regulations
IPCC   Intergovernmental Panel on Climate Change
IPTF   Influenza Pandemic Task Force
IRGC   International Risk Governance Council

MERS-CoV	Middle East Respiratory Syndrome Coronavirus
NFP	National Focal Points
NGO	Nongovernmental organization
NIC	National Influenza Centers
OECD	Organization for Economic Cooperation and Development
OEF	Oxford Economic Forecasting
OIE	World Organization for Animal Health
PHEIC	Public Health Emergency of International Concern
PIP	Pandemic Influenza Preparedness
SARS	Severe Acute Respiratory Syndrome
SAR	Special Administrative Region
SEARO	Regional Office for South-East Asia (World Health Organization)
SHOC	Strategic Health Operations Centre
TEPHINET	Training in Epidemiology and Public Health Interventions Program Network
UNICEF	United Nations Children's Fund
UNSIC	United Nations System Influenza Coordination
vCJD	Variant Creutzfeldt-Jakob Disease
WFP	World Food Programme
WHA	World Health Assembly
WHO	World Health Organization
WPRO	Regional Office for the Western Pacific (World Health Organization)

Introduction

Risk[1] is about interdependence.[2] Risk has become a central and complex feature in the development of our interconnected and globalized world. Large-scale disasters are often referred to as "mega risks," (4 p. 3) "systemic risks," (4) or simply as "global risks." Examples include hurricanes or floods, effects of climate change, new diseases such as severe acute respiratory syndrome (SARS), food-related diseases such as bovine spongiform encephalopathy (BSE), terrorist attacks such as September 11, disruptions of critical infrastructures, such as cross-border power grids, and disruptions to air travel, such as the 2010 eruption of the Eyjafjallajökull volcano. These risks are complex and highly uncertain. They are characterized by the great speed with which they occur and the magnitude of their potential effects in terms of geographic coverage and impact on human lives, as well as economic and social costs. If the nature of these risks is not new, then the context within which they occur has changed. Intensification of trade and travel, greater intangible transborder exchanges, and demographic trends and migrations, as well as environmental changes have made societies more vulnerable to events that occur in other parts of the world.[3]

The development and intensification of international travel and tourism represents a more rapid vector for the propagation of infectious diseases. In 2003, the SARS virus spread across continents within a few days, putting the world at risk of a pandemic for which no treatment or cure was effective. The growth of international trade accentuates the dissemination of food safety issues and related diseases. For example, BSE, which initially affected cattle in the United Kingdom, quickly reached other countries first within and then outside Europe, due to exports of cattle and cattle feed. Pathogens such as *Escherichia coli* and parasites also constitute growing sources of transborder foodborne illness. In the technological field, greater transborder data flow, using technologies such as the Internet, communication satellites, and telephones has made societies more vulnerable to technical failure or cyberattacks, such as the one that hit Estonia in 2007. Similarly, technical failures of the global financial system could have immediate and significant consequences for the worldwide economy. For example, a deficient algorithm in the electronic system resulted in amplification of the financial crash of 1987. (5 p. 13) Demographic trends, such as the extension of urban zones and an increase in human activities, represent another source of the multiplication and diversification of risk. Mass migrations of people for security, social, or economic reasons, and the resulting concentration of these displaced populations in certain areas, represent an important factor in risk development. Poor living conditions and promiscuity may not only favor the development of diseases but also generate fundamental changes in the natural environment. Decreasing energy and dwindling water supplies are also expected to be intensified sources of risk. Finally, climate change contributes to the emergence of newly identified risks that may harm the living conditions and health of populations worldwide. For example, global warming is expected to provoke the displacement of millions of people, as well as increase the number and magnitude of natural disasters.

As globalization continues to blur borders and increases interdependence, risk transcends national borders, causing major challenges in risk governance. Recent risk literature converges on one aspect: risk assessment and risk management pose major challenges in all fields of our interconnected societies. The roles and responsibilities of actors and the structures and processes to assess risk, design responses, and apply measures, however, are often not clearly defined. While risk interdependence and the increased complexity of the international environment require the formulation of global responses to global risks and risk governance processes to cope with them are emerging (2).

While governance has become a very popular topic over the past 20 years and implies that at all levels governance outputs are based on the interplay between governments, industries, academia, and civil society, (2 pp. 8–9) risk governance, and in particular global risk governance, remains a discipline in its infancy. Risk governance has emerged as a concept over the past ten years, and is meant to include more than risk analysis practices that have traditionally encompassed in various degrees of separation, risk assessment, risk management, and risk communication. Risk governance includes consideration of the legal, institutional, social, and economic contexts in which a risk is evaluated, and involvement of the actors and stakeholders who represent them (6 pp. 8–9), and they can be applied at all levels. This concept is intimately linked to the complexity of modern risks, the role of science and experts, and the importance of trust and stakeholder participation. (7) In its report "Emerging Systemic Risks in the 21st Century: An Agenda for Action" (4), the Organization for Economic Cooperation and Development (OECD) proposed recommendations to improve the governance of the "new risks," or "systemic risks," and argued for a coherent and common risk approach. In parallel, the development by a nonprofit organization based in Switzerland, the International Risk Governance Council (IRGC), of a risk governance framework that may be applied by various stakeholders, also represents an attempt to provide a response to these challenges. However, these writings focus on potential improvements to current models of risk governance, or propose the implementation of a new model, but they do not emphasize the respective roles of the actors within the process and how it could be organized at the global level.

Risk analysis models that have been developed and applied over the past 30 years have become insufficient to address modern risks. First, models may fail to account for risk uncertainty, environment complexity, and human behavior simultaneously. The special issue of the *Journal of Risk Research* of April 2011, dedicated to risk management, underlines the current difficulties in assessing uncertainties, establishing adequate risk steering mechanisms and processes, and forming balanced responses with regard to scientific knowledge about the risk, its origins and consequences, the logic of precaution, and the costs of action. Risk governance processes suffer from a lack of adequate risk frameworks, a shortage of risk harmonization procedures, and an interdisciplinary deficit in the approach to risk. In this environment, the Red Book Risk Analysis Framework that was developed in the United States in 1983 and updated in 2009 (8) has progressively been recognized as an international standard. This framework is used by governments, international organizations, and other entities worldwide, and is composed of three interrelated components with various degrees of separation: risk assessment (science-based evaluation of risk), risk management (development and evaluation of regulatory options and/or decisions), and risk communication (both internal and external).

In 2002 and as a result of the BSE crisis, the European Union's risk framework was developed based on the joint Food and Agriculture Organization (FAO) / World Health Organization (WHO) risk framework that relied on the Red Book Risk Analysis Framework. (9) Risk assessment was clearly separated from risk management functions, and expertise was selected based on excellence, independence, and multidisciplinary criteria. In parallel, following the Weissmann report, substantive research programs were launched at the European level to increase knowledge about the disease and reduce the uncertainties surrounding the risk to humans and the origins of BSE. The BSE crisis was the first crisis of this nature and this magnitude in Europe, and served as a learning case to improve risk assessment and risk management in the European Union (EU). It was also a case study for risk managers in different organizations or governments, and is often referred to as an example of risks that could generate significant consequences due to the increase of trade exchanges and interconnectedness of societies. (4) The reduction of casualties in animals began in 2003 and in humans in 2004. However, the objective of eradication of BSE remains unachieved, and the decrease in Variant Creutzfeldt-Jakob Disease (vCJD) cases should be interpreted with caution as the disease is not detected easily and the incubation period is long.

Second, risk approaches are often based on past experience, which is not sufficient to address risks that depart from past data, such as terrorist attacks or new infectious diseases. (4 p. 16) In addition, risk assessment and risk management processes are often fragmented and performed on an ad hoc basis rather than integrated in the regular perimeter of activities of the actors involved in the governance processes. This renders the performance of a comprehensive risk assessment and the deployment of international responses to global risks more difficult. Also, the integration of technical/natural science-based knowledge is privileged, while interdisciplinary knowledge, including sociology, psychology, and economics, seems essential to better and more completely understand the continuously changing environment (4 p. 25) and the risk's impact upon it. Finally, the identification, capturing, and analysis of the contributing factors to the emergence of such risks also represent an additional difficulty for practitioners. (10 p. 5) The possibilities of estimating risks (risk assessment) and reducing and controlling them through policy measures (risk management) are under pressure (11 p. 401) due to the increased level of uncertainty prevailing in the emergence of a new disease, the development of a new technology, and large-scale disasters of various natures. This is particularly well illustrated in the assessment of pandemic risks under WHO.

The questions of responsibility and accountability have not been solved yet. Which bodies should be ultimately in charge of the risk governance process and handle the consequences of the risk is not always clearly established. For example, WHO has neither the enforcement means nor the risk compensation mechanisms in regard to states. For example, Indonesia's refusal to provide its avian influenza viruses to the network of laboratories, or a situation wherein peasants hide sick animals, cannot be directly addressed by the institutions. In this context, worldwide mobilization of stakeholders to address global risks is necessary, but engaging in costly activities remains a difficult enterprise when risks may not be perceived as equally significant by all parties or are seen as less significant compared to other risks. Although governments become one actor among others in global risk governance, the commitment of states in assessing risk and deploying adequate responses is more and more critical to the success of the actions undertaken.

Finally, a lack of trust, which is intimately linked to the credibility of the actors in charge of risk governance processes, renders risk management strategies ineffective, as food crises in the EU have shown. (12 p. 218, 13 pp. 1107–1122) Communication among risk governance actors and toward external parties, such as the public or the media, has not systematically been open and consistent, has failed to garner the full support of all parties concerned, and has been unable to prevent certain behaviors, such as the imposition of unilateral trade restrictions in the case of the BSE crisis.

Over the past 15 years, multilateral institutions have been increasingly involved in assessing and managing risks. They have also developed capacities in terms of international leverage, access to information, human and financial resources, and infrastructures, in addition to networks of experts to address international issues. They have gained independence from their constituent bodies, the states, and have emerged as actors with the capacity to initiate, inform, and drive globally relevant projects. They are also embedded in larger, intertwined networks with other institutions and partners in the public and private sectors and civil society, which bring to these institutions a greater variety and representation of ideas and means of actions. Finally, they have built expertise networks that are sources of information exchange and advice across fields of activities and countries. Driving global governance processes is within their capabilities and scope of action, as demonstrated by the leading role WHO played in tobacco control. WHO was able to mobilize a broad range of stakeholders, including representatives of states, scientific experts, international institutions, and members of the civil society, in order to federate their views and coordinate the process that led to the adoption of the Framework Convention on Tobacco Control (FCTC) in 2003 (14 p. 208).

Multilateral institutions have positioned themselves as important players in global risk governance processes, (15) responding to the growing needs for more international consultation and cooperation in dealing with emerging global risks. They have been shaping guidelines and policies aimed at containing or reducing risk; they have also contributed to the development of international regulatory approaches that were developed in a coordinated and cooperative manner, integrating the work of external experts from different sectors of activities. For example, the Codex Alimentarius (or the Food Code) has become the global reference point for consumers, food producers and processors, national food control agencies, and the international food trade. (16 p. IX) These international standards have served as the basis for developing national food-quality and food-safety policies, as well as for benchmarks in international food trade. In public health, the implementation of the revised International Health Regulations (IHR) (17) set the rules for WHO and its member states to identify, evaluate, and manage outbreaks of infectious diseases. The development of these regulations involved member states, multilateral institutions, and other partners in a novel approach that departed from a fixed set of measures for a predefined list of diseases and resulted in a set of procedures for defining the steps to assess and address any health event. In the environmental field, assessment reports of the Intergovernmental Panel on Climate Change (IPCC) that have a significant impact on international and national policies (18 p. 191) constitute another example of multilateral institutions' activities to address global risks. These risk assessment and management initiatives have been carried out to respond to the growing needs for more international consultation and cooperation in dealing with global risks. They have contributed to the increasing acceptance that national sovereignty may not be relied upon exclusively to respond to problems of global significance (19 p. 35) and have shown the emergence of global risk-governance processes in which multilateral institutions have played a key role. However, the study of these risk-analysis practices has been neglected in the global governance literature, and in particular insufficient attention has been given to examining risk assessment and management activities carried out by multilateral institutions.

The effects of globalization render the question of risk governance and the role of multilateral institutions[4] in this emerging process particularly relevant. This is especially well illustrated in the health sector. Epidemics and pandemics know no borders and are often characterized by a high level of uncertainty regarding the causality of risk and its potential social and economic consequences.

In this book, we seek to show how WHO positioned itself as a leading organization in the governance of pandemic risks and to shed light on the essential organizational features of these emerging global risk governance processes. In particular, we will explain how WHO gained the capacity and legitimacy for action in pandemic management and how it conducted a science-based risk assessment that set the basis for the formation of the international responses to SARS and the avian influenza (H5N1). These processes, instruments, and mechanisms provided the bases for WHO's governance of the A (H1N1) influenza pandemic, revealing the limits of the organization in the deployment of its strategy and resources, as well as its governance processes and instruments. The lessons that can be drawn from the analysis of the SARS outbreak, the avian influenza H5N1, and the 2009 H1N1 influenza pandemic go beyond their single histories, emphasizing the importance of the role of WHO and the modalities of its action within global risk governance processes in health.

In addition, this study may shed some light on risk-analysis practices carried out within or under the lead of multilateral institutions in order to address global risks. It may increase understanding of the functioning of multilateral institutions and risk-analysis mechanisms as well as identify the role of these actors in the emerging field of global risk governance. It may also provide some evidence about the learning process within multilateral institutions in addressing global risks that pertain to the same domain of activities.

Finally, it may challenge assumptions regarding the primary role of states in risk governance by illustrating that other forms of governance are in place and effective in dealing with global risks. It may reveal that multilateral institutions are in a position to obtain more optimal outcomes in dealing with risk as they have legitimacy to act globally, benefit from networks of international experts, and leverage resources and infrastructures worldwide. It may also show that risk strategies carried out by governments, for example, publication of recommendations or adoption of regulations, find their origin in measures proposed by multilateral institutions.

This book includes the results of two empirically based case studies that were completed between 2005 and 2009 and integrated in a PhD thesis (15) – the SARS crisis that took place from February 26, 2003 to July 5, 2003 and the avian influenza (H5N1), still ongoing, from February 2003 to December 2008 – by drawing on the past experience of the BSE crisis management in Europe. Our study is based on a qualitative analysis of documents (with a focus on official documents of organizations) and interviews. For each case study, we conducted a total of about five to ten semidirected interviews of WHO personnel and other actors in the field of global risk governance. All the interviews contained in this book have been anonymized. Secondary sources such as news articles, studies, and books were also consulted in order to add another perspective to the analysis. To a lesser extent, complementary sources such as information gathered during conferences and communications with certain experts were included as well. The analysis of the H1N1 pandemic mainly relied on the study of documents and constitutes an outlook on the results of the processes, instruments, and mechanisms that WHO put in place in terms of global risk governance for the SARS and the avian influenza H5N1.

This book is divided in four chapters. The first chapter is dedicated to a description of the analytical framework that will be applied to the case studies. The next two chapters consist of two empirically based case studies. Chapter 2 examines the risk analysis performed by WHO in the containment of the SARS outbreak in 2003. Chapter 3 studies the influence of risk analysis in the preparedness activities from 2004 to 2008 to face a human pandemic of avian influenza H5N1 origin. Chapter 4 compares the two stories in relation to the proposed framework and explains how the management of the H1N1 influenza pandemic relied on the structures, processes, and tools set up to address the SARS and avian influenza H5N1 diseases. The concluding remarks provide a perspective on the policies and procedures that were in place and the changes that occurred after the H1N1 pandemic, with comments and a synthesis of the common features and differences.

1
Thinking the International Response to a Global Health Risk

This chapter provides the theoretical basis for the empirical casework that follows. It firstly draws on the definitions of key concepts and theoretical elements presented in the literature review to provide the analytical framework on which this research is based. It then provides an overview of the process and key dimensions of the analysis of risk and the formation of an international response to it. It ends with a brief description of our approach.

Our framework is original in the sense that it introduces additional elements such as the notion of legitimate basis for the action of the multilateral institution and the existence of a risk assessment method, and it focuses on the existing and newly established risk assessment mechanisms and combines scientific risk assessment techniques with economics-based tools such as cost analysis in order to reach a more comprehensive approach. The combination of these elements allows for an evaluation of the quality of the risk analysis and, in turn, to determine whether these elements contribute to the quality of the response. Our framework borrows elements from both the technical approach to risk (in particular from the Red Book risk analysis framework) and business risk management techniques commonly used in companies, which consist of reducing uncertainty in order to understand more precisely and estimate the risk, thus allowing for more targeted action. In particular, the procedure of hazard identification, dose-response assessment, and exposure and risk characterization was used as guidance to analyze the activities of multilateral institutions, along with cost analysis, monitoring, evaluation of implementation problems, continuous improvement, and iterative characteristics of the business risk management process.

At a specific moment in time, one actor issues a risk warning. This actor may be an inside or outside agent of the multilateral institution, and its warning may or may not be revealed in the media.[1] For the purpose of our study, we consider this warning that is captured by the multilateral institution as the triggering fact for the risk analysis process. This warning initiates the performance, within a multilateral institution, of a risk analysis in order to identify and evaluate the risk. The actors who participate in the risk analysis process, in identifying and evaluating the potential risk drivers and risk consequences, feed the risk analysis process with their theoretical and empirical knowledge. Risk analysis is based on a method, and it may take the form of an institutionalized, structured, and formalized process with predefined procedures, milestones, and requirements, or it may consist of a more informal and participative forum. Risk-related activities of multilateral institutions should appear legitimate to its members, thus relying on a formal agreement or recognition of action. The multilateral institution uses existing or establishes new risk analysis mechanisms in order to complete the risk assessment.

The process will result in a quantitative or qualitative estimation of the risk, or a combination of both, and a proposal of measures to be taken to reduce the risk. The appropriateness of this response that is provided by the multilateral institution will depend on the existence and the quality of the risk analysis performance. This response is designed to ensure the highest level of preservation of collective interest or, in other words, the highest level of risk reduction based on the information available at the time of the decision. The risk reduction level will translate into lower casualties in terms of impact on human lives, on other countries, and with respect to economic costs. This response should be the result of consultations that are formalized (documented), publicly communicated, and implemented. The implementation of the response is based on mechanisms that are internal and external to the multilateral institutions. While the multilateral institutions ensure the compilation and communication of information, regular reassessment of the issue and monitoring of the implementation of the response states are instrumental in reporting information to the multilateral institution and carrying out the measures that are recommended. Other actors such as nongovernmental organizations (NGOs) or private companies can also contribute to the completion of the response.

The monitoring of the response's implementation is a key element of the risk management process. Risk analysis is not linear, with a beginning (a risk) and an end (a solution to that risk). It is, rather, a continuous process of regular reassessment of the situation, the potential consequences, and the validity of the measures adopted in light of any new information acquired by the scientists and professionals dealing with that particular risk. Global risks often are characterized by uncertainty due to a lack of knowledge about the likelihood of occurrence of an event (e.g., the probability of a human influenza pandemic), its magnitude or damage (e.g., the number of persons infected and the number of deaths, as well as economic costs), its initial location, and its timing (where it could arise and when). Information about these elements may evolve over time and result in reviews of the previously adopted measures. These measures can be confirmed, modified, or canceled depending on the results of this continuous risk analysis.

The level of knowledge is not the only element driving this process. The success or the failure of an international response is another aspect of the continuous process. An evaluation of the response (whether the measures were applied and how effectively they were applied) should be performed to determine whether the objectives set have been met, not met, or partially met, and why. Measures that are not implemented or are partially implemented may be a sign that they are not accepted or understood by the concerned populations, are too costly, or are not adequate for the situation. The outputs of this evaluation should be used to feed the risk analysis process so as to continue to analyze the risk and formulate new responses. This continuous and iterative process can be illustrated as follows:

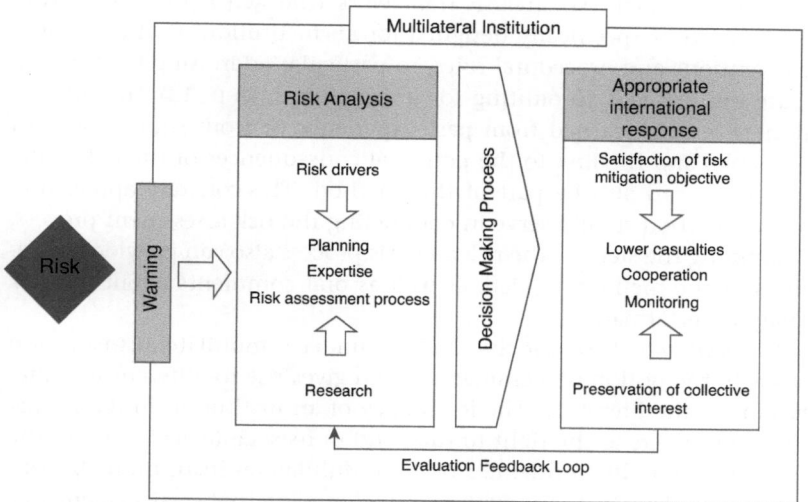

Figure 1.1   Iterative risk analysis process

1.1   Analyzing risk

Within this framework, risk analysis is based on the scientific assessment of an issue that ultimately aims to gain more knowledge about the issue and reduce uncertainties (whenever possible), including conducting a cost analysis and benefiting from the multilateral institution's legitimacy of action. Risk analysis, for the purposes of this study, is defined as *an expert-based deliberative and participative process that takes place within or under the lead of a multilateral institution, consisting of the performance of a scientific assessment of the risk according to a predefined plan or an organized method and addresses possible risk sources and their potential consequences* and is characterized by three key dimensions: planning, expertise, and the risk assessment process. We will use these dimensions as key milestones to analyze each empirical case.

First, the *planning* dimension provides for the general conditions under which risk analysis can take place. It is composed of a predefined plan or an organized method, and rests on a legitimate basis for the multilateral institution's action. The *method* that is used as the basis for the risk analysis can take the form of a conceptual formalized model (a predefined and documented risk analysis method, model, structures, and processes) or an empirical (and informal) method. This plan is built to track the risk, identify its source(s), and establish a risk causal chain. It can be inspired from existing frameworks such as the American National Research Council risk analysis framework (the Red Book risk analysis framework) or specifically designed for an institution. It also includes conventions and procedural rules, in particular addressing how to estimate the risk and accounting for uncertainties. (2 p. 13) The integration of lessons learned from past experience or from similar cases (if available) and the link to the potential consequences of the risk materialization can also be part of this method. The concrete application of this method should serve in conducting the risk assessment process. Examining the steps of the risk analysis process also can provide indications of the method applied, as well as oral comments about the risk analysis performance.

The *legitimate basis* for risk analysis under a multilateral institution refers to the notion of legitimacy, which gives rise to different interpretations in the literature. The legitimacy of an institution in its normative sense refers to the right to rule, and in its sociological sense to the belief in the right to rule. (22 p. 405) Multilateral institutions historically have derived their right to rule from international agreements.

States delegate certain competences to the organization to issue rules and to ensure their compliance by the parties to these regulations. The IHR are an example of such agreements that confer rights to the WHO to use nonofficial sources to detect disease outbreaks and to issue recommendations to handle them. The European treaties also confer rights to the EU to issue regulations in specific areas, and the European Court of Justice represents one instrument of compliance available to the institution to ensure compliance with the European regulations. This legitimacy is important, as it defines the frame within which the institution can act, but the perception of other actors that the institution has the right to rule matters as well.

Believing that an institution is legitimate is an essential element in supporting its actions. Legally accepted bases for action are a necessary but insufficient condition of legitimacy. Formal legitimacy may be ineffective if no broad-based support from the public is associated with it. Keohane and Buchanan combine normative and sociological aspects to define legitimacy as "the right to rule, understood to mean both that institutional agents are morally justified in making rules and attempting to secure compliance with them and that people subject to those rules have moral, content-independent reasons to follow them and/or avoid interfering with others' compliance with them." (22 p. 411) We share with these authors the idea that formal delegation of competences granted to an organization is a necessary but insufficient condition for legitimacy. But focus remains the multilateral institution and the support granted to its action by member states, as states are considered the primary partners of the multilateral institution in implementing the response to a global risk, and stakeholders' concerns are not analyzed here. Legitimacy essentially will be derived from the application and compliance by the states to the measures adopted by the multilateral institution.

Our approach considers both "rule-based" and "action-based" legitimacy. Legitimate bases for action are derived from two nonexclusive sources: the multilateral institution's constitutive agreement (e.g., treaty or constitution), regulations, or rules accepted by member states, and generally accepted practices within a multilateral institution. For example, certain WHO practices in response to the Severe Acute Respiratory Syndrome (SARS) outbreak, such as the use of nonofficial sources of information, generally were accepted by member states, although they were formally accepted as rules by the World Health Assembly later in the process, and then in the revised IHR in 2005.

Second, the *expertise* dimension combines the requirements for a diversified and internationally recognized background of the expertise involved in risk analysis, as well as the integration of the latest research, results in the risk estimation and proposition of measures. The *background* refers to the quality of scientific expertise involved in risk analysis, including the best-available scientific knowledge. There is no agreed-upon definition of expertise, but it seems generally accepted at the international level that it should be multidisciplinary and highly qualified in order to ensure that the best-available and more comprehensive scientific knowledge is used in a balanced way to analyze risk and propose measures. International expertise can be analyzed through excellence in performance or based on nomination. An expert is considered to be a skilled performer and recognized as an expert in his/her field. This recognition is based on several dimensions, including education, practical experience, and organizational role (23 p. 602).

In our approach, the quality of expertise is determined by its *background diversity*, which is defined by multidisciplinary, institutional, and geographical broad-based origin and an international track record. The combination of theoretical knowledge, knowledge of risk approaches (quantitative assessment and qualitative assessment such as scenario techniques), and past experience gained in different disciplines is considered to enrich risk analysis. For example, teams may be composed of individuals who are active worldwide in research institutions, universities, or laboratories, high-level professionals with field practical experience, internal expert officers working for the multilateral institution, and experts from other organizations. The review of the professional background, the institution of origin, and the country, as well as the level of experience of the key participants involved in the risk analysis process, will be based on public documents such as lists of participants, minutes, and reports regarding specific risk analysis meetings, complemented by interviews. The international track record of participants can be derived from the estimation for the group of the quantity and quality of international publications in peer reviews.

The *research* part of the expertise dimension is dedicated to the capacity of the multilateral institution to obtain and integrate the latest research results available into the response. It is important that the risk analysis encompasses the most recent research developments, particularly in the case of situations of uncertainty, when knowledge about the risk is progressing regarding the origin of the disease, its symptoms, its transmissibility, and its clinical course. Research findings can contribute to a more precise risk assessment that in turn may result in more targeted and effective measures. Evidence on how research is conducted to reduce uncertainty, the publication of results, and the integration of these results in recommendations can be found in meeting minutes, press releases, public communications, and documents of multilateral institutions and secondary sources that have analyzed the cases under study, as well as interviews. When available, it is also interesting to consider which resources were allocated to research and how they were split among the participants, when, and for which results.

Third, the *risk assessment process* dimension is composed of a series of steps that lead to the risk estimation and proposed risk management measures combining scientific assessment and cost analysis techniques. We consider the presence of an observation system, risk analysis mechanisms, and cost analysis as essential components of this process. The risk assessment process relies on the presence of a continuous *observation system* that reports information on a regular basis about risk issues that serve as a basis for the risk analysis. This system may report a warning concerning a potential risk or a new risk, and the development of that risk. This observation system (also called surveillance system) can be human or system based, or both. It may encompass different mechanisms and tools in order to achieve its mission of providing information. For example, it can take the form of computerized surveillance systems that compile facts reported in a particular field (such as disease outbreaks), human activities of observation in the field, or an international forum for professionals who exchange knowledge about a particular issue. This observation system can be internal or external to the multilateral institution, or a combination of both. The Global Public Health Intelligence Network (GPHIN), which represents one element of the WHO observation system, provides this organization with information about disease outbreaks that occur worldwide.

Risk assessment mechanisms mainly relate to how risk analysis is performed in terms of activities, resources, and tools. Risk analysis mechanisms consist of activities carried out to identify the risk source(s) and evaluate the relationship between the risk source(s) and the potential consequences of the risk, including the determination and exposure of the populations at risk. These activities should result in an estimation of the probability of occurrence and the seriousness of the consequences of the risk, a communication of uncertainties, and a proposal of measures to reduce the risk. The mechanisms are often contained in the risk analysis method, but can also be a current practice that is not documented. They also can be adapted or customized upon the identification of a new risk. Risk assessment mechanisms are mainly science based and may operate using different tools such as modern telecommunications or top-level research infrastructures.

In our analysis, risk assessment mechanisms are essentially science based and borrow elements from the technical risk framework, as well as the American National Research Council risk analysis framework. Based on the latter framework, WHO defines risk assessment as "the process of evaluating the probability and consequences of injury or illness arising from exposure to identified hazards," hazard being the potential to cause harm and risk being the likelihood (or probability) of harm or damage occurring from exposure to a hazard, as well as the possible consequences. (24 p. 10) Based on this definition, WHO would carry out three main steps: identification of the source, vulnerability assessment, and estimation of the consequences. In practice, risk assessment mechanisms include risk-tracking or risk-tracing activities to determine the cause(s) of the risk (the hazard) by investigating different presumptions or intuitions based on the available knowledge about the issue at a particular time.

Proceeding to a risk assessment can be particularly difficult in situations that present a high level of uncertainty, as risk characteristics may be completely unknown or partially unknown. One challenge of any risk assessment process is to take into account the fact that knowledge about a particular risk is still in construction. When the level of uncertainty is complete or remains high, the technical approach to risk shows certain limits. The absence of sufficient and relevant historical data, as well as the gaps in knowledge to confirm the causal relationship between the hazard and the risk may prevent the calculation of a relevant probability of occurrence and the estimation of the consequences. Instead of quantitative mechanisms, more qualitative mechanisms are applied to combine elements of developing risk knowledge such as experimental or empirical references, analogy thinking, integration of lessons learned from past experience, and formulation of best estimates of probabilities and damages or use of scenario-building techniques. However, one should be aware that psychology judgment biases such as availability, anchoring and adjustment, representativeness, and overconfidence may influence the judgment of experts with respect to risk and the estimation of its probability (25 p. 111).

The scenario technique consists of "thinking about every scenario possible and its consequences". In most cases, the assessment proposes three scenarios: a best-, a middle range-, and a worst-case scenario. As risk assessment is a continuous process, the experts can revise their assessment based on the latest experimental and/or empirical studies, aiming at increasing knowledge about the risk and establishing a link between one or a few risk source(s) and the risk under study. For example, the risk of an influenza pandemic has been analyzed on a national basis, taking into consideration different scenarios that are mainly based on different estimations of the percentage of the population affected and the number of deaths estimated in order to evaluate the burden on health care resources, as well as the potential socially disruptive impacts. Computerized models using parameters from previous pandemics have supported these evaluations in order to produce quantitative figures, although the virus is not yet known. Official documents published by the multilateral institutions, such as the existence of references to or documented scenarios, risk estimates or risk-related information such as documented risk cartography, lists of risk drivers or risk sources, and analysis of their possible consequences provide information about the concept and practices of risk assessment mechanisms. Findings communicated by the experts (e.g., communications, recommendations, reports) who perform the risk analysis and have published studies (e.g., articles in peer reviewed journals) are valuable sources of information as well.

The risk assessment process entails a *cost analysis*, which refers to cost-benefit analysis that is commonly performed in the business sector to determine the most profitable option. However, cost-benefit analysis cannot systematically be performed, as cost considerations may be prohibited by law (25 p. 84) (e.g., safety regulations) or be considered unethical when dealing with risks in which human lives are at stake, such as health and food safety risks. (6 p. 18) In addition, concerns also have been raised with respect to the fact that cost-benefit analysis could dominate the debate and the decision-making process to the detriment of exchanges about conflicting values regarding the risk. (25 p. 104) However, some sort of cost-benefit analysis is a complement to informed decision-making about risk, but can take different forms according to the risk fields, as the EU recognizes in its impact assessment guidelines.

This cost-benefit analysis often is replaced by cost-effectiveness analysis in order to evaluate and compare the relative costs and effects of two or more measures. For example, WHO has developed the approach CHOICE (CHOosing Interventions that are Cost-Effective) to evaluate and compare the costs and effects of an intervention with the burden that would exist in the absence of that intervention. (26 p. 12) This method is often referred to as "cost-effectiveness analysis" (CEA) (27, 28) and results in the calculation of a cost-effectiveness ratio. This ratio is taken into account in the decision made on the implementation of measures to deal with a specific risk and can be compared to the ratios of other programs. However, this approach requires a large number of available data and is time consuming and difficult to communicate. (28 p. 241) In addition, although the level of uncertainty has been reduced in the model, it cannot be eliminated.

Although this cost-effectiveness analysis cannot be applied as such to global risks in which the level of uncertainty remains high, insufficient data are available, and time pressure is growing, the performance of some sort of cost analysis is a key element of the risk analysis. The proposed measures that result from the risk assessment process represent costly actions that must be undertaken upfront in order to become prepared to deal with the risk if it materializes. These upfront measures are expected to enable more costly future actions to be avoided that will have to be taken in an emergency without prior preparation once the risk materializes. The costs to be incurred in the present time should lead to the avoidance of higher future costs, considering that these measures would reduce the risk. This cost-saving relationship depends on the probability of occurrence of the risk and the discount rate used to evaluate the future costs. (6 p. 18) This cost-saving relationship can be expressed in monetary terms and nonmonetary terms, such as human lives saved, in official documents, press communications or articles.

1.2   Responding to risk

The combination of legitimacy and the capacities of the organization and the quality of this analysis is expected to influence the quality of the international response to risk through the implementation of measures that increase net benefits to human societies by preventing or reducing harm to humans and the things they value. In that context, the appropriate international response shall be understood as *a concerted, formalized, and publicly communicated risk reduction measures that aim to ensure the highest level of preservation of collective interest and that are adopted and implemented in a cooperative manner, as well as continuously monitored.*

First, the dimension *lower casualties* refers to the reduction of the consequences. The multilateral institution's response contributes to the supply of risk reduction (that can be considered as a global public good), which ensures the preservation of the collective interest on a worldwide basis. The preservation of collective interest raises the question of a society's acceptable level of risk. Reducing risks (for example, limiting the severity of consequences) entails costs as well as benefits. In most cases, it is reasonably stated that there may be an optimal level of risk at which costs and benefits are in balance. However, there may be too much uncertainty to evaluate these costs and benefits with a sufficient degree of confidence as is the case for emerging pandemics such as SARS or influenza. Alternatively, disagreements may arise regarding the threshold to be applied to determine the acceptable level of risk.

The acceptable level of risk is often defined by a technical threshold that triggers specific actions, or by balancing the cost-benefits of variable options, or through cooperation in accepting a risk level. First, a technical threshold in terms of costs and benefits is difficult to apply to health-related issues for ethical and social considerations. (4 p. 261) For example, WHO does not apply thresholds that are expressed in terms of acceptable cost of human life; rather, it uses thresholds stated in absolute terms, such as preventing a pandemic from occurring or reaching a flu-free world (or a SARS-free world), and therefore promotes containment and eradication measures to manage these diseases. Second, balancing the cost-benefits of variable options with a sufficient degree of confidence remains difficult in situations that involve a high level of uncertainty. This approach has been partially adopted by WHO in long-term health programs, but not for emerging pandemics such as SARS or influenza in which estimates may vary significantly. Third, cooperation in accepting risk level necessitates the inclusion of stakeholders. Thresholds are the result of negotiations and are reviewed periodically, which is more practical at local or national rather than global levels. For these reasons, we focused on casualties as an indicator of the preservation of collective interest that would express how the multilateral institution performs in providing measures to reduce the risk or eliminate it. A decrease in casualties following the implementation of proposed measures would be interpreted as a sign that the containment and eradication of the disease are progressing. This decrease in casualties contributes to preserving the collective interest by reducing the occurrence and/or the severity of consequences of the risk.

Lower casualties can be evidenced by three indicators: spread, impact on human lives, and economic cost. First, *spread* can be evaluated by the number of new countries affected by the risk event (e.g., a disease). In practice, the preservation of the worldwide collective interest if a new infectious disease emerges could be expressed in terms of the geographical spread of the disease by recording and comparing the number of new countries affected by the disease since the alert was given, until the measures were implemented; or after the measures were taken up, until the first deadline set for an evaluation of these measures; or up to the stage at which no more new countries are affected. The evolution of the spread can be derived from reported data published on the websites of the multilateral institutions. Risk reduction is considered to be achieved when there are no new countries affected, and when countries affected can be declared progressively risk free.

In addition, the impact on human lives can be measured by the evolution of the *number of cases* and/or case fatalities. These data often are published by the multilateral institution based on reporting from the member states. When sufficient and relevant data are available, the mortality rate[2] and the case fatality ratio[3] also could be used as measures of the impact on human lives. A decrease in the number of additional cases and a decline in the epidemiological curve (total number of cases) are considered to be risk reduction. The indicator of the reproduction[4] number R_0 often is used as a metric to evaluate the spread of a disease among a population. When R_0 falls below 1, the epidemic is considered to be contained. The international geographical spread and the evolution of cases among populations are both necessary in order to evaluate the level of casualties. A disease with a high R_0 may result in a large number of cases localized in one specific area and no international geographical spread due to the implementation of rapid and effective containment measures. In contrast, a disease with a low R_0 still could spread to a lot of countries and result in a significant number of cases over time, although it may not result in high numbers of cases locally.

Finally, the actual *economic cost* of the actions taken can be compared to the planned cost and/or the cost of inaction. Economic cost sometimes also is compared to that of previous similar events in order to evaluate the impact of the different measures taken to determine the most cost-effective ones. For example, a simulation using the Monte Carlo model estimated the economic impact of a pandemic in the United States of between USD 71.3 and USD 166.5 billion, excluding disruptions to commerce and society, and projects' net savings or losses, depending on the price of the vaccine and the number of persons vaccinated. (30) These cost comparisons between the vaccination and the lack of vaccination are based on computerized computations, taking into account different parameters. These indicators often are produced by computerized mathematical models. The scenario analysis may also provide a basis for comparison between the worst-case scenario (e.g., the risk materializes and no prior action was taken) and the costs of measures proposed to prepare for the risk for a medium- or best-case scenario.

Second, the *cooperation* dimension relates to the way in which decisions are made. To a certain extent, it can be extended to the relationships with other organizations when the design and implementation of the response require the contributions of different – and sometimes competing – international organizations. The decisions with respect to risk reduction measures are the result of a dialogue (consultation process), are reached by consensus (collegial decision), and are publicly communicated (public decision). These decisions are sometimes expressed as deliberative or participative processes and considered an interactive and mutual learning process, resulting in a more democratic decision.[5] The group of experts mandated by the multilateral institution to perform the risk analysis decides collegially with respect to the risk reduction measures that will then be proposed to the multilateral institution's top management for adoption. The decision is the action of a group, not one individual. These measures are the result of a consultation process and are publicly communicated, generally on the institution's website. Such a process reinforces the binding effect of the decisions: the actors have the opportunity to address the issues and to defend their propositions and solutions (the dialogue phase); they are involved in the decision-making process (each voice has its importance); and the decisions are publicly communicated (every actor has access to the same final information). Cooperation is said to improve communication by allowing exchanges of information, the creation and reinforcement of confidence, conflict resolution, and training with respect to the risk (6 p. 203).

The existence and performance of a *consultation process* shows the presence of a dialogue. Consultation processes can take the form of general or technical meetings dedicated to the risk analysis. The consultation process is supported by the multilateral institution's general rules and procedures, and the evidence of its presence can be derived from official documents, such as the minutes of these meetings or the regulations, guidelines, or procedures issued as a result of these meetings. Such documents often describe the themes that were discussed and the manner in which the decision was reached. Information from interviews can complement the analysis.

The *collegiality of the decision*, the fact that the decision is a group decision and not that of one individual, can be attested by documents showing that the group has been working on the issue and that this discussion resulted in the production of a common document to which everyone agrees. It also can be based on the multilateral institution's bylaws or procedures stating the decision-making rules (e.g., a decision made by an assembly or a committee).

The *public communication* of the decision can be verified by analyzing measures posted on the institution's website, press releases published, or information disseminated by the media.

Third, the *monitoring* dimension of the response refers to the follow-up with respect to the implementation of the measures and their evaluation. A *reporting system* is established to track on the implementation of the measures adopted regarding the risk that was tackled. This reporting system is administered by the multilateral institution, but different sources provide the system with information. These sources include the institution itself, state authorities, stakeholders, and laboratories for health-related issues. Conclusions about the effectiveness of this reporting system can be derived from the analysis of the information it publishes.

In addition, an *evaluation of completion* of the measures adopted represents also a key element of the international response monitoring. This evaluation can consist of self-assessment reports of the entity concerned or of an external evaluation of the measures implemented. For example, the multilateral institution can carry out evaluation missions with a selected team of experts, obtain audit reports, or receive oral or written communications about different actors involved in the process (state parties, NGOs, etc.). Field mission reports, self-assessment reports, and a multilateral institution's communications, as well as dissemination of information from other sources such as the media or NGOs are the privileged information providers for analyzing whether countries applied the proposed measures.

Finally, *enforcement tools* refer to the capacity of the organization to have the measures complied with. This is a complex aspect, as multilateral institutions may issue recommendations that do not have a legally binding character and with which no penalties can be associated in monetary terms. For example, an agreement such as the IHR is self-enforcing and based on the good will of its state parties. Enforcement mechanisms can be prescribed in legally binding documents such as the bylaws, the constitution, or specific regulations, but they also can be based on informal means such as generally perceived incentives to cooperate, for example to maintain, restore, or improve international reputation and credibility.

Multilateral institutions can be confronted with not only free-rider problems but also moral hazard issues. Moral hazard is a notion from the insurance field whereby the expected payout for a loss unintentionally encourages excessively risky or fraudulent behavior. (31 p. 219) More generally, one actor may act less carefully (or even fraudulently) considering the fact that another actor is taking the responsibility for the consequences of the actions of the first actor. For example, countries may not declare an outbreak of an infectious disease (or deny the existence of such an outbreak) and take no preliminary precautionary measures such as infection control measures and social distancing measures, knowing that WHO will identify the disease, send expert teams to the field, and organize the response globally. Such behavior may jeopardize the ability to contain the disease worldwide, and WHO has to find strategies to encourage the cooperative behavior of states. Strategies of cost sharing, randomization, and regulation have been applied in the insurance sector and expressed in monetary terms. (31 pp. 227–232) Transposed to a context of global risk, the strategies may be difficult to carry out, in addition to the fact that units of measurement may be different. Cost sharing between the careless actor and the multilateral institution is difficult to establish when no monetary penalties have been established upfront for such behavior. In the case of WHO, it could implement strategies such as withholding assistance interventions. However, these actions, while targeting a state behavior, may have negative consequences not only for the population of this state but for other populations as well. Randomization consists of adding uncertainty about payouts to reduce risky behavior. Again, this strategy would be difficult due to the already high level of uncertainty existing in global risk situations, and vagueness about a possible intervention would make a difficult difference within that context. It also would increase exposure of the population to the risk. Finally, regulations can be established to limit the payout to the actors that behave responsibly. Although regulations provide expected rules about behavior, if these rules have not been agreed upon upfront, such strategies are difficult to put in place. For example, the IHR do not prescribe penalties for states that fail to report outbreaks. Therefore, WHO could, with difficulty, grant assistance only to countries that report outbreaks and leave unattended countries that do not.

Therefore, incentive-based strategies appear to be more powerful tools than coercive strategies and provide additional enforcement leverage for the institutional frame of regulations to foster cooperative behavior. For example, in accordance with the IHR, the fact that WHO will know about outbreaks from nonofficial sources of information may influence states positively to spontaneously report them in order to benefit from direct consultation before any public communication and early assistance. In addition, the incentive of confidence-gain or confidence-loss may be strong in an interdependent world in which reactions can be immediate in a response to a behavior that is considered deviant from the norm.

Stopping trade relationships could have important repercussions, and it might be beneficial to avoid them through immediate collaboration.

The process of thinking the international response can be represented in the figure below, which summarizes the key features of the risk analysis and the formation of an international response to a global risk:

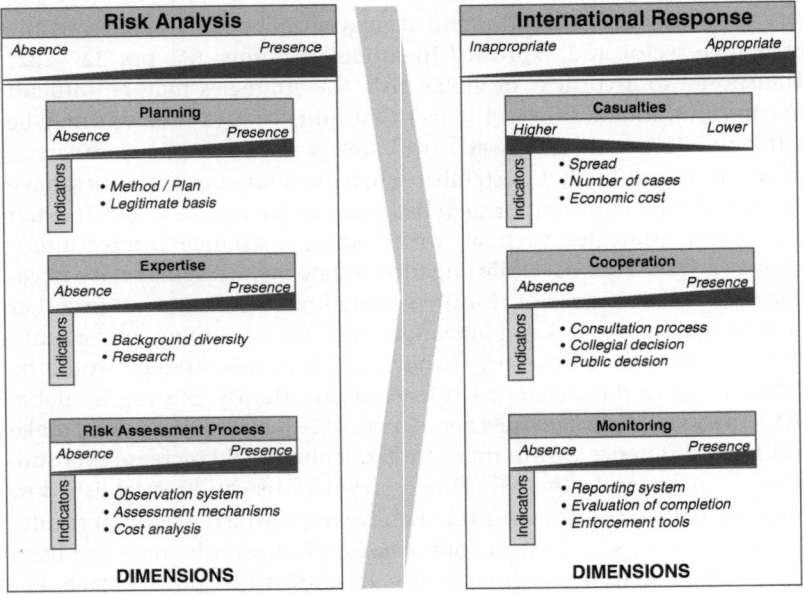

Figure 1.2   Thinking the international response

These dimensions were applied as pillars to organize our analysis of the selected empirical case studies in the field of health addressed by WHO. The absence of one dimension, be it planning, expertise, or the risk assessment process challenges the presence of risk analysis. Risk analysis depends on the legitimacy and methodology, on the work of the experts, and on risk assessment mechanisms developed to address the risk. The same is true for the international response. An appropriate international response includes cooperation and response monitoring and results in lower casualties. The first case addresses WHO's guidelines with respect to SARS and the recommendations issued by WHO from February 26, 2003 (date of the first reported emergence of the disease in Hanoi, Vietnam), to July 5, 2003 (WHO announcement that the last human chain of transmission was broken). And the second case analyzes WHO's preparedness activities for facing a risk of human influenza pandemic that could arise from the avian influenza H5N1 outbreaks from February 19, 2003, to December 31, 2008. These cases were analyzed using a qualitative approach based on content analysis of documentation – mainly primary sources – and interviews of actors and researchers.

2

Severe Acute Respiratory Syndrome: Analysis of a Successful Containment

SARS, a human infection caused by a coronavirus, is considered to be the first severe infectious disease to emerge in the twenty-first century that poses a serious threat to global health security, the livelihood of populations, the functioning of health systems, and the stability and growth of economies. (32) Its outbreak and rapid international spread through Asia, North America, and Europe in 2003 represented major challenges for people's health, economies, and international trade.

The outbreak took place from November 2002 to July 2003, and led to 8,096 cases and 774 deaths in 29 countries and regions, with an overall case-fatality ratio[1] of 9.6%. (33) When WHO alerted the world about SARS on March 12, 2003, there was still substantial uncertainty about the disease. Its cause and how it had developed were unknown, treatments were ineffective, and tests for all known causes of respiratory illness turned up negative. (34 p. 49) In various Asian hospitals, people who were dying from this mysterious disease presented similar symptoms, confirming fears of a worldwide spread of the disease that could have a devastating human, social, and economic impact.

The SARS outbreak occurred in an international context of growing concern about infectious diseases as a resurgent public health issue. Several infectious disease outbreaks, such as cholera in South America in 1991, pneumonic plague in India in 1994, and Ebola hemorrhagic fever in Africa in 1995, had demonstrated the need for stronger international cooperation in forming and implementing responses and in sharing the latest accurate information during the course of the outbreak in a timely way. (35 p. 92) In 1996, WHO began setting up a new emerging infectious disease program to better detect and respond to such outbreaks.

(36) This initiative resulted in the establishment in 1999 of the Global Public Health Intelligence Network (GPHIN),[2] which scanned newsfeeds in English and French, and in the launch in 2000 of the Global Outbreak Alert and Response Network (GOARN),[3] which brought together some 120 partners.

Over the course of a few months, the world was put on alert regarding this new disease, which many observers feared would become a pandemic with a severe economic and social impact. Although the total number of fatal cases remained low in comparison, for example, to the 3.7 million estimated deaths from respiratory diseases and the 2.8 million estimated number of deaths from HIV/AIDS in 2003, (39 pp. 154–158) the special features of SARS made it a global public health risk. First, its spread from person to person required no specific vector. Second, it incubated silently for about one week and presented the symptoms of many other diseases, particularly endangering hospital staff. Finally, it killed about 10% of those infected. These features meant that the disease could spread easily along the routes of international air travel, placing every city with an international airport at risk from imported cases (40).

According to some authors, the perception of risk of a SARS pandemic resulted in a disproportionate economic impact. Nevertheless, the necessity of contending with SARS was considered an historic moment in the governance of risks of global infectious disease. (41 p. 7) The effort represented the first successful management of an emerging infectious disease in globalized societies and economies of the twenty-first century.

2.1   SARS risk analysis

The account of the SARS story brings into focus several aspects of the performance of a risk analysis by WHO. WHO verified information about possible outbreaks of a new disease, activated an influenza surveillance network that could perform laboratory tests, led field investigations early in the process (except in China) to learn about the cases being detected in affected areas, and evaluated these results and the regional and then the international spread of the disease in order to issue recommendations. Estimates of the SARS risk were based on qualitative elements, for the probability of risk and the consequences could not be precisely quantified given the high level of uncertainty. This initial assessment was done in the context of nearly complete ignorance about the disease, so that fear of an influenza pandemic led to the global alert of March 12 and March 15, 2003. This alert was followed by a series of measures designed to acquire knowledge about the virology, epidemiology, and clinical aspects of the disease and pursue the risk assessment during the SARS crisis.

2.1.1   Method and legitimacy

WHO used a risk assessment method that was developed prior to the SARS case and adapted it to the specificities of the disease. In parallel, WHO gained legitimacy for its actions by issuing recommendations that were largely followed and validated later in the process by the World Health Assembly.

2.1.1.1   Risk assessment method

WHO developed risk assessment methods that could be used jointly to address SARS at different levels: at the organizational level in assessing the public health event and leading the scientific assessment of the disease, at country levels in improving national public health policies, and at the disease level in formulating guidelines to be used as standard protocols for known diseases. WHO's risk assessment of SARS was based on consistently combining its overall risk assessment framework, its alert and response method, and elements of the influenza plan of 1999. In the case of an outbreak of an infectious disease, the alert-and-response method, in compliance with the overall risk assessment framework, focuses on assessing the infectious nature of the disease and therefore its potential to spread internationally, taking into account the need to effectively cope with the disease as quickly as possible.

In its World Health Report 2002, "Reducing Risks, Promoting Healthy Life," (26 p. 8), the organization defines risk as "a probability of an adverse outcome, or a factor that raises this probability," and provides a framework for risk assessment consisting of "a systematic approach to estimating the burden of disease and injury due to different risks." This approach is based on the "Red Book" framework of risk analysis developed by the American National Research Council (described in Chapter 1), and seeks to guide countries and the organization itself in assessing risk in order to take effective countermeasures and improve health.

WHO's risk assessment framework consists of four major steps. (26 p. 10) The first step is hazard identification (i.e., virus X causes disease Y). Second is an exposure assessment to estimate the extent to which a given population is exposed to the hazard. Third is a dose-response (or cause-effect) assessment that relates the probability of a health effect to the degree of exposure. Fourth is a risk characterization that consists of calculating the estimated health risk, such as the number of people predicted to experience a particular disease for a particular population. This step also includes the estimation and the communication of uncertainties. This risk assessment framework was applied in the case of the SARS outbreak.

For outbreaks of infectious diseases, this framework is used in conjunction with the *Guiding Principles for International Outbreak Alert and Response* (42) published by the Epidemic Alert and Response,[4] which is the method used by WHO to identify and evaluate health events. This method will be integrated into the revised IHR 2005 and formalized in the *WHO Event Management for International Public Health Security*. (24 pp. 8–13) It is based on surveillance, detection, verification, and risk assessment of the event to determine whether it does indeed represent an international public health risk. A notification instrument about events that may cause public health emergencies of international concern that will be included in the revised IHR as Annex 2 was available for use for the SARS case. This annex is a roadmap for assessing the seriousness, unexpectedness, and potential for international spread and for trade and travel restrictions related to a disease or an event that could be a public health emergency of international concern, and is included as Appendix 1. How the disease is spreading internationally; whether it is a known or an unknown disease; its incidence, morbidity, and mortality; the vulnerability assessment of populations, infrastructures and healthcare capacities – all of these factors inform initial decisions about how to handle the event. Since WHO considers risk assessment to be an iterative process, the method suggests continuous investigations to increase the level of information, which is of particular importance when new diseases emerge such as SARS. (24 p. 10) At the time of the SARS outbreak, there was no risk assessment method specific to the disease, the nature of which was then almost completely unknown. In 2004, WHO published a SARS-specific method of risk assessment (43 p. 31) to be used as a protocol in case SARS should resurge.

The Influenza Pandemic Plan 1999 (44) also provided some guidance for WHO's actions. Since SARS was at first mistakenly associated with A (H5N1) influenza and only later confirmed to be a new disease, the initial response included activating the influenza surveillance network. Although it may not have been directly applied once influenza was finally ruled out, the methodology of the influenza pandemic plan may have influenced WHO staff who were working on the SARS outbreak, for these personnel had also been involved in the influenza program.[5] The 1999 influenza preparedness plan included guidelines for tracking the risk and its possible sources, as well as for determining the causal chain of a pandemic risk; these guidelines were also followed in the SARS case. As prescribed by the influenza plan, WHO coordinated laboratory research to determine the characteristics of the new virus and of the SARS disease, enhanced surveillance, and developed a case definition. WHO also provided guidelines to national health authorities regarding the surveillance, risk groups, and case management, including guidance on the best available drugs. In addition, WHO set up a SARS task force as prescribed for preparedness level 3 of the influenza plan, which coordinated the SARS risk assessment process and response.

2.1.1.2   Legitimate basis for action

Two major instruments would provide the basis for the legitimacy of WHO's management of the SARS crisis: the 1969 IHR and the resolutions of the World Health Assembly of May 2003. While the resolutions adopted by the World Health Assembly for the most part validated WHO's actions, which largely relied on provisions contained in the revision project of IHR, IHR 1969 did not apply to SARS.

International Health Regulations.   The SARS case raises an important issue. In 2003, the IHR of 1969 (revised in 1981), which were the only legally binding international instrument for managing infectious diseases with the potential to spread internationally, did not apply to SARS. In fact, these rules prescribed the implementation of mostly sea and air transportation measures to prevent the international spread of only three communicable diseases: cholera, plague, and yellow fever.

In 2003, IHR was under revision to produce a more adequate instrument for responding to the challenges posed by infectious diseases in a globalized world, and thus could not yet provide a legally validated basis for action. An early draft of the revised IHR was only a working document that was not yet published.[6] Nevertheless, its major provisions were summarized in the International Health Regulations Revisions Project published by WHO in 2002, and would inform WHO's response to the SARS outbreak.[7] On the one hand, WHO's actions during the SARS crisis went beyond the IHR revision project; on the other hand, the practice developed during the SARS outbreak anticipated rules that would be included in the revised IHR as finally approved in 2005. For instance, the scope of diseases would be extended to include public health emergencies of international concern. But authority to respond to emergencies of international relevance that could lead to the issuance of WHO recommendations under the International Health Regulations Revision Project of 2002 (45) (and that were applied in the SARS outbreak) was amended in the final version of the revised IHR 2005 to require consultation with state parties before the issuance of WHO's communications. This consultation was perceived as one way to better preserve the sovereignty of states in the process, although it does not preclude WHO from issuing recommendations without the state's consent.

Thus, IHR, the legally binding instrument, did not support and justify WHO's actions during the crisis, actions that complied mostly with a non-legally binding draft of rules. However, WHO's actions can be regarded as generally accepted practice, since member states effectively applied its recommendations and guidelines. Moreover, states generally complied with the obligation to report daily cases (as even China did, albeit in a later stage of the outbreak management) and with travel-related measures. Although some states, such as Canada, openly complained about the economic impact of the travel restrictions, they nevertheless complied with reporting requirements and did not engage in legal action against WHO.

In addition, the May 27, 2003, World Health Assembly Resolution on SARS and the IHR resolution, which were approved by member states, converted WHO's practices in SARS risk assessment and case management into formal rules. For example, the SARS resolution urged state members to apply WHO-recommended guidelines on surveillance, case definitions, case management, and international travel; to report cases promptly and transparently and provide other requested information to WHO; to enhance and strengthen cooperation with WHO; to request WHO support and assistance for the control measures; and to exchange information within the networks. The IHR resolution also authorized WHO to employ unofficial sources as a starting point in its outbreak verification process. A posteriori, member states approved WHO's actions and confirmed an action-based legitimacy that it gained through its management of the SARS outbreak.

The IHR revision enlisted the efforts of all 192 member states of WHO over several years, was approved by the World Health Assembly on May 23, 2005, and went into effect on June 15, 2007. The SARS story speeded completion of a revision begun in 1996. The revised IHR seeks effective surveillance of and protection from cross-border transmission of diseases, in the hope of avoiding unnecessary disruption of trade and travel. (45 p. 1) Its explicit goals are "to prevent, protect against, control and provide a public health response to the international spread of disease in ways that are commensurate with and restricted to public health risks, and which avoid unnecessary interference with international traffic and trade." (46 p. 15, Article 2) It enlarges the scope of diseases covered under the regulations, reduces dependence on country notification, improves mechanisms for collaboration, and provides incentives to encourage compliance by member states and the development of risk-specific measures to prevent the international spread of disease.

Another purpose of the revised IHR is to provide WHO with a more adaptive tool for internationally disseminating information, one based on a cooperative rather than a coercive approach as member states facing outbreaks of infectious diseases. Under the 2005 revised IHR, SARS is on the list of diseases – along with smallpox, poliomyelitis, and new subtypes of human influenza – the occurrence of which must trigger notification of WHO. However, a preliminary version of Annex 2 of the 2005 revised IHR was circulating in 2003, and SARS met the criteria of a public health emergency of international concern. These criteria consider the seriousness of the disease (in terms of morbidity and mortality), its unexpectedness, its potential to spread internationally, and the risk of restrictions on international travel and trade.

If member states fail to spontaneously report public health emergencies of international concern under IHR 2005, it would then be incumbent upon WHO to investigate rumors to determine whether there is or is not an outbreak, how serious it is, whether the disease can easily spread internationally, and whether it might require restrictions on international travel and trade. Based on this assessment of the situation, the organization determines what measures are appropriate to contain the outbreak. WHO then sets up a special task force and communication networks (including phone and email networks) to ensure that it is being constantly updated about the evolution of the disease, and conducts missions to evaluate the situation in the field. Based on the results of these assessments, WHO issues recommendations.

This is the procedure that was applied in the SARS case. After the first GPHIN and GOARN alerts, WHO requested more information from China and, based on initial reports, suspected an influenza outbreak. (47 p. 93) The investigations continued after the alert of February 11, 2003, when WHO received reports of a severe respiratory disease. Unofficial sources were the starting point for WHO's process of verifying the emergence of this new disease. Authorization for such an information investigation was not part of the IHR 1969, but would be folded into IHR 2005. The recommendations issued, as well as the surveillance system put in place, also anticipated IHR 2005. The 2002 project was thus modified by actual practice during the SARS crisis to result in IHR 2005, which was now the legally binding instrument for addressing public health emergencies of international concern.

IHR 2005 resulted from a consensus reached among WHO member states, which suggests that some requirements included in the draft revision of 2002 were softened (or even abandoned) in order to reach that consensus. The most important difference pertained to once legally binding measures that were now only recommendations. The list of diseases requiring that WHO be notified was not suppressed but extended to other diseases, and the list was complemented by the concept of a state's notifying WHO of any public health emergency of international concern. More consultation with a concerned state is generally required before the recommendations can be issued.

Most provisions included in the revision project of 2002 were put into practice during the SARS case, but there was an important difference in the decision-making process. This project did not prescribe any procedure, but during the SARS crisis, the highest level of the organization was involved in the decisions on assessing and controlling the SARS outbreak. For example, it was the WHO Director-General, Dr. Gro Harlem Brundtland, who finally decided to issue a global alert on March 15, 2003. In addition, a WHO task force was created and experts were consulted before WHO made major decisions. This practice contributed to the creation of an Emergency Committee, selected from a roster of experts, in the revised IHR 2005.

The IHR revision project of 2002 largely served as the basis for action and cooperation regarding the measures to be taken in the case of an international public health emergency like SARS. Although this document lacked formal legal legitimacy, the measures that WHO promulgated during the SARS crisis were inspired for the most part by the revised IHR draft, and were largely followed and applied by governments, organizations, and individuals. Moreover, some of these measures were validated at the time of the crisis by the World Health Assembly, which, both a posteriori and prospectively, recognized the authority and competence of WHO to use unofficial sources, to issue case management and travel recommendations, and to coordinate field actions among member states.

Resolutions of the 56th World Health Assembly in May 2003. The Fifty-sixth World Health Assembly (WHA) took place during the SARS crisis in May 2003, and adopted two important resolutions that justified WHO's role in handling the SARS outbreak and that consolidated its role as global coordinator in assessing and managing public health emergencies: the Severe Acute Respiratory Syndrome (SARS) resolution[8] and the Resolution on the Revision of the International Health Regulations.[9]

The SARS resolution. The SARS resolution constituted a formal recognition by the member states of WHO's actions during the SARS outbreak. It provided a formal and legal basis, prior to completion of the IHR revision, for further action by WHO should a SARS outbreak recur. Through the SARS resolution, member states committed themselves to intensified cooperation with the organization and among states and partners with respect to assessing the risk and undertaking the appropriate responses; making themselves extensively available if charged with operational responsibilities; providing timely, transparent, and complete reporting (for example, of the occurrence of an outbreak and the number of cases); and reinforcing surveillance systems.

At the time of the SARS outbreak, WHO lacked a mandate to act as an international health police that could force countries to report. (48) This resolution not only confirmed the practices WHO followed during the SARS crisis but also represented a commitment by the states to comply with its requirements. Until the revised IHR could be finalized, it would help prevent certain uncooperative state behavior that could jeopardize the global response. Certain affected member states, like Vietnam, Singapore and Hong Kong provided daily reports of the number of cases, replied promptly to requests for information, and cooperated in the management of the crisis since its beginning. China began to fully cooperate on April 1, 2003, and after some episodes of incomplete reporting, Canada also began to fully comply. During the SARS crisis, international cooperation reached an unprecedented level with the deployment of field teams (upon the request of countries such as Vietnam and Taiwan) and the coordination of scientific efforts around the world. WHO wished somehow to institutionalize this cooperation in preparation for responses to future crises. Passage of the resolution showed that, for the most part, states supported its actions in the SARS crisis, which reinforced the role of the organization.

Finally, the SARS resolution strengthened WHO's risk assessment and risk management mechanisms. It requested the strengthening of the Global Alert and Response Network and the collaborative networks, further development of research and country assistance programs, and the application of lessons learned from the SARS experience to revisions of the International Health Regulations. After the outbreak was declared over in July 2003, WHO carried out initiatives to build on the knowledge it had acquired and to increase preparedness levels should SARS resurge. As IHR was revised, standardized guidelines in aviation were also updated. Aid and loan reallocations were provided to improve the surveillance and response capacity of some national health

The resolution on the revision of IHR.   The resolution on the revision of IHR acknowledged the inadequacy of the current (1969) IHR to cope with the emergence and rapid international spread of SARS, and it treated the revision of IHR as a top priority. It first established "an intergovernmental working group open to all Member States to review and recommend a draft revision of the International Health Regulations for consideration by the Health Assembly under Article 21 of the WHO Constitution." Within this new structure, WHO was in charge of completing the technical work of IHR, keeping member states informed about the work in progress, and facilitating the reaching of an agreement. Participants from other organizations and observers could be invited to attend the work sessions of the intergovernmental group in which the participation of developing countries was to be facilitated. The establishment of focal points[10] on the basis of the SARS resolution for public health emergencies in general was also determined, as were the terms of enhanced cooperation with veterinary, agricultural, and other relevant agencies involved in planning and implementing preventive and control measures. For example, joint research with other agencies was carried out with regard to animal reservoirs of SARS and risks of resurgence of the disease. This acceleration of the revision of IHR resulted in its voluntary early adoption in 2005. It came into effect on June 15, 2007.

In addition, WHO became a more independent and rapid risk assessor, since a state's notification of an outbreak was no longer the single recognized channel of information. One major provision of the resolution, which would also be included in the revised IHR of 2005, was the possibility for WHO "to take into account reports from sources other than official notifications, to validate these reports according to established epidemiological principles." (48) This resolution confirmed WHO's practice in the case of SARS, when the organization verified the rumor picked up by GPHIN. Ultimately, the revised 2005 IHR will oblige states to respond in a timely manner to WHO's requests for verification in the case of a suspected public health emergency of international concern; this was not the case with respect to the Chinese government, which withheld information at the beginning of the outbreak, controlled the media, and refused international access to SARS victims (48).

The resolution on the revision of IHR also recognized WHO's right to alert the international community after having informed the government most directly concerned. In the revised IHR 2005, this provision requires consultation with the affected state party before WHO can issue an alert. This modification indicates that states wish to retain a certain degree of control over the organization's decisions by being able to

Finally, this resolution formalized the collaboration of WHO with willing state members to assess the severity of the threat and the adequacy of control measures, and it proposed "on-the-spot studies" by WHO teams to evaluate the implementation of control measures. During the course of the SARS crisis, WHO was finally able to send field missions to China, but the late and reluctant consent of Chinese authorities delayed the risk assessment. Vietnam, by contrast, requested such intervention immediately. Under the resolution and the revised IHR 2005, WHO can still intervene, but, as before, only upon being invited to do so by the member state.

WHO practices during the SARS crisis, largely inspired by the 2002 IHR revision project, led to official recognition and acceptance of those practices by member states in the form of the adoption of two resolutions in late May 2003. Nevertheless, at the time the global alerts and travel recommendations were issued, there was no formal and documented delegation of this authority to WHO. WHO's actions preceded the enactment of formal authorizing rules, but this usually takes place the other way around.

2.1.2   Mobilization of expertise

The multidisciplinary composition and international track record of the experts involved in the SARS risk assessment process and the integration into the risk assessment of the latest research results available in the course of the outbreak characterized the expertise that WHO mobilized to address the risk of a pandemic. SARS expertise consisted of a WHO SARS task force composed of officers and staff from headquarters, the Western Pacific Region Office in Manila, country offices, and external experts.

The WHO SARS task force, led by Dr. David Heymann, managed the outbreak in close collaboration with the WHO Western Pacific Regional Office in Manila. SARS-dedicated teams made use of operations rooms with all modern means of communication, both at headquarters and at the WHO Western Pacific Regional Office in Manila. At WHO headquarters, a team of about 30 to 40 people worked on the SARS outbreak, forming an intelligence network group and a risk assessment group staffed by experts on international health regulations and specialists on diseases such as influenza or cholera.[11]

On March 7, 2003, the WHO Western Pacific Regional Office formed an ad hoc team to deal with outbreaks that might be public health emergencies of international concern and to establish a Surveillance and Response Unit responsible for coordinating two teams: the SARS Response Group to support teams in the field in affected countries, (34 p. 61) and a SARS Preparedness Group to operate in vulnerable countries in order minimize the risks of importation of the disease to other countries.

This task force at headquarters and regional offices played a key role in both risk analysis and response coordination and implementation. In affected areas, the key activities of the SARS Response Group focused on hospital and infection control; surveillance; quarantine; laboratory testing; human resources, logistics, and supplies; and public information. (34 p. 61) The SARS Preparedness Group, for its part, sent public health and infection control experts to vulnerable countries to strengthen surveillance and develop contingency plans. Field support was provided for countries suffering from local transmission, including Hong Kong, China, Singapore, Vietnam, and the Philippines. In the meantime, experts were sent to vulnerable countries like Malaysia and Laos to help them prepare for a SARS outbreak.

In 2003, WHO requested support from the GOARN overarching network that linked in real time 115 experts from 26 institutions in 17 countries. (49 p. 185) These institutions have the capacity and resources to detach specialized and experienced personnel to provide data and perform laboratory tests. GOARN's broad geographical base enabled it to send field teams to five countries. However, the WHO regional office in Manila also organized teams of experts and consultants, since GOARN could not respond to every need and WHO had a stronger presence in America and Europe. The WHO regional office in Manila requested support from other networks as well, including the Training in Epidemiology and Public Health Interventions Program Network (TEPHINET), Field Epidemiology Training Programs (FETPs), and various academic institutions (34 p. 62).

WHO also hired consultants to act in the name of the organization in field missions, and who were often assimilated into WHO personnel. The three virtual collaborative networks created to work on the SARS outbreak gathered external experts in their respective fields (see further details on virology, clinical aspects, and epidemiology networks). WHO also mobilized and integrated local expertise in the hospitals, universities, and state agencies of affected countries.

2.1.2.1 *Background diversity*

When examining the SARS outbreak, a key requirement is attentiveness to broad-based expertise – scientific, technical, geographic, and institutional. Such expertise is manifested in teams, field missions, scientific networks, and technical meetings.

Multidisciplinary teams   The two poles of expertise – internal WHO expertise and external expertise – were combined for interventions in the field. These teams were composed of persons with expertise that ranged from clinical management, communication, epidemiology, and public health to infection control, laboratory work, logistics, psychology, and animal health. They came from many different organizations based in many different countries, and included WHO headquarters, regional offices and country offices, NGOs such as Médecins sans Frontières (MSF; Doctors Without Borders), hospitals, laboratories, universities and research institutes, ministries of health and health agencies, centers for disease control, animal research institutions, independent experts, and private companies.

To deal with the SARS outbreak, 16 institutions of the GOARN network from 12 countries offered the assistance of clinicians, data managers, infectious disease experts, epidemiologists, laboratory experts, logistics experts, medical epidemiologists, microbiologists, media experts, pathologists, public health specialists, and virologists.[12] The GOARN teams that worked on the SARS epidemic were composed of 60 experts representing 20 organizations and 15 nationalities. They collaborated with national authorities on case management, infection control, surveillance, and laboratory and epidemiological investigations in China, Vietnam, Singapore, and Hong Kong. (51) Field missions also included experts from both WHO and other organizations.

WHO has published a list of about 300 technical staff and consultants (including GOARN experts) who provided support during the SARS pandemic for the region's response.[13] The list classifies people by type of intervention, country of intervention, field of expertise or area of work, organization, country base of this organization, and duration of their intervention. Table 2.1 shows the proportions of the professional backgrounds of those experts who worked with WHO between March 12, 2003 and July 16, 2003 (52).

Most of the experts came from the field of epidemiology and public health (32%), infection control (15%), and laboratories (6%). Data are missing about the fields of expertise of the WHO headquarters' staff (19%) involved in dealing with the SARS outbreak, and also the WHO and USA CDC personnel involved in field missions (9%). But the data show that the 22 American CDC staff members were exclusively involved in the Taiwan mission. The analysis is more precise when the field missions specifically are considered.

About 244 (53 p. 1731) of these 327[14] technical staff and consultants were assigned to field missions. Epidemiologists represented 43% of

Table 2.1 SARS technical staff and consultants by area of work and field of expertise

Area of work / field of expertise	Number of experts	Experts in %
Epidemiology and public health	106	32.4%
WHO Headquarters	61	18.7%
Infection control	49	15.0%
Unspecified USA CDC / WHO	29	8.9%
WHO other regional and country offices	22	6.7%
Laboratory	19	5.8%
Communication	15	4.6%
WHO country office	12	3.7%
Logistics	6	1.8%
Clinical management	2	0.6%
Animal health	2	0.6%
Psychology	1	0.3%
Administration	1	0.3%
Funding	1	0.3%
Other	1	0.3%
Total of experts involved in SARS outbreaks (Feb.–July 2003)	**327**	**100%**

the staff, infection control specialists 20%, laboratory experts 8%, and communication 6%. Experts in logistics, clinical management, animal health, psychology, administration, and funding remained in the same proportion as shown in the table above. Teams were multidisciplinary and combined expertise from different areas. A psychologist and a communication specialist might collaborate to ensure that messages about protection measures were effectively promulgated among the populations affected and the medical community. Thus, missions were rarely composed entirely of technical experts but also included social, psychological, and communication experts.

The field missions in Vietnam, Hong Kong, and China integrated multiple fields of expertise and a range of institutions from different countries. The team that intervened in Vietnam was composed of about 30 experts who were active in five different fields and associated with ten different organizations located in eight countries.[15] The team sent to Hong Kong was composed of 23 experts who were active in four different fields and associated with 12 institutions located in seven countries. The largest mission in China was composed of 77 experts from 27 institutions and 16 countries, who were active in seven fields.

All three missions included a majority of epidemiologists in order to better track and understand the behavior of the disease, as well as a significant proportion of infection control specialists to evaluate the situation and the implementation of control measures. However, the composition of the teams and therefore of the fields of expertise varied from one mission to the next, depending on the local needs and capacities in affected areas. Laboratory experts were sent to China to cope with the lack of resources in certain areas, for example. Both Hong Kong and Singapore received smaller teams with fewer fields of expertise, since more specialists were available locally and authorities had more resources and ability to deal with the outbreak than was true in other affected countries. The participation of psychological and communication experts showed that not only technical aspects of the disease but also behavioral aspects relevant to communication about measures to combat the crisis and explanations about risk were also crucial to the success of the intervention. The participation of NGOs such as MSF in Vietnam also permitted more precise evaluation of the situation and better dissemination of the measures to be applied. Animal health expertise was concentrated in China, where investigators sought to learn whether the virus had an animal origin.

Thirteen missions were conducted in affected areas, including the preparedness missions carried out in vulnerable areas. Although the teams were diverse, resources were not abundant enough to allow all relevant fields of expertise to be systematically represented in each mission. In particular, expertise was underrepresented in the field of social sciences. While economic and funding aspects were taken into account from a macro-perspective, field missions did not systematically address financial considerations nor enlist economists to assess the impact of the disease and countermeasures on local economies. Similarly, no legal experts participated in critical missions to ensure respect for local laws by the field teams, as well as compliance with international regulations in the fields of health and trade. Neither sociologists nor anthropologists, who could provide input on risk perception and cultural approaches to health risks, were involved in field missions. Finally, although logistical planning was carried out essentially from the WHO Western Pacific Regional Office, logistics specialists were not systematically involved in supporting field missions.

International track record.   Both experts from WHO and external experts in charge of risk assessment had an international track record in their area of expertise, including publications in prestigious journals like *The Lancet* or *The New England Journal of Medicine* or referenced in MedLine. Most could point to practical experience in the field in managing infectious disease outbreaks.

WHO set up a SARS task force of highly qualified and internationally recognized professionals to lead the risk assessment and the response to SARS. This task force benefited from the solid track record of three key individuals who played an important role in dealing with the outbreak and in recommending action to the Director-General: Dr. David L. Heymann, Executive Director of the WHO Communicable Diseases Cluster; Dr. Michael J. Ryan, Coordinator of WHO's Global Alert and Response program; and Dr. Klaus Stöhr, Coordinator of the World Health Organization's Global Influenza Program. They had published over 200 scientific articles on infectious diseases and related issues in peer-reviewed medical and scientific journals, and authored several chapters on infectious diseases in medical textbooks.

Another example is the first global conference on SARS epidemiology that was held at the WHO headquarters in Geneva from May 16 to 17, 2003. About 100 participants from 16 countries gathered face to face and via video and audio linkups to share their experience. They represented academic institutions, health agencies, centers for disease control, representatives from all regions experiencing SARS outbreaks, and WHO itself (about 40 persons). Leading international experts in the fields of communicable disease epidemiology, mathematical modeling of public health, and clinical virology attended the meeting. The work of the epidemiology network was documented in the *WHO Consensus Document on the Epidemiology of SARS*, (53 p. 1731, 54 p. 115) which summarized the current understanding of SARS epidemiology, identified gaps in knowledge in order to launch further epidemiological studies, and determined how the SARS epidemiology network could support these initiatives. This meeting fostered discussion about and dissemination of the latest knowledge about SARS by scientists who were members of renowned organizations around the world, even as the SARS outbreak was getting under control.

Some indication of the international track record of the participants is shown by the fact that over a ten-year period ending in 2003–2004, *The Lancet* published 98 articles by the participants and *The New England Journal of Medicine* published 21 by them.[16] The eminent specialists in epidemiology who gathered at the Geneva meeting represented the whole range of expertise involved in the risk assessment of SARS.

2.1.2.2 *Integration of latest research results*

The quality and transparency of research is a key aspect of quality risk analysis. When the first global alert was published on March 12, 2003, almost nothing was known about the disease except that it was a contagious respiratory infection that could spread internationally and cause death rapidly. The acquisition and sharing of knowledge was essential to the design of a risk assessment that could inform an appropriate international response. During the SARS outbreak, WHO defined and coordinated the efforts in three areas of research: laboratory identification and testing of the SARS virus, epidemiology of SARS, and clinical aspects of the disease.

WHO played an instrumental role in rapidly setting up a collaborative network that included qualified personnel from institutions located across continents. Although this way of working was new, these institutions had international credentials and resources, and most had benefited from a history of collaboration with WHO. Risk assessment was updated as research about the disease progressed, whether as a result of the discovery of the new virus at the end of March, improved knowledge about the symptoms and reactions to treatments, or better understanding of the transmission routes of the virus. Secure Internet-based exchanges of information and regular video conferences were privileged forums for cooperation among these experts. Later in the course of the outbreak, WHO organized technical meetings. The first meeting of experts, held in Geneva on May 16–17, 2003, was thought to reflect the "latest and best scientific knowledge."

Virology laboratory network.   On March 17, 2003, the GOARN, led by Dr. Michael J. Ryan was coordinating 11 laboratories[17] in 9 countries in an international multicenter effort to identify the causative agent of SARS. Identifying this agent would permit resort to more specific measures than merely isolation and quarantine – for example, the development of a vaccine in the case of viral origin, or the administration of more specific drugs for treatment. Dr. Klaus Stöhr, who had been running the Global Influenza Program, was in charge of creating that network. The decision to set it up was made on March 15, 2003, the day the emergency travel advice was published. The institutions were selected on the basis of their outstanding experience in detecting a wide range of viruses and other microorganisms, history of collaboration in international investigations coordinated by WHO, access to SARS samples, high-level facilities, and capacity to fulfill the six criteria of Koch's postulates[18] required to establish a virus as the cause of a disease. Over the weekend, the network was constituted on the basis of the influenza network[19] and the capacity of these laboratories to ensure virtual collaboration.

The partners in this network shared the results of their investigation of clinical samples from SARS cases (e.g., virus identification and characterization) in real time by email and on a secure website, as well as through daily teleconferences. Samples from the same patient could be analyzed simultaneously in several different centers, employing different techniques, and the results could be compared rapidly. The research rapidly progressed toward the identification of a new virus. On March 27, WHO announced on its website that scientists of this lab network had identified a new member of the coronavirus as the causative agent of SARS. Already, on March 21, the Hong Kong University team of Dr. Malik Peiris had announced its isolation of the virus and communicated it to Dr. Klaus Stöhr at the WHO headquarters. (53 p. 1731) The Hong Kong team provided evidence that a virus in the coronavirus family was the causal agent of SARS, (57 p. 1324) working with a sample of 50 patients, all ethnic Chinese, of whom 8% had recently traveled to mainland China. (57 p. 1320) They also made available their virus isolate to members of the network for further checking and confirmation, which was obtained from the Netherlands partners (58).

Dr. David Heymann, Executive Director, Communicable Diseases, publicly recognized that the Hong Kong team was the first to discover and identify the SARS virus, which was collectively announced once all tests had been performed on April 16, 2003. (53 p. 1732) While international collaboration appeared necessary to tackle the global risk of a pandemic, the initial idea of a collective publication of research findings did not come true. Competition among the institutions to publish the results first in academic reviews remained an issue, although the collaboration did lead to the identification of the causative agent in a relatively brief period of time.[20] The Hong Kong team was the first to publish its results, which appeared in *The Lancet* on April 8, 2003, garnering international recognition. (54 p. 121) The other teams published in equally renowned publications; the American CDC and a group of scientists in Germany and the Netherlands published articles in *The New England Journal of Medicine* on April 10, 2003. (54 p. 121) This race to publish showed that it was a difficult enterprise to set up these collaborative networks and make them function. Even so, the latest knowledge available about SARS was originating in this network coordinated by WHO.

The discovery of the virus was considered to be a turning point in the research, for it uncovered the cause of SARS and allowed for a more precise risk assessment and more focused recommendations. The latest available knowledge contributed to the refinement of the risk assessment due to a better apprehension of the contagious properties of this virus. This progress in knowledge about the disease, together with the observation that sick people were continuing to travel, contributed to the issuance on March 27 (the same day that the discovery of a new corona-virus was publicly announced) of a WHO travel advisory to international travelers and airlines. WHO recommended the screening of passengers departing from airports in affected areas. In addition, the viral origin of SARS opened the door for new research to develop diagnostic tests (to replace case definitions), vaccines, and drugs. These research tracks were expected to generate targeted measures for improved detection, contain-ment, and treatment of SARS. The virology network results would have an even greater impact in the long run if they could lead to the produc-tion of a vaccine or specific drugs. Based on the network's results, WHO could envisage the development of alternatives measures of contain-ment to isolation, quarantine and health-care staff protection, measures that were very costly and time consuming in affected areas.

Epidemiological network. On March 28, 2003, the GOARN set up an epidemiology network that included 32 epidemiologists from 11 institutions (57 p. 1324) in nine countries and that was coordinated by Dr. Mark Salter from WHO.[21]

The objective of the epidemiology network was to provide data and to share the results of its work in order to reach a consensus on the epide-miology of the disease and then, on that basis, to design the appropriate public health response. The key elements to agree upon were the incu-bation period, the period of communicability, the modes of transmis-sion of the virus, and the identification of risk groups and factors. While Canada had epidemiologists, GOARN epidemiologists were dispatched to other affected areas, such as Vietnam, Singapore, and Hong Kong.

Evolution of knowledge about the epidemiology of the disease had consequences for the measures adopted by WHO. For example, the discovery that a coronavirus was the source of the disease confirmed that it was spread by droplets or by direct and indirect contact, although airborne and fecal-oral routes of transmission could not be ruled out. It was established that transmission was essentially limited to close contacts via droplets, although some routes of transmission had not been fully determined in some clusters, such as the Amoy Gardens or Metropole Hotel outbreaks. (34 p. 189) In the cluster of cases originating in the Metropole Hotel in Hong Kong, the air conditioning system could have been a vector of transmission, or, as Hong Kong Health Department director Dr. Margaret Chan speculated, (59) "perhaps they all stood outside the elevator at the same time and someone sneezed or coughed." These elements of analysis contributed to the issuance of the screening recommendation of March 27, 2003 and, what is more important, to the travel advice of April 2, 2003 recommending that unnecessary travel to Hong Kong and Guangdong be postposed.

Clinical network. On March 17, 2003, WHO set up a collaborative network of 50 clinicians (60 p. 13) in 14 countries[22] to acquire knowledge of symptoms, diagnosis, and treatment of SARS from the hospitals in the affected countries and territories. The objectives of this network were to gather, compile, compare, and archive case management data from all affected hospitals (including x-ray, laboratory, and other findings); update the case definition; prepare guidance for clinical diagnosis; and develop treatment guidance, including discharge criteria. (61) On March 26, the first "ground rounds"[23] consultation on SARS symptoms, diagnosis, and management initially gathered 80 clinicians from 13 countries in real time (62).

On a daily basis, hospitals in this network exchanged and reviewed diagnostic and treatment results, as well as case management. The results of this consultation were published immediately on the WHO website so that they could be readily accessible to WHO members, partners, and the general public. This network helped produce the latest insights into the disease, to search for an effective cure, and to improve hospital infection control measures and clinical guidelines for the management of SARS cases and their contacts. (50) During the press conference on April 11, 2003, Salter explained its benefits: "We now know from their work and bringing it together, again on a secure website, that of those who contract SARS, 96% are getting better; 4% are dying; 10% of all the numbers are requiring admission to intensive care units, of whom approximately 50% are requiring mechanical ventilation" (58).

This information was further used as the basis for a continuous risk assessment to better prepare the health-care structures to deal with these patients in affected countries. Progress in learning about the symptoms and treatments enabled a consensus about the clinical signs of SARS. This knowledge also made it possible to refine case definitions (last updated on May 1, 2003) and case management guidelines (last updated on April 24, 2003).[24] But at that time, uncertainty remained about the clinical indicators that would allow distinguishing between the 90% of people who could recover from the disease and the 10% who would require intensive therapy and die from it (58).

The results obtained from the studies on the characteristics of SARS, such as its means of transmission and control, were shared within the network of clinicians, making it possible to refine the risk evaluation and the content of the SARS disease control guidelines. The clinicians' network produced infection control guidelines and contributed to the development of case definitions (60 p. 13) that were periodically revised. Clinicians were asked to provide clinical records about chest X-rays, clinical courses, laboratory data and incubation periods, all of which was information required in order to understand the natural course of the disease and its clinical presentation. Such data, which was made available through the network, led to the development and revision of the guidelines. For example, as a result of the investigation in the Guangdong Province in the beginning of April, case definitions were updated with more precise elements developed by Chinese scientists, who had been confronted with the disease for a longer period of time than other researchers.

WHO also regarded this collaborative work as a way of fostering the development of more effective infection control measures, which had been fundamental in halting the transmission of SARS in many countries. (58) The network improved knowledge of the disease's symptoms and diagnosis, thereby making possible more adequate treatments. The results of the ground rounds, combined with the assessment of the WHO team in China that the cases were most probably SARS, and the identification, on March 27, of the causative agent of SARS, generated the second travel advisory of March 27. The new advisory went beyond that of March 15 in prescribing the screening of air passengers who were departing from a small number of affected areas for another country.

In summary, WHO and teams in the field used the latest results of researchers who were participating in the SARS-dedicated international collaborative networks focusing on virology, clinical management, and epidemiology. WHO's risk analysis thus encompassed the latest insights about SARS. This was particularly critical in the context of such an emerging disease, the combating of which involved making decisions and proposing measures despite chronically high levels of uncertainty, for which no specific standard protocol was in place and that necessitated innovative ways of addressing the risk.[25] WHO relied on the continuous and rapid acquisition of knowledge about the disease, and efficient integration of its latest state of knowledge into the recommendations that would be publicly communicated. For example, the identification of the virus enabled the refinement of case definitions and case management guidelines. Similarly, the exchange of descriptions of cases, courses, and diagnostics provided input for updating case definitions that could then be submitted to health authorities for screening.[26] WHO could not rely on preestablished strict guidelines due to the fact that the disease was hitherto unknown. The risk could not be calculated upfront due to the lack of sufficient data to quantify it with a satisfactory level of confidence. WHO followed the research closely and adapted its guidelines on the basis of each new element, motivated by a constant concern to prevent a global epidemic.

2.1.3 Risk assessment process

Planning, the mobilization of expertise, and the integration of the latest available research are essential but not sufficient conditions to complete a risk analysis. Risk assessment mechanisms have to be deployed in order to identify and evaluate the risk.

2.1.3.1 *Observation system*

The SARS risk assessment was based on an observation system consisting of three pillars that each contributed to better-informed decisions: rumor surveillance at the initial stages of the outbreak, the influenza surveillance network when an influenza outbreak was suspected, and SARS-specific virology, clinical, and epidemiological networks set up in the course of the outbreak.

Rumor surveillance. The rumor surveillance process relied on two major sources: the GPHIN for media sources and rumors promulgated by anonymous individuals. The GPHIN raised the first alert about the SARS outbreak, as it did for other outbreaks between 1998 and 2001.[27] The GPHIN is an early warning system that scans rumors and reports of suspicious diseases (34 p. 51) that are the basis of a daily risk assessment performed at WHO headquarters in Geneva. The interest of such a system in the case of a new disease outbreak such as SARS was to report unofficial information about unusual events relevant to public health that governments might be reluctant to report and to speed up the exchange of information to promote early international action to contain a possible epidemic. However, the system was overwhelmed during the SARS outbreak, encountering access problems. In addition, the GPHIN was limited to French and English news. Its efficiency in developing countries, where little information is posted on the Internet, and information is often subject to government censorship (64 e14) has been questioned. Since the SARS outbreak, this system has been further developed in order to upgrade its platform and cover more sources in several additional languages.

The second source of rumors was individuals. A first email sent on February 10, 2003, to Alan Schnur, Communicable Disease Team Leader of WHO China, by the son of a former WHO staff member reported a "strange contagious disease" that "left already 100 people dead...in Guangdong Province, in the space of one week." (34 p. 75) The email was followed by anonymous emails of members of the public or NGOs reporting to WHO that people who had contracted an infectious disease had been admitted to different hospitals in various regions. WHO then contacted governments to obtain up-to-date and accurate information about the outbreaks. Two-thirds of the rumors were confirmed (34 p. 70).

These two major unofficial sources supported WHO in its SARS risk assessment by providing information on the local and international spread of the disease. The system of rumor surveillance also provided WHO with more accurate and updated information when countries delayed in reporting SARS cases to minimize the economic consequences. In terms of the verification process, it appears that WHO remained dependent on the response of national governments to its information requests to allow field evaluation missions in the affected regions. The verification process of the first rumor was impaired by information biases and by organizational and structural factors. (65) First, an atypical pneumonia is not rare in the Guangdong Province in China. Second, rumors were not unusual in China, but often appeared to be false. Third, a bias occurred in the analysis, since the Guangdong Province is associated with a risk for avian influenza. Fourth, the delay in Chinese responses after numerous tentative efforts to obtain information (information requests initiated by the WHO report of Dr. Alan Schnur to Dr. Hitoshi Oshitani, WHO's Regional Adviser for Communicable Disease Surveillance and Response, and then to WHO headquarters, which sent an official letter from WHO to the Chinese Ministry of Health, which did not immediately reply). Fifth, incorrect identification of chlamydia as the source of the disease by the Chinese scientists – and cultural pressure to stick to that response even when scientists in Beijing identified a new virus late February 2003 – revealed structural deficiencies in the scientific analysis of health issues in China.

The rumors surveillance system captured initial information that was analyzed by WHO and verified with authorities of the states concerned. In the case of SARS, this information about rumors initially fed the risk assessment process, and China's attitude, along with the rapid international spread of the disease, increased the risk for the organization. The process of verifying the rumor was key as it was the first analysis that determined the presence – or absence – of a potential risk, and the necessity of launching the disease identification process. This identification process was biased by the false intuition about possible avian influenza cases, which probably delayed investigation of other possible sources of the disease. In addition, the reluctance of the Chinese authorities to provide critical information (such as the identification of a new virus at the end of February) and to allow teams of experts to visit the Guangdong Province prevented the possibility of identifying the cause of the disease sooner. It was only after the disease had spread to Hong Kong and Vietnam that analyses became easier and similarities could be found and eventually traced back to Guangdong Province.

Global Influenza Surveillance Network. The GOARN placed the WHO Global Influenza Surveillance Network under alert in late November 2002, following the GPHIN report of an influenza outbreak in mainland China. (47 p. 93) This was the first time in the SARS outbreak that the influenza surveillance network was solicited. Influenza surveillance, which had been established in 1947, is the oldest disease control program at WHO, and is one major partner in the GOARN. (47 p. 93) This network of laboratories was set up to gain a global view of influenza viruses and their implications for human health. These laboratories freely share influenza viruses collected from around the world and related documented analysis among themselves and with vaccine manufacturers. In 2003, the network consisted of 112 national influenza centers in 83 countries and the four WHO collaborative centers for reference and research on Influenza.[28]

The national centers collect influenza viruses and send them to the four collaborating laboratories for investigation and analysis. These four centers are able to compare virus samples to historical data that they have stored and to provide diagnostic support for the countries experiencing unusual influenza cases, such as the ones caused by the H5N1 virus. These comparisons are useful for confirming the type of virus and determining its evolution and possible instances of human-to-human transmission.

As a result of the first alert, the laboratories of the WHO global influenza surveillance program verified the December 12, 2002, report of Chinese surveillance sites in Beijing and Guangdong. This verification confirmed Chinese reports of cases of influenza B. In fact, as would become known only after WHO's team of experts visited Guangdong Province to review the outbreak of atypical pneumonia in the province, there had been two disease outbreaks: an outbreak of influenza from an avian origin, and an outbreak of what would become known as SARS.

The SARS outbreak intensified, giving rise to the second rumor of February 10, 2003, and generating the second alert of the WHO Global

Influenza Network. Since the outbreak concurred with the detection of the A (H5N1) virus in two persons in Hong Kong, it also resulted in the activation of the WHO Pandemic Preparedness plan. The laboratories analyzed the specimens of a patient in Hanoi, while the GOARN teams in Vietnam and Hong Kong collected information about this patient and a growing number of others with similar symptoms. (53 p. 1730) The work of the Global Influenza Network activated on February 19, 2003, enabled the gathering of enough clinical and epidemiological information to warrant the issuing of the first global alert about a new infectious respiratory disease on March 12, 2003. The network also ruled out all influenza virus strains and other known causes of pneumonia from the samples taken in Hanoi, Singapore, and Hong Kong, thereby bolstering the assessment that SARS was a new disease. After this first alert, and concurring with the emergency travel advisory of March 15, 2003, this network was supplemented by the establishment of three SARS-dedicated epidemiological, clinical, and virological networks that were instrumental in the risk assessment.

SARS dedicated networks. The SARS dedicated networks also served as surveillance networks, knowledge sharing forums, and research production networks.

The SARS virology laboratory network was closely linked to the already existing WHO influenza network. It included WHO national influenza centers and WHO collaborating centers, which reinforced continuity of collaboration and developed synergies with the regular influenza surveillance program. This closeness arises from the fact that both diseases are infectious, with comparable characteristics and that the influenza network had already been alerted in response to the suspicion of an avian influenza. This virology laboratory network was in fact composed of thirteen institutions, of which eight[29] were national influenza centers (NICs) and three were WHO collaborating centers (CCs) and NICs simultaneously.[30] This network, which was initially modeled on the influenza surveillance network, evolved into a specifically designed SARS network according to the characteristics of the disease.

This surveillance network was essentially based on preexisting cooperative structures of WHO in the field of influenza, which were used to unravel the nature of the new disease in order to protect populations from it. The network worked and communicated its results about the causative agent of the virus and its characteristics, which, in turn, enabled the refinement of the risk assessment and the design of more precise recommendations and guidelines. These clinical and epidemiological networks were also set up to enhance the surveillance of the disease and its evolution. The mission of these centers was to discover what caused the disease, how it spread, and how it could be treated (54 p. 93).

The observation system deployed for the SARS disease acted on both national and international levels. National health authorities gathered information from their national surveillance systems (some of them, through partners of WHO's influenza surveillance program) about a new emerging infectious disease, information that they transmitted to WHO. At the international level, the GPHIN raised the alert, and the WHO influenza surveillance system and, later, the SARS dedicated networks were used to watch closely the development and spread of the disease. Information communicated by national authorities, combined with the information from experts involved in the virtual networks and in the field, was key to advancing knowledge of the disease and to refining the risk assessment in order to issue further travel recommendations and case definition and management guidelines.

The existence and effectiveness of surveillance systems in developing countries was often mentioned as needing improvement. In China, laboratories that joined the surveillance system of WHO shortly before the outbreak of SARS had difficulty being effective and communicating clearly due to the country's policy of secrecy. In China, investment was made in an electronic reporting system based on the national existing surveillance system during the SARS crisis in order to produce more accurate and updated reports of cases on a daily basis. (66) Vietnam requested assistance, and it promptly and spontaneously reported SARS cases to WHO. Hong Kong and Singapore installed detection and reporting of cases as soon as the outbreaks started, and voluntarily reported their cases to WHO as well. Usually, WHO case definitions were used as the basis for both national and international reporting.

Although the observation system was imperfect at the WHO level and at national levels, it contributed to the risk assessment of SARS by providing information about the start of the outbreak and its evolution. First, the identification of a new emerging disease was accomplished, thanks to concurring information from two WHO-related observation systems. Second, the evolution of the disease was closely watched, thanks to national surveillance systems of countries that reported their information to WHO so that it could update the global surveillance system (e.g., Vietnam, Singapore, Hong Kong). Finally, the SARS dedicated networks provided one common channel of information for discussing and assessing the global risk of SARS and proposed SARS disease management solutions. WHO in cooperation with national health authorities (except for those of China, at the beginning of the outbreak) was able to centralize relevant information about the disease in order to establish possible connections between the outbreaks in different countries (China, Hong Kong, and Vietnam). It was able to estimate on the basis of reported symptoms that the infection could be the same disease, and that this disease presented the capacity to spread via international air travel.

2.1.3.2   Risk assessment mechanisms

The risk assessment mechanisms applied by WHO included the application of its general risk assessment method, the decision instrument for the assessment and notification of events that might constitute a public health emergency of international concern – the future Annex 2 of the revised IHR – and the *Guiding Principles for International Outbreak Alert* (42) to identify the risk source and estimate the risk and the seriousness of its consequences. WHO used a combination of new mechanisms such as the networks of experts and the ground rounds, supported by modern technological tools like web-based technologies and videoconferences, with older mechanisms like contact tracing also supported by such new technologies as electronic mapping. The risk assessment mechanisms resulted in an estimation of the risk that was not expressed as a probability, but rather as a scenario that took into account the disease characteristics, the virus characteristics once they became known, and the level of uncertainty. In this analysis, actions to protect populations and reduce uncertainty played a key role. The absence of knowledge at the initial stage was addressed by early decisions on standard precautionary measures such as isolation of patients and quarantine until the disease and its modes of transmission could be better known, which were expected in turn to help evaluate and potentially reduce the global impact of the disease. Subsequent discoveries allowed for more targeted measures to reduce the risk.

Application of risk assessment method. The *Guiding Principles for International Outbreak Alert* sets forth more specific guidelines that are compliant with the general risk assessment framework and that specifically apply to outbreaks of infectious diseases. They include detection, verification, and communication of the outbreak, as well as risk assessment steps. In this risk assessment, WHO considers elements such as context, the fact that the disease is unknown, its rapid international spread, its serious health impact (contagious disease causing death), its transmission capacity, it potential impact on travel and trade, and the capacities of infrastructures and health care to handle the disease and make initial decisions on how the event should be handled.

Detection usually functions based on the Outbreak Verification List, a daily list containing reports on rumors of outbreaks that have ben identified by national or regional offices, national governments, and media. After WHO verifies that there is a public health event, this list is made available on a confidential basis to public health professionals around the world. (67 p. xv) Once the outbreak is confirmed by the country, WHO publicly announces the presence of the outbreak. In the case of SARS, on February 10, 2003, WHO received a report about 300 cases, of which five were deaths from an atypical pneumonia in the Guangdong Province that the Chinese authorities, in a press conference, said was under control. The context of the spread of a new contagious and deadly disease, China's refusal to cooperate, and the situations reported in Vietnam and Hong Kong made the presence of an outbreak in China likely. But information was still missing.

WHO used other information sources (media, NGOs, other United Nations agencies, and partners in its GOARN to identify areas in which there might be new cases. Once cases were suspected, WHO and its partners followed up with countries to establish whether cases were actually occurring and what measures were being implemented to ensure containment. An epidemiological team systematically analyzed data and conducted risk assessment. (50) This analysis also entailed contact tracing to identify index cases and possibly all secondary cases in order to learn more about the transmission of the disease, and, in the end, about its origin.

Hazard identification included identification of the risk source or causative agent and the assessment of the cause-effect relationship. At first, very little epidemiological information was available. A severe respiratory disease could cause death quickly, and occurrences of nosocomial transmission and household transmission seemed to imply that prolonged contact was necessary to transmit the disease. Risk tracking, including laboratory research and testing, was performed in order to identify possible sources for the disease and points of origin. When Hong Kong reported two human cases of avian influenza, WHO activated in response to this new fact its global influenza laboratory network to perform tests about the disease. Based on the laboratory tests results, the suspicion of a form of influenza, including an H5N1 avian influenza, was replaced by the presumption of an unknown severe respiratory disease designated as an "atypical pneumonia." Analyses in China were negative about influenza. Later in the process, anthrax, pulmonary plague, leptospirosis, and hemorrhagic fever were also eliminated as possible causes of the disease. The fact that patients did not react to antibiotics caused investigators to think that the causal agent could be a virus, and this track was further investigated until the novel coronavirus was discovered.

Finding the cause of the disease (in this case, a new coronavirus) and obtaining enough evidence that this virus caused SARS were the primary tasks of the virology network. The identification of the causative agent was essential in preventing further international spread and developing emergency plans. (53 p. 1730) First, such identification could result in the production of diagnostic tests to facilitate the early identification, isolation, and treatment of patients, without researchers' having to rely exclusively on case definitions. Second, it would allow a better clinical management of patients with the use or development of adequate drugs. Third, and on a longer time horizon, it could lead to the development of a vaccine. Finally, virology discoveries would also help epidemiologists enhance their understanding of the origin of the disease, its incubation period, its infection rate, and its transmission patterns. A further step would be to discover where this virus came from. Although research determined that particular animals were a reservoir of the virus, as of today, it has not been shown whether the virus is animal or human in origin. Progress toward identifying the virus was the result of the collaborative work of different partners in the virology network (Germany, Singapore, Hong Kong, the Netherlands, and the United States) that further built knowledge based on the findings of their colleagues. (53 pp. 1731–1732) The network stimulated research and accelerated medical discoveries regarding the virus type and characteristics.

The exposure assessment consisted of estimating how humans could be exposed to the virus and with what effects, and resulted in the conclusion that the groups at risk were health-care workers and other individuals who had close contact with the patients, mainly in households. The populations at risk could not be precisely estimated due to the lack of sufficient and relevant data, but the ability of the disease to kill quickly and the rapid international spread indicated that world populations could generally be at risk, in particular, health-care personnel. In the risk assessment, the case fatality ratio is an indicator of the severity of the disease, but should be interpreted with caution. The case fatality ratio remains approximate up to the point at which data are sufficient to provide a more reliable estimate and better knowledge about the disease is acquired. Computing it using only cases for which the final outcome – death or recovery – is known leads to overestimation, because the average time from onset of illness to death for SARS is shorter than the average time from onset of illness to recovery (68).

Based on our calculations, the effective case fatality ratio was around 3% when the alert was given, about 8.5% when the coronavirus was identified, and steadily increased until it reached the reported 9.6% at the end of the outbreak. This effective case fatality ratio can be compared to WHO estimates that ranged from 4% on March 25, to 6%–10%, and finally 15%, the last revised estimate published by WHO during the crisis. Even heavily affected countries such as Vietnam continued to exhibit this average ratio. This difference was explained by the immediate and consistent application of infection control measures to contain the disease and by the persevering work of the field teams in close cooperation with local health-care staff and authorities in order to ensure the better possible treatment for the patients. However, age and general health condition would later prove to be important risk factors in the death of patients as well.

By tracing the cases and working on the identification of the index case (first case), the epidemiology network established that the virus could travel by air, which was a determining factor in the issuance of the March 15 travel advisory that was mainly intended to limit the spread of the disease. Also, it was investigated whether the virus could be transmitted by feces in air sewage (69 p. 122) after a certain number of cases appeared in the same block of flats in Hong Kong, or through air conditioning in a hotel in Hong Kong. It was determined, for example, that the disease was less contagious than influenza, generated fever, and presented a relatively short incubation period, which rendered control measures such as isolation and quarantine more effective at early stages of the epidemic when the number of cases was less important. (70 p. 1969) It also led to temperature checks that were applied in airports (e.g., in Singapore) and in the streets (e.g., in China).

Dose-response or cause-effect assessment depends on the amount of exposure necessary to cause the disease. Is the small quantity of virus diffused while talking sufficient to infect the other person engaged in the conversation? This aspect was difficult to establish, for knowledge of the disease was progressing at the same time that the outbreak was developing. The cause-effect or dose-response relationship remained unclear until the very end of the outbreak, but it was suspected that SARS could be transmitted easily from human to human by droplets,[31] which led to additional precautions in dealing with patients. The key factor was that the hospital staff seemed to be the group at highest risk, accounting for 20% of total reported cases. (71 p. 7) It later appeared that members of the health-care staff were often not aware of the risk and/or were not taking adequate protection measures when dealing patients suffering from SARS. The clinicians' network was instrumental in gaining knowledge about the symptoms and linking them with the epidemiological factors to improve protection for the hospital staff. For example, WHO issued a series of guidelines to improve the handling of SARS patients in hospitals and to decrease the risk of health-care personnel's catching the disease.

Risk characterization should result in a risk estimate derived from the calculation of a risk, such as the number of people who could catch SARS in a particular population. This phase can give rise to a quantitative result mostly in the form of a probability or to a qualitative result expressed by scenarios. The reproduction number, defined as the average number of secondary cases generated by one primary case in a susceptible population, is one measure of the risk of an infectious disease in terms of potential spread and consequences among a population. The basic reproduction number of a known disease such as influenza measures the risk and drives the measures to be taken to limit the spread of the disease. The effects of control measures reduce transmission, resulting in an effective reproduction number that decreases relative to the basic reproduction. Once the effective reproduction number passes below 1, the epidemic is considered to be contained. Therefore, the reproduction number is simultaneously an indicator of risk and an indicator of the effectiveness of the measures taken to control the risk. If experts agree that the reduction of the reproduction number is a key measure for evaluating the effectiveness of intervention measures, (70, 72, 73, 74) they also recognize that complete and accurate data need to be available, and that the models used to predict the transmission potential of a disease need to be further developed.

Spread-modeling studies were completed during the course of SARS with the first results published on line on May 23, 2003, by two teams, one from the Harvard School of Public Health and one from the Imperial College. Both gave a reproductive number of R_0 between 2.2 and 3.7 – Lipsitch's team of 2.2 to 3.6 with an average of 3.0 (excluding superspreading events) (70 p. 1967) and Riley's team of 2.2 to 3.7 with an average of 2.7 (including superspreading events). (73 p. 1963) It was the first quantitative assessment of the risk of the epidemic and of the effectiveness of control measures. These results could lead to optimistic conclusions about the transmissibility of the disease compared to influenza (R_0 around 10) or measles (R_0 between 15 and 20), but both studies agreed that the SARS infectious agent could provoke a pandemic if no control measures were implemented. For Lipsitch's team, the relatively low value of R suggests that an achievable combination of control measures – including shortening the time from symptom onset to the isolation of patients, and effective contact tracing and quarantine of exposed persons – can be effective in containing SARS. Indeed, such measures appear to have formed the basis of effective control in Singapore and Vietnam and have, on a smaller scale, likely contributed to the prevention of major outbreaks in other countries.

Wallinga and Teunis (74) have proved that timely alerts, coupled with the rapid and consistent implementation of control measures, have prevented approximately three-quarters of all potential secondary infections of SARS. Their major contribution has been to show that the reproduction number decreased from about 3 before the alert to 0.7 after the WHO alert of March 12, 2003, for regions in which infection had been introduced in late February 2003 (in particular Hong Kong, Vietnam, Singapore, and Canada showed a higher reproduction number) (74 p. 512).

The three teams agree that in the absence of such effective measures, SARS can spread widely, independently of its initially low reproduction number. It could easily spread and become endemic, like AIDS. Nevertheless, the intervention measures are costly and not sustainable over the long run for most public health infrastructures. Lipsitch's team insists that considerable effort is necessary to implement such infection control measures in settings where transmission is ongoing, but that such efforts are essential to quell local outbreaks and reduce the risk of further global dissemination.

Although the studies of Lipsitch et al. and Riley et al. were conducted using data gathered in selected areas at early stages of the spread of the disease with a history of about two months, they provided an estimate of the risk of SARS that can be used to design control measures, and also to evaluate their effectiveness. In addition, these studies suggest that modeling the geographical spread of an epidemic is possible if the reproduction number is known, (75 p. 81) which requires that the disease be known and that sufficient data are available.

In the case of SARS, the reliability and relevance of modeling studies results remained fragile due to the quantity and quality of data available. The studies refined their results once the outbreak was over. WHO set up a modeling group, bringing together ten institutions on a secure website during the SARS outbreak, but it remained unclear whether these estimates of the reproduction number were made available to WHO before Pr. Anderson and Pr. Lipsitch presented the results of their modeling studies at the first global meeting on the epidemiology of SARS, which was held at WHO in Geneva on May 16–17, 2003. (76 p. 26) This suggests that a major concern of WHO was whether such models can serve to better assess the risk and to implement adequate control measures, as well as to adjust the response to the evolution of the reproduction number.

Uncertainty reduction. WHO mechanisms to reduce uncertainty and improve risk characterization were essentially information based. New cases and new outbreaks were reported by countries or other sources, which indicated the spread of the diseases and the acquisition of knowledge through the newly set up communication forums, leading to such advances as the identification of the hazard. Proceeding to the SARS risk assessment was particularly challenging due to the high level of uncertainty that experts were facing and the initial lack of cooperation, and therefore a lack of information, from China. At the beginning of the outbreak, the disease was completely unknown. It could not be related to any familiar disease (e.g., influenza or pneumonia). Before the global alert of March 15, 2003, SARS was an unknown infectious disease that was probably airborne transmissible, presented a high case fatality ratio of around 10%, and for which no vaccines or effective treatment existed. (40 p. 3115) WHO knew that it could be transmitted easily and could kill quickly. The organization mostly applied a scenario approach to handle the high level of uncertainty. It essentially worked on a worst case scenario in which SARS could turn into a pandemic with a significant impact on human health and human lives worldwide, but which did not provide a range for the magnitude of these expected effects. In this perspective, the establishment and follow-up of epidemic curves, case fatality ratios, and contact tracing were essential tools in the risk assessment. WHO also heavily relied on scientific research to find the cause of the disease so that the measures could be more effectively targeted.

WHO and areas such as Vietnam and Hong Kong that were initially affected lacked information about the "atypical pneumonia" in the Guangdong Province. Although the relevant health authority conducted an expert investigation, its report, dated January 23, 2003, apparently circulated to a limited audience that included neither WHO nor Hong Kong authorities. (77 chapter 3, p. 14) This report pointed out the possibility of a new disease of probable viral origin and provided information about its epidemiology, clinical features (such as an average incubation period of 4 days in a range of 1 to 11 days), treatment, preventive meas-

patients, protecting health-care staff with masks and hand washing, and communication within the province to enhance intensive care structures). (77) Knowing that Guangdong Province had a low case fatality ratio of 3.8%, (78 p. 1115) could have helped improve clinical and epidemiological measures more quickly. There is no evidence that this information was made available to WHO experts during the field mission in the Guangdong Province undertaken between April 3 and April 5, 2003, although case definitions were updated following that mission.

Before the issuance of the global alert, uncertainty was mainly due to ignorance about the disease, as shown in Table 2.2, which illustrates the balance between facts known and unknown by WHO:

Table 2.2 Balance between known and unknown facts for SARS

Known	Unknown
Severe respiratory disease caused by a virus, also referred to as "atypical pneumonia"	Causative agent of the disease (bacteria, virus, chemical or biological agent from terrorist origin)
Potential for rapid international spread	Transmission (close contact, airborne transmission, environmental contamination ...)
Potential global impact	Magnitude of impact (burden on health systems, number of deaths, economic and social costs)
Highly lethal	Case fatality ratio
Symptoms	Infection rate, incubation Cure, treatment (medicine, vaccine)

After an assessment by WHO teams in Hanoi, Hong Kong, and Beijing, Dr. Heymann, Dr. Ryan, and Dr. Rodier from WHO were concerned about the similarities in the clinical aspects of the patients hospitalized in Hong Kong and Vietnam, and concluded that the disease qualified as a public health emergency of international concern. (79) These conclusions led to the Director-General's issuing the first global alert about an atypical pneumonia on March 12, 2003. This alert said that "no link has so far been made between these outbreaks of acute respiratory illness in Hanoi and Hong Kong and the outbreak of "bird flu" H5N1 in Hong Kong," in fact, clearly showing that WHO was considering the possibility that the Vietnam and Hong Kong outbreaks were linked to the atypical pneumonia reported in Guangdong.

In terms of risk assessment, the major difference between the alert of

spread internationally by air travel, which constituted a key reason for issuing the emergency travel advisory. (41 p. 78) On March 15, WHO had received reports from seven countries with declared SARS cases: Canada, China and Hong Kong, Indonesia, the Philippines, Singapore, Thailand, and Vietnam. (80) In addition to difficult internal discussions, to complete the evaluation of the risk of spread (41 p. 78) urgent teleconferences were conducted among WHO headquarters, regional offices, and Singapore, (34 pp. 15, 101) as well as with contacts in Hong Kong and Vietnam, to discuss the situation. Any link that could be established between air travel and the spread of this mysterious and lethal disease would involve substantial repercussions for the travel and tourism industry. In addition to the international spread of the disease, the following factors also influenced positively the issuance of the second global alert (81): the uncertainty about the possibly high potential of transmission of the disease, the fact that health workers were particularly at risk, the inefficiency of the drugs administered to patients, and the proportion of patients who had suffered respiratory failure.[32] The result of this risk assessment was that this disease was probably new, highly pathogenic, transmissible from person to person, and had the characteristics to become the first severe new disease of the twenty-first century with global epidemic potential, (53 p. 1730) although no one could predict its magnitude. Therefore, WHO determined that the world should be warned, and issued the second global alert on March 15, 2003. The next day, this travel advisory was followed by the issuance of case management guidelines aimed at supporting hospitals in affected countries in order to better protect health-care staff.

The identification of the causative agent at the end of March 2003 reduced uncertainty about the disease, but did not eliminate it. At this stage, it still remained unclear how the disease had developed and where it had originated. A hypothesis led to animal reservoirs, but no evidence could be found to confirm it. In the clinical field, the virus was identified, but diagnostic tests were insufficient and no treatment appeared to be efficient, so that about 10% of patients died. On April 16, 2003, WHO summarized the remaining uncertainties: "It cannot be predicted when this [SARS] outbreak will end but the world is on high alert, is better prepared and is acting in a true global alliance to protect the health of the world's population against a threat of as yet unknown dimensions." (50). In May 2003, the causal chain was partially identified, and experts attempted to provide some estimates about the reproductive number and the case fatality ratio.

As the level of uncertainty remained significant during the outbreak, the risk assessment was a continuous process in which experts relied on the latest experimental and empirical studies to increase their knowledge about the disease, establish the causal link, and propose measures. Uncertainty remained after the outbreak was declared over. The networks that had contributed to rapid progress in knowledge about the disease during the outbreak also continued to work on SARS after the outbreak. Numerous articles were published in the second half of 2003 and in 2004 about the epidemiology, virology, and clinical aspects of the disease. Research in areas that remained uncertain, such as the origin of the disease, its transmission modes, and its treatment has been undertaken, as has the development of drugs and the tests for the production of a vaccine in the coming four years (69).

Even at the end of the outbreak, the SARS risk did not qualify as a "known risk." The initial host of the disease and how it had developed remained unknown. Superspreading events were supposed to be caused by individuals who were more infectious than others, and the probability of SARS to resurge remained difficult to establish. Knowledge had progressed, and risk can be more precisely estimated, thanks to studies such as the ones mentioned above on predictions of the spread of the disease. However, a resurgence of SARS remained a distinct possibility, and WHO and other experts were convinced that vigilance should be maintained given the capacity of the disease to spread and the lack of a cure and vaccine.

Epidemic risk assessment. Following the alert, WHO implemented a procedure for the daily reporting of probable cases, for which a standard format was provided to countries. This information was mainly sent by emails to the WHO Regional Office or the Headquarters for compiling and producing epidemic curves and making dynamic electronic distribution maps to serve as bases for the analysis. This database remained confidential, and member states did not have access to it. The WHO headquarters posted situation updates and reports of the accumulated number of cases on a daily basis on its website. Based on these data, WHO assessed the risk of epidemic and international spread, and classified countries by level of risk based on the pattern of local transmission. (34 p. 69) For each country in which an outbreak was verified and/or for each country that reported SARS cases, WHO assessed the local transmission level, assigned a rating, and published the list of affected areas on its website. An area or a country would be rated as low (imported SARS cases with one generation of local cases), medium (more than one generation of local cases among identified known contacts of SARS cases), high (high transmission pattern with local cases occurring among persons who had not been contacts of SARS cases), or uncertain (insufficient information available to specify areas or extent of local transmission).[33]

WHO's first published list on March 16, 2003, included China (Guangdong Province, Hong Kong), Vietnam (Hanoi), Singapore, and Canada (Toronto, Vancouver) as affected areas. (82) This system was refined during the SARS crisis to indicate the recent local transmission of the disease.[34] Recent local transmission has occurred when, within the last 20 days, one or more reported probable cases of SARS have most likely acquired their infection locally, regardless of the setting in which this may have occurred. Accordingly, on May 2, 2003, WHO reclassified the "affected areas" as "areas with recent local transmission" (34 p. 262).

WHO's criteria for assessing the risk to international public health were the magnitude and the dynamics of an outbreak, including both the number of prevalent cases and the daily number of new cases; the extent of local chains of transmission; and evidence that travelers were becoming infected and were exporting the disease to other areas, possibly seeding an outbreak in those other areas. (83) Epidemic curves, case fatality ratios, and risk maps based on contact tracing were the main sources of information used for the risk assessment. Travel advice was issued on the basis of this set of epidemiological criteria, including the risk rating allocated to an area by WHO. Starting on May 10, 2003, the risk rating list included a link with the travel restrictions; regions or countries for which WHO recommended, as a precautionary measure, that all but essential travel be postponed were marked with a distinctive symbol. These travel advisories were reassessed every three weeks, a period that corresponded to twice the incubation period of SARS.

Information reporting was crucial to the risk assessment, but difficult for WHO to obtain. China, one of the most affected areas, began to cooperate only late in the process, while Thailand's delay in providing information to avoid the economic impact, mostly in the tourism sector, did not prevent it from being rated and included in the list. Canada provided incomplete and incorrect information, revealing inadequacies of the public health system and hospital sector in Ontario, as well as problems arising from an unclear division of responsibilities among federal, provincial, and territorial authorities. (84 p. 378) In addition, Canada (Toronto) strongly complained about the fact that it had not been informed of the WHO decision to put Toronto on the affected areas list before the information was made public. However, WHO had extended its travel advisory to Toronto on April 23, 2003, after the Ontario government had declared SARS a provincial emergency on March 26, 2003, and emergency plans had been activated in hospitals to suspend nonessential services and concentrate on the SARS outbreak. (85 pp. 63–71) WHO decided to include Toronto in the travel advisory based on the facts that the outbreak was growing and had affected groups outside the initial risk groups of hospital workers, their families, and other close person-to-person contacts, and that a small number of persons with SARS who had traveled to other countries had acquired the infection while in Toronto.

WHO used this transmission risk assessment as an incentive-based strategy to foster cooperation. It considered a lack of information about a country, a reluctance to provide, or a delay in providing this information as in itself a risk indicator. Information was sometimes shared on a confidential basis if the context had high political or economic impact. Countries therefore had an incentive to limit their risk by cooperatively providing adequate and timely information, reducing the potential economic impact of any travel restrictions.

Information sharing and communication. In addition to structures such as the GOARN, or the Global Influenza surveillance program (investigation and data reporting) – which played an important role by sending experts for field assessment missions, laboratory testing, and reporting activities – WHO set up new technology-enabled structures to better inform the risk analysis process, that is, virtual networks of experts and ground rounds. These ground rounds were video conferences and phone conferences organized at regular intervals that gathered experts, WHO personnel, field mission participants, consultants, and local and national authorities to share information and determine the next steps. The WHO regional office SARS task force organized daily meetings for all team members and for human resources planning and logistics, as well as teleconferences with all country teams and Headquarters. It also held weekly meetings with WHO teams in affected countries, with three global groups of technical experts (epidemiological, clinical and laboratory), as well as separate teleconferences with WHO representatives in Asian countries, Pacific countries, and countries not directly affected by SARS, and with senior WHO management at Headquarters and in the five other regional offices (34 p. 60).

This new mechanism operated at the global level in a cooperative and participative manner, enabling real-time sharing of data and experience about SARS on a worldwide basis. These ground rounds were not only privileged channels of communication that coordinated responses by guaranteeing that all participants would receive the same content and level of information, but they were also key instruments in assessing and reassessing the risk of SARS in light of the stream of new information. For example, concerns about travel advisories were discussed and reassessed within the WHO teams through global teleconferences conducted every evening. (86) These videoconferences provided valuable information for WHO's risk assessment of the situation of a region, a country, and globally, and their results served as basis for the issuance of WHO reports and guidelines.

The advantages of these ground rounds were that they made possible more transparent and complete information that was updated in real time and equally shared among participants. The challenges of such a system were to avoid routine or the presence of people who were not adding value or were even slowing down the process, in order to keep the teams motivated and moving ahead with the latest knowledge. Rivalries among teams of experts were difficult to manage in order to ensure that all information was adequately disclosed, a prerequisite for planning the most appropriate measures (see discussion above regarding the dispute over the merit of the discovery of the coronavirus). Although this innovative global risk governance mechanism was less than perfect, subject as it was to certain technological problems and occasionally being overwhelmed, it still served to combat a disease that could affect all countries.

WHO also organized international meetings during the outbreak to work on SARS risk assessment. WHO had already organized international consultation meetings, but these were generally part of a consultation process that was not done in an emergency situation. In collaboration with FAO and the World Organization for Animal Health (OIE), WHO gathered a meeting of concerned scientific experts in Madrid on May 8–9, 2003, to exchange information about the survival of the virus and further investigate the potential modes of transmission of the SARS virus. Until that date, it was believed that its most important mode of transmission was close personal contact, in particular exposure to droplets of respiratory secretions from an infected person. (87) After reports on the cluster of SARS cases in an apartment block in Hong Kong, sewage was believed to have played a role in transmission.

In addition, a potential risk for infection by ingestion (food and water) had to be assessed. On April 11, 2003, WHO did not prescribe any measures on its website related to goods, products, or animals, since these were not considered as posing a risk to public health. WHO nevertheless invoked as a precautionary measure the need to reinforce procedures to ensure food worker hygiene, including active assessment for diseases. (87) Finally, the group of experts gathered in Madrid was organized into a research network, as part of the international effort to coordinate the collective scientific understanding of SARS. The purpose of the meeting was to prevent SARS from becoming endemic and to agree on a research agenda, including studies on the resistance, persistence, and inactivation of the virus under conditions commonly found in food and water processing, as well as sanitation and sewage treatments and studies related to fecal-oral transmission.

The first global consultation on SARS epidemiology was held at WHO headquarters in Geneva from May 16 to May 17, 2003, and it brought together in person and via video and audio linkage more than 40 leading epidemiologists from 16 countries, including representatives from all areas experiencing significant outbreaks and from WHO teams at these sites. (52) This meeting aimed at sharing the experience of representatives of the centers (institutions, national and regional public health authorities, and other health protection agencies) that had dealt with outbreaks of SARS, as well as leading international experts in the fields of public health and communicable disease epidemiology, mathematical modeling, and clinical virology (76 p. 2).

In terms of risk assessment and adaptation of the global response to SARS, the objectives of this meeting were to understand the dynamics of SARS transmission and to evaluate the appropriateness of recommended measures of control. In the plenary session, the participants presented data on incubation period, infectious period, case-fatality ratios, routes of transmission, exposure dose and risk factors of transmission, the presence and significance of subclinical information, reproduction number in different transmission settings and under different control strategies, and animal and environmental reservoirs. (76 p. 2) A smaller group consisting of the WHO secretariat and external experts synthesized the discussions into a *Consensus document on the epidemiology of severe acute respiratory syndrome (SARS)*[35] that specified the current stage of knowledge about the SARS disease, the recommended control measures, and areas for further research. (50) It also provided member states with a basis for establishing preparedness plans to ensure that infrastructure and mechanisms were in place to prevent an outbreak should a case be imported (50).

The conclusions of the meeting were that there was no evidence that persons without symptoms had transmitted SARS to others and no evidence that SARS had an animal host or reservoir in the environment.

The pattern of outbreaks in different countries was similar, and the measures proposed by WHO showed consistent effectiveness. These measures included identification and isolation of patients, contact tracing, management of close contacts by home confinement or quarantine, and public information and education to encourage prompt reporting of symptoms. At this stage and based essentially on data provided by China, Hong Kong, Taiwan, Singapore, Vietnam, and Canada, the overall case fatality ratio was around 14% to 15%, and seemed to vary greatly according to age, sex, and general health condition of the patients (76 p. 11).

Based on these revised risk assessment results, WHO updated its recommendations in the *Definition of a SARS Contact in Management of Contacts of Probable SARS Cases*, (88) in a web document dated April 11, 2003, to include new facts about transmission such as precautionary recommendations in confined spaces and revised information about incubation and infectious periods. (89) In addition, WHO continued to be in charge of coordinating research on the transmission of SARS, reviewing guidelines for hospital cleaning and disinfection, conducting case studies of individuals who appeared to make a special contribution to the spread of SARS, supporting modeling studies to better assess the impact of control measures, analyzing the case fatality ratio for health-care workers, and coordinating further international collaborative research on SARS (81).

This meeting consolidated WHO's position in organizing international collaboration and showed the ability of the organization to deal with the global risk of SARS. The conclusions of the meeting were that the response put in place by WHO was appropriate and that the measures proposed for case management (health care), containment (identification and isolation of patients, vigorous contact tracing, management of close contacts by home confinement or quarantine, advisories of travel restrictions) and communication (public information and education to encourage prompt reporting of symptoms) were effective. This meeting also helped feed the risk assessment process with additional questions about the characteristics of the disease. Although the disease had stopped its progression, WHO continued to assess risk in order to be ready in case it should come back.

2.1.3.3   Cost analysis

It was not made public whether WHO proceeded to in-house evaluations of the total cost of SARS to worldwide economies as part of its risk assessment. However, WHO cited total SARS cost estimates resulting from studies done by others as ranging from USD 11 billion to USD 30 billion.[36]

In April 2003, WHO publicly referred to the estimated cost of USD 30 billion for the SARS disease, (90 p. 2) and to figures published in the *Far Eastern Economic Review* in April 2003 that estimated initial SARS-related damage to Far East GDP growth at USD 10.5–15 billion.[37] These computations included the economic effects due to the decrease of retail consumption, as well as trade activities and tourism. In comparison, this amount was close to the annual donor spending necessary to significantly reduce the global infectious disease burden in the poorest nations, and the yearly budget of WHO was around USD 800 million (90 p. 2).

Different organizations and academic institutions used modeling techniques to estimate the economic impact of SARS on GDP in Asia. These models mostly presented two scenarios that differentiated themselves by the expected duration of the SARS outbreak and the corresponding expected duration of the shock to the economies ("low scenario" SARS lasts about one quarter, and "high scenario" SARS lasts about two quarters). The cost expressed in GDP loss varies from 0.5% to 3.0% in the upper scale of the "low scenario" and from 1.5% to 4.0% in the "high scenario" according to the different studies. While the figures differ due to the varying assumptions made and the methods of computation applied, they all represent a significant amount of loss (mostly expressed in GDP loss in percentage to allow comparisons) for the areas affected by SARS. East Asian economies are particularly affected, but these studies show that the economic impact is global, affecting, for example, American and European countries as well. These financial estimates remained "best estimates" based on the available information at the time and subject to the assumptions made. The major driver of these analyses was the loss in confidence that the SARS crisis generated among the public on a worldwide basis. Although Asian economies had been vulnerable in the first half of 2003 due to the effects of the terrorist attacks in Bali and the start of the war in Iraq on March 19, 2003, SARS further eroded confidence in financial markets, as well as in tourism and consumer activities. In addition to the estimates of USD 11 billion and USD 30 billion, the Asian Development Bank foresaw an income loss ranging from USD 12.3 to 28.4 billion for East and Southeast Asia as a whole under two scenarios (SARS lasts through the 2003 second quarter or third quarter), in which Hong Kong and China represented about 43% of these losses under both scenarios.[38] The largest impact was in most cases on Hong Kong and China and was rather due to the effect of the SARS disease on the behavior of many people within the economies than to the disease itself (92 p. 129).

The estimated SARS cost of USD 30 billion in relation to the 8,096 reported SARS cases resulting in 774 deaths could be regarded as high compared to other diseases, such as tuberculosis, which killed 1.7 million people for 9.2 million new cases in 2006. (93) However, experts agree that the total cost might have been far higher, and models have been further developed to evaluate the cost of a future pandemic as a point for comparison. For example, a "small" influenza that infects 0.5% to 1.0% of the population (compared to 2% to 3% for SARS and around 25% for the 1918–1919 Spanish influenza), resulting in up to 65 million people infected and lasting around two to three years, would generate economic losses of USD 1 to 2 trillion dollars per annum based on 2005 GDP data (Asian GDP loss of USD 150–200 billion). (94 p. 23) Therefore, one can conclude that the measures enabling containment of the SARS outbreak in about three months on a worldwide scale were cost effective.

Comparisons in terms of lives saved provide additional arguments for cost effectiveness. Although the means of transmission of AIDS and SARS are very different, they had a comparable basic reproduction number (R_0) of between 2 and 5, (95), which can let one think what could have happened had no measures been taken and had SARS become endemic, such as AIDS. Another parallel can be drawn with the case fatality ratio of the Spanish influenza, which resulted in a case fatality ratio in the United States of about 2.2%; Spanish flu in modern America would kill about 1.8 million people. (96 p. A03) In comparison, the overall case fatality ratio of SARS was 9.6%. Although the transmissibility of the disease was less important than for an influenza, it provides an idea of the number of deaths SARS would have been able to cause worldwide had no measures been taken to contain its spread. According to WHO, "[I]n retrospect, spending to get rid of the new public-health threat was infinitely more cost effective than having to apply resources continuously over time to control the disease. No further outbreaks occurred, neither in winter of 2003–2004 nor in the next one. If SARS had become endemic, the resources required to root it out would have been enormous, especially in the winter months, and the impact on the health system would have been incalculable" (34 p. 252).

Regarding public health costs, WHO had to assign a budget from its emergency fund to handle the outbreak and support the field missions, a fact that was not made public. WHO's intervention in the SARS outbreak required additional funding from agencies and the reassignment of available funds, to which donor governments responded quickly and generously. For example, the Japanese government's grant of USD 3 million (97 p. 76) covered logistic support and supplies for both affected and unaffected countries (personal protective equipment, including masks, collection materials for blood and respiratory samples, and internationally approved containers for shipment of samples).

WHO included in its risk assessment cost elements from other evaluations, suggesting that USD 30 billion represented the total cost of SARS. If the cost side was thoroughly investigated using different costing models and WHO openly referred to them, they were not further analyzed or compared to the total expected cost of the epidemic to justify containment action. The notion of cost per life saved was not applied, as the expenditures on SARS were for an emergency situation and not part of a long-term public health program.[39] Effectiveness was justified by the fact that the absence of these measures, which were more significant in terms of potential economic impacts than solely in terms of public health costs, would have led to a far more costly situation. While WHO has not measured this cost effectiveness in terms of human lives saved or economic costs saved, it has relied on analyses of the cost of a pandemic as a benchmark to estimate the costs of a far larger economic impact, up to USD 1–2 trillion dollars per annum, which could apply to a SARS pandemic as well.

2.2 SARS international response

WHO's international response to SARS was based on the new concept of containment that was applied after 2002. This approach to SARS aimed at sealing off opportunities for further spread, both within countries reporting cases and internationally, to support the overall objective of preventing SARS from becoming widely established as another new disease in humans. (98) WHO's international response to SARS in the form of recommendations and guidelines was organized around three main activities, case detection, patient isolation, and contact tracing, in order to reduce the number of people exposed to each infectious case and eventually to break the chain of transmission, both locally and internationally. (99) WHO's response also included the monitoring of research activities, extending support to affected countries, and communicating information to health authorities and to the public (100).

The four recommendations that put the world on alert until WHO declared the outbreak over in July 2003 are as follows:

- *March 12, 2003. WHO issues a global alert about cases of atypical pneumonia.* (79) The alert confirmed outbreaks of a severe form of pneumonia in Vietnam, Hong Kong, and the Guangdong Province in China, and recommended isolation of suspected cases.

- *March 15, 2003. WHO issues an emergency travel advisory.* (101) This recommendation declared SARS to be a worldwide threat given its rapid spread to several countries, and provided guidance for travelers, airline companies, and crews on how to recognize symptoms of the disease (defining suspected cases and probable cases). Travelers suffering from the symptoms were advised not to travel. Airline companies were instructed to report any passenger or crew member who was suffering from the symptoms to the airport health authorities, who would assess the situation.
- *March 27, 2003. WHO recommends new measures to prevent travel-related spread of SARS.* (102) This travel advice sought to reduce the international spread of the disease and recommended that airline passengers departing from declared affected areas be screened. It was complemented by recommendations to airlines on what steps they should take if they detected a suspected case of SARS during flight.
- *April 2, 2003. WHO issues new travel advice for Hong Kong and Guangdong.* (103) WHO recommended that persons traveling to the Hong Kong Special Administrative Region of China and to the Guangdong Province, China, consider postponing all but essential travel.

In addition, on May 28, 2003, the World Health Assembly adopted a resolution on SARS (48) urging state members to continue their efforts to control SARS, apply WHO guidelines, ensure transparent and complete cooperation, and foster communication. In parallel, a resolution on the revision of the IHR authorized WHO to verify unofficial sources that reported an outbreak of a disease, evaluate the seriousness of a reported risk, and lead field investigation missions. These resolutions represented a formal acknowledgement of the extensive actions undertaken by WHO during the SARS outbreak, and provided a basis for future WHO actions until the adoption and enactment of the IHR. Finally, these recommendations were accompanied by guidelines for clinical management and the handling of specimens, as well as by a list of reported cases and affected areas. These documents were available on WHO's website and provided the most up-to-date information about how to handle the cases and protect health-care workers from contracting the disease. The list of the number of confirmed cases published and the list of affected areas – based on countries' reporting – indicated which regions were riskiest based on the criteria of effective local transmission, which provided information about the evolution and the international spread of the disease.

2.2.1 Reduction of casualties

WHO measures taken to contain SARS contributed to reducing the risk of the disease, mainly by limiting its global impact. The limitation of the international spread, the rupture of local chains of transmission, and the decrease in the number of new cases, combined with a cost-effective analysis, were completed in a few months.

2.2.1.1 Spread limitation

The preservation of the global collective interest in the case of SARS includes the limitation of the geographical spread of the disease both locally and internationally. We evaluated the limitation of the international geographical spread of SARS by considering the evolution of the number of new countries affected by SARS. SARS was regarded as contained when the local chain of transmission of the disease was ruptured, which resulted in local containment but also prevented the contagion of additional regions. We studied the effects of two kinds of measures: recommendations aimed at limiting the international spread of the disease by acting on travel (mostly air travel) through the screening of passengers at the airports in affected areas and travel restrictions based on the risk assessment of the local transmission level. These two sets of measures were complementary insofar as they reduced the number of new SARS cases both locally and internationally, with local containment contributing to global containment and vice versa.

International spread of SARS. The map overleaf (97 p. 75) shows about 30 countries and regions affected by SARS, along with the total number of cases due to outbreaks of the disease and imported cases.

As shown in Figure 2.1, in absolute terms, China and Hong Kong were the most affected areas in a worldwide number of cases that remained small. China is considered as the epicenter of SARS, and the first case of SARS was retrospectively traced back to November 16, 2002, in the Guangdong Province. At the time that WHO made the decision for the first alert on March 12, 2003, the outbreak was regional: all reported cases were in China, Hong Kong, and Vietnam, and the suspicion was that they originated from the same disease. (34 p. 58) By March 15, 2003, new cases were identified in Singapore and Toronto (Canada), and on flight SQ25 from New York to Singapore (patient intercepted in Frankfurt, Germany), which showed that the disease had already traveled by plane. The first list of affected areas (areas with recent local transmission) was issued on March 16, 2003, and included Guangdong (China), Hanoi (Vietnam), Hong Kong, Singapore, Toronto (Canada),

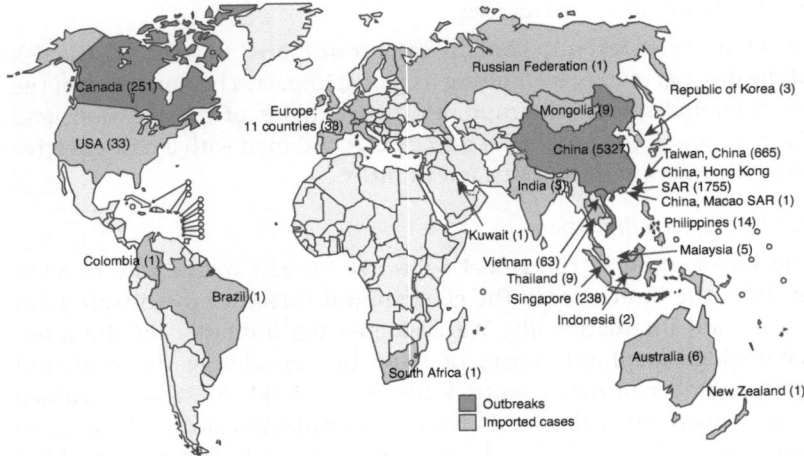

Figure 2.1   Probable cases of SARS worldwide, August 7, 2003

and Vancouver (Canada). Other countries have had SARS cases, but these remain imported cases with no local transmission (e.g., Germany).

Table 2.3[40] shows the evolution of the geographical international spread of the disease by country and date of reporting (case identification could have occurred earlier), indicating the presence of local transmission. Local transmission occurred when one or more reported probable cases of SARS most likely acquired their infection locally, regardless of the setting in which this may have occurred.

According to the table, major outbreaks occurred at the beginning of the crisis and for the most part before the second global alert of March 15, 2003, including the first travel recommendations. Of the eight areas with local transmission, three areas were infected by SARS before the March 12, 2003, alert and six before the issuance of the second global alert and travel advisory of March 15, 2003. Since March 15, only one major outbreak (Taiwan) occurred, and two other countries were added to the list of affected areas, but very few areas were rated "areas with recent local transmission."

Importation of cases continued, but the rapid development of international awareness about the risk and the implementation of infection control measures, coupled with a disease less infectious in nature than had originally been thought, helped limit the international spread and prevent local transmission. Of the about 30 areas or countries where imported cases were reported, only China, Vietnam, Hong Kong,

Table 2.3   International spread of SARS

Nr	Area / Country	First formally reported case(s)	Local transmission
1	*China*	*Feb-11-03*	*yes*
2	*Vietnam*	*Feb-28-03*	*yes*
3	*Hong Kong*	*Mar-11-03*	*yes*
4	Thailand	Mar-11-03	none
5	*Singapore*	*Mar-13-03*	*yes*
6	*Canada*	*Mar-14-03*	*yes*
7	*Taiwan*	*Mar-14-03*	*yes*
8	Germany	Mar-15-03	none
9	Switzerland	Mar-17-03	none
10	United Kingdom	Mar-18-03	none
11	Slovenia	Mar-18-03	none
12	United States	Mar-19-03	none
13	Spain	Mar-19-03	none
14	Italy	Mar-21-03	none
15	Republic of Ireland	Mar-21-03	none
16	France	Mar-24-03	none
17	Romania	Mar-27-03	none
18	Australia	Apr-01-03	none
19	Belgium	Apr-01-03	none
20	Brazil	Apr-03-03	none
21	Malaysia	Apr-05-03	none
22	Kuwait	Apr-10-03	none
23	South Africa	Apr-11-03	none
24	Japan	Apr-11-03	none
25	*Philippines*	*Apr-14-03*	*yes*
26	Sweden	Apr-14-03	none
27	Indonesia	Apr-14-03	none
28	*Mongolia*	*Apr-17-03*	*yes*
29	India	Apr-17-03	none
30	Bulgaria	Apr-24-03	none
31	Republic of Korea	Apr-29-03	none
32	Poland	May-01-03	none
33	New Zealand	May-02-03	none
34	Colombia	May-06-03	none
35	Finland	May-08-03	none
36	Russian Federation	May-31-03	none

Singapore, Canada, Taiwan, the Philippines, and Mongolia encountered local transmission. Countries with imported cases after March 15, 2003, were able to prevent outbreaks from happening in their communities or to limit their extent and duration. For example, Mongolia and the Philippines encountered small outbreaks that were quickly brought under control. After the SARS outbreak that began in Mongolia on April 17, no other area would suffer the same fate, which is only about one month after the issuance of the first global alert.

The communication about SARS outbreaks, the publication of the list of affected areas, and the application of airport screening recommendations[41] contributed to reducing the number of symptomatic persons with SARS traveling internationally and containing the international spread of SARS. After May 31, no new SARS case was identified in the areas known to have been affected – which is about 2.5 months after the issuance of the global alert. It was interpreted as a sign that the outbreak was now contained, although it was officially declared over only at the beginning of July 2003.

Travel restrictions effects.   Since the screening of international travelers – by asking questions and possibly checking their temperature as they departed from areas with local transmission in the B or C rating (adopted on March 27, 2003) – did not prove to be effective in reducing the travel of infected persons from some of the affected areas and resulting in exportation of cases, WHO raised the level of alert by publishing the first travel restrictions against the Guangdong Province and Hong Kong on April 2, 2003. Since that date, travel restrictions have been reevaluated daily based on the results of the risk assessment and the determination of "areas with recent local transmission."

Table 2.4 shows the relationship between the risk rating of an area as an "area with recent local transmission" and the issuance of travel restrictions, and the lifting of these restrictions once the area has been declared free of recent local transmission. This table is based on the publication on WHO's website of issuances of travel restrictions (107) and a summary table of affected areas (105). The starting date corresponds to the date of onset of the first imported case, which is the case that most likely started a local chain of transmission. An exception is China, where the date of onset corresponds to the first identified case in Guangdong on November 16, 2003. The ending date is 20 days after the last reported, locally acquired probable case either died or was appropriately isolated (105).

There is a link between the risk rating and the travel restrictions. Once an imported case was reported, WHO evaluated whether the case remained limited or whether there was a chain of local transmission. Then, if there was a local transmission and therefore an outbreak, the area was classified as an "area with recent local transmission" with a rating of *A, B, C* or *Uncertain*. Finally, WHO issued travel restrictions for

Table 2.4 SARS travel restrictions

Country	Area	Area with local transmission of SARS		Travel restriction	
		From	To	Issued	Lifted
Canada	Greater Toronto Area	Feb-23-03	Jul-02-03	Apr-23-03	Apr-30-03
				May-26-03	Jul-02-03
Canada	New Westminster	Mar-18-03	May-05-03	none	none
China	Beijing	Mar-02-03	Jun-18-03	Apr-23-03	Jun-24-03
China	Guangdong	Nov-16-02	Jun-07-03	Apr-02-03	May-23-03
China	Hebei	Apr-19-03	Jun-10-03	May-17-03	Jun-13-03
China	Hong Kong SAR	Feb-15-03	Jun-22-03	Apr-02-03	May-23-03
China	Hubei	Apr-17-03	May-26-03	none	none
China	Inner Mongolia	Mar-04-03	Jun-03-03	May-08-03	Jun-13-03
China	Jilin	Apr-01-03	May-29-03	none	none
China	Jiangsu	Apr-19-03	May-21-03	none	none
China	Shanxi	Mar-08-03	Jun-13-03	Apr-23-03	Jun-13-03
China	Shaanxi	Apr-12-03	May-29-03	none	none
China	Tianjin	Apr-16-03	May-28-03	May-08- 03	Jun-13-03
China	Taipei	Feb-25-03	Jul-05-03	May-08-03	Jun-17-03
China	Taiwan	Feb-25-03	Jul-05-03	May-21-03	Jun-17-03
Mongolia	Ulaanbaatar	Apr-05-03	May-09-03	none	none
Philippines	Manila	Apr-06-03	May-19-03	none	none
Singapore	Singapore	Feb-25-03	May-31-03	none	none
Vietnam	Hanoi	Feb-23-03	Apr-27-03	none	none

areas that were classified *C* or *Uncertain*. On May 10, WHO indicated on its website that nonessential travel should be postponed to countries rated *C* and *Uncertain*, clearly showing the relationship between this risk rating and the travel recommendations. (108) China (including Hong Kong and Taiwan) was rated C (except for Inner Mongolia and Tianjin, rated "uncertain"), indicating that travel to China should be avoided, while Singapore, Canada, and the Philippines incurred no travel restrictions, thanks to their *B* classification.

However, being rated as "areas with recent local transmission" did not systematically lead to travel restrictions, since other factors are also considered in the analysis. On March 16, 2003, Vietnam and Singapore found themselves on the first list of affected areas, but did not face travel restrictions. In fact, both countries managed to rapidly limit the number of new cases and the local chains of transmission due to strict infection control measures. Hong Kong, however, which also implemented strict control measures, could not be easily contained because of its proximity to mainland China and the entrance of additional infected persons into its territory. Canada incurred travel restrictions at two stages of the outbreak mainly due to inadequate infection control measures that were put in place at the beginning of the outbreak, which allowed for contamination among different hospitals. The first travel advisory was nevertheless contested by Canada, which considered its outbreak to be under control. James G. Young and the minister of health and long-term care, and several other personages, made the trip to WHO headquarters in Geneva to argue that the travel advisory was inappropriate, but without success. (109 p. 37) In fact, a second wave of SARS cases soon occurred, peaking at the end of May, and as a result Canada landed on WHO's second travel advisory, in force until July 2, 2003.

Although the traveling of exposed or infected persons is considered to have been a major source of the spread of SARS, the effect of travel restrictions and airport screening of passengers remains difficult to evaluate. Initial studies suggested that travel directives were effective in limiting the international spread of SARS, highlighting the fact that implementing airport screening, early detection, and isolation and quarantine are very costly measures that are difficult to maintain over long periods of time and with an ongoing large number of new cases. (72 pp. 75–76) WHO estimated that protection measures limited in-flight transmission of SARS and showed that cases due to in-flight exposure were no longer being reported after March 27, 2003. Between March 15, 2003, and March 27, 2003, twenty-seven persons on 4 of 32 international flights carrying symptomatic persons with SARS appear to have been infected (one flight alone on March 15 accounted for 22 of these 27 cases), and these occurred before March 23. (110) The fact that the majority of the infections due to symptomatic persons traveling by plane occurred before March 23, 2003, may indicate that travel restrictions helped reduce the potential number of travelers from and to affected areas, and therefore helped reduce the number of infected persons and areas affected. The sensitivity to travel restrictions is evidenced by the way travel through Hong Kong International Airport rebounded once travel restrictions were lifted on May 23, 2003 (111 p. 243).

2.2.1.2 Impact on human health

The reduction in new cases of SARS indicated that the risk of a SARS pandemic had been lessened. The evolution of the effective reproduction number based on the measures taken could also provide an indication of the reduction of the pandemic risk. Since the evolution of the total number of cases depends on the rate of new cases per day, we assessed the effectiveness of the measures proposed by examining whether the number of additional cases decreased once the measures began to be implemented.

Evolution of the number of SARS cases. After the global alert of March 12 and the travel advisory of March 15, coupled with the issuance of case definitions, and as the global epidemic curve of SARS below shows, the number of new cases continued to increase, with the highest peak early in April before the trend fluctuated down and up again at the end of April, to finally decrease until the outbreak was declared over on July 5, 2003[42] (Figure 2.2).

Two main factors can explain this evolution. On the one hand, there are time lags between the issuance by WHO of alerts and recommendations, their implementation, and their effects, as well as the reporting of these effects. On the other hand, China and Taiwan – where reporting and measures were implemented later – encountered a significant increase in the number of cases up to May 2003, which significantly influenced the total epidemic curve. After April 2, once the four major WHO recommendations were issued and started to be implemented, the percentage of new cases decreased consistently right up to the end of the outbreak. After April 30, the additional number of cases stayed below 6%, varying between 0%–1% from May 13 onward. After June 2, new SARS cases were no longer reported.

The peak that was registered on April 2, 2003, with 419 new cases driving the travel advisory of April 2, can be explained as a response

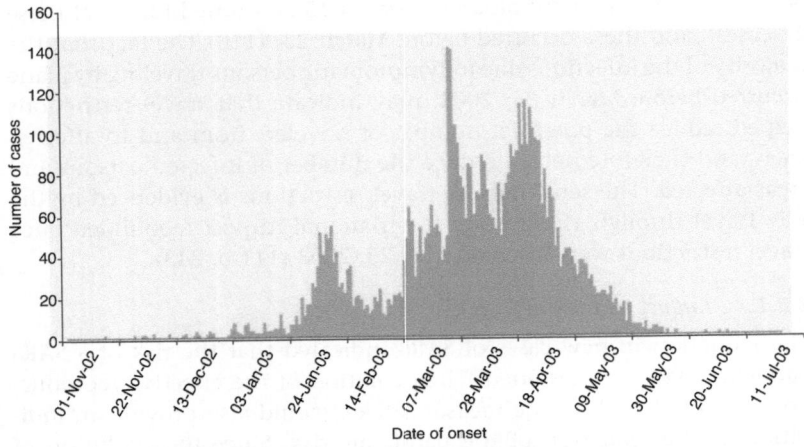

This graph does not include 2,257 probable cases of SARS (2,521 from Beijing, China), for whom no dates of onset are currently available.

Figure 2.2 Probable cases of SARS by week of onset worldwide (n = 5,910), November 1, 2002–July 10, 2003

to a continuous export of the virus, spread at Amoy Gardens in Hong Kong and with further outbreaks in Vietnam and Singapore. There was evidence of an increase in the number of cases in Hong Kong and of the continuing travel of sick persons, as well as more precise information about the infectious characteristics of the newly discovered coronavirus. In addition, a local outbreak occurred in another Vietnamese hospital on April 3, 2003, and an increase of the number of cases among health-care workers and family members in Singapore contributed to the peak of this period. Case reporting of China also strongly influenced the epidemic curve in early April. On March 26, 2003, China reported 792 cases and 31 deaths from atypical pneumonia from November 16 to February 28, although it reported only 305 cases and 5 deaths up to February 9. China officially started daily reporting of probable SARS cases both nationwide and by province on April 1, and reported an increase of 384 cases from April 1 to April 2. This spike may have contributed to the increase of reported cases up to mid-April, although cases were supposed to be reported and classified based on the actual date of onset.

The measures prescribed to identify SARS cases and manage them through isolation and specific protection measures for health-care workers proved effective, although peaks in epidemic curves occurred after the issuance of the global alerts and the first travel advisories. According to

WHO reports, after the issuance of recommendations, all countries with imported cases (with the exception of provinces in China) were able either to prevent further transmission or keep the number of additional cases very low through prompt detection of cases, immediate isolation, strict infection control, and vigorous contact tracing (113 p. 2).

The first measures proposed by WHO were intended to reduce the spread of the disease locally (guidelines to protect health-care staff and persons close to the patients) and internationally (reduction of travel, detection, and isolation of cases). In fact, hospital staff constituted the primary population at risk, and the measures aimed at protecting them from catching the disease from their patients required some training before they could be implemented correctly and consistently. Case definitions and protection measures were regularly updated to integrate the latest findings of the collaborative multicenter, such as the cautious manipulation of respiratory systems. Early detection and isolation of patients were evaluated as positive measures to reduce the spread of the disease in light of the fact that no further transmissions of the disease beyond those initially identified were reported after March 24 (34 pp. 22–24).

For a more detailed analysis of the evolution of total SARS cases, the data of the following areas have been grouped into six graphs based on the cumulative number of reported suspect and probable cases of SARS that are available on the WHO website and that were published on a daily basis. (34 p. 80) These data include confirmed SARS cases of the "affected areas" or "areas with local transmission" based on the WHO case definitions.

Evolution of SARS cases in areas with local transmission. The application of WHO control measures helped reduce the number of new daily cases of SARS in areas with local transmission – China, Hong Kong, Taiwan, Singapore, Vietnam, Canada, Mongolia, and the Philippines – and achieve its worldwide containment by early July 2003. The evolution of the additional number of cases per day in the areas with local transmission for China, Hong Kong, Taiwan, Singapore, Vietnam, and Canada (Mongolia and Philippines were not analyzed, since these were outbreaks of minor importance) followed two trends, as shown in Figure 2.3.[43]

The first trend consisted of one wave of cases that was progressively brought under control (occurring in China, Hong Kong, Taiwan and Vietnam), while the second trend shows an outbreak in two waves (occurring in Singapore and Canada). These trends took place in different

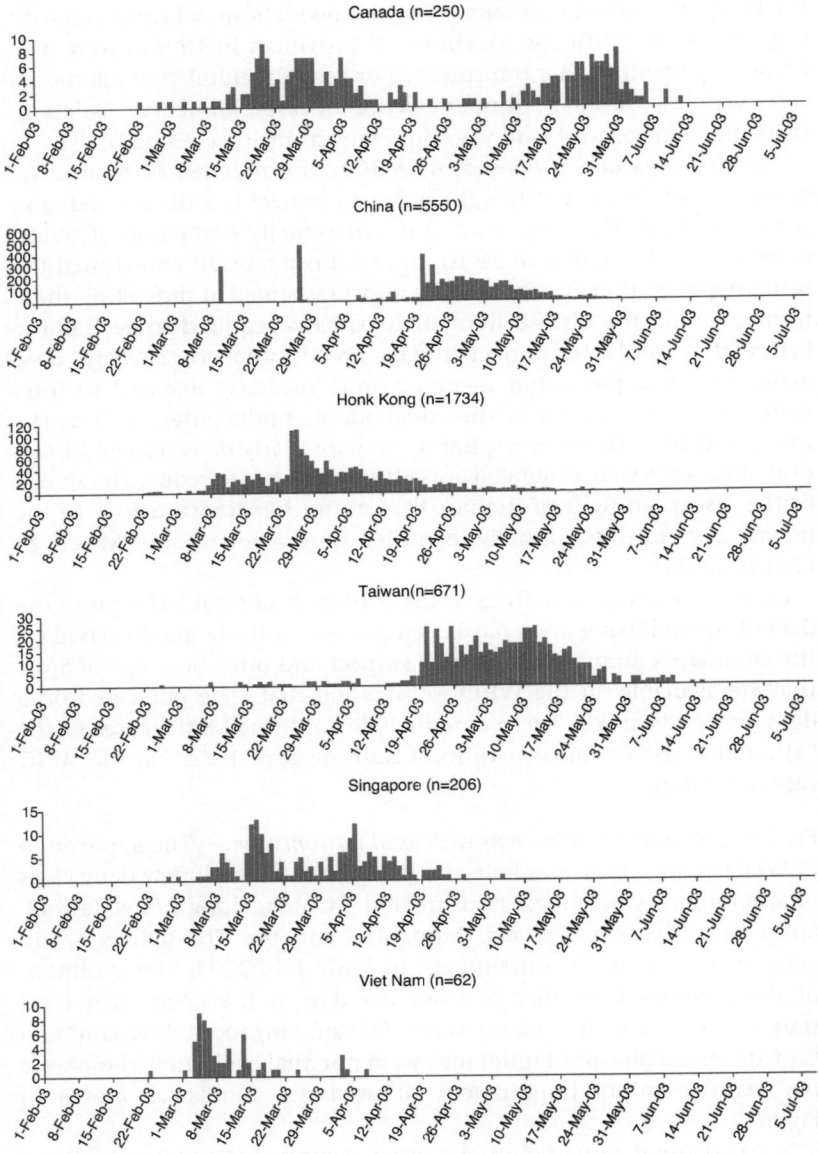

Figure 2.3   Evolution of SARS cases in areas with local transmission

transmission settings, but the rebounds in various waves did not undermine the capacity to finally contain the disease, although in particular cases it may have required more effort over a longer period of time.

Within the first group of countries, the evolution of the additional number of cases followed a similar pattern, but with a time difference attributable to the delayed application of the response in China and Taiwan. Although China's and Taiwan's[44] application of the response to SARS was delayed and China started to report cases only at the end of March, the overall pattern remains similar to the ones in Hong Kong and Vietnam. As the outbreak in Hong Kong was about to come under control, China's outbreak was growing fast and significantly. On May 12, 2003, about two months after the global alerts, while China was passing the cap of 5,000 cases (5,013 cases) with a daily increase of 129 cases (+2.6%), Hong Kong's new cases were decreasing overall from the peak of 155 additional cases reached on April 1 to 9 cases on that date. Hong Kong took measures as soon as the outbreak was declared and closely monitored the containment of the disease with the support of WHO.[45] China started to cooperate later in the process, but implemented larger scale, strong containment measures such as temperature checks, airport screening, isolation of patients, closure of public places, and quarantine. However, the last probable case of SARS in Hong Kong was recorded on May 31, 2003, as opposed to June 3, 2003, for China.

The containment of SARS in mainland China was critical to the global containment of the disease and the reduction of its global effects. WHO officials were concerned about the spread within the country and the cases that it could export worldwide. Hong Kong incurred new cases due to the proximity and exchanges with the Guangdong Province, a circumstance that contributed to the export cases abroad. Data for mainland China were incomplete, and the reliability of their reporting was questioned during the outbreak, which is reflected in the figure above with two isolated large numbers of additional cases. On February 11, 2003, 305 cases of "atypical pneumonia" had been reported by Guangdong health authorities that were later attributed to SARS. On March 26, the WHO team concluded that the Guangdong outbreak was an outbreak of SARS, which would be acknowledged as such by Chinese authorities on March 28, 2003, when it started to report cases to WHO. The global alerts and the travel advisories previously issued, designating China and Hong Kong as regions to be avoided, triggered significant economic consequences. These consequences and increased international pressure helped change China's attitude toward multilateral cooperation.

This date of March 28, 2003, represented a reversal of China's policy in three ways. First, it was a break with the previous reluctance to accept investigations conducted by international experts and WHO experts on Chinese territory. After weeks of being put on hold, a WHO mission was now authorized to investigate the outbreak in Guangdong. In all, around 80 experts from around the world intervened in China to assist WHO in its work. Second, it marked a complete change in conclusions about the source of the disease. China now accepted that SARS could be caused by a new virus. In fact, Chinese CDC officials announced that chlamydia was a source of the disease and maintained that position firmly, even though evidence inland and abroad was already challenging these results, which appeared to be difficult to combat for cultural and political reasons. Third, it marked a radical change in Chinese policy, which was that the SARS crisis would now be managed both internally and in cooperation with the international community. Finally, it triggered the resignation of high-ranking Chinese officials, including Health Minister Zhang Wenkang and Beijing mayor Meng Xuenong, who were accused of responding inadequately to the SARS outbreak on April 20, 2003, and the launch of a centrally led mobilization campaign to contain SARS in China. In the Chinese system, health is managed in the provinces, but from now on, strong direction would be coming from the central government.

Starting on April 1, China mobilized resources to contain the disease and worked in close cooperation with WHO, allowing different visits in various provinces and applying WHO recommendations. As a result of its visits, WHO concluded, for example, that the outbreak in the Guangdong Province had been appropriately managed, but that this was not the case in Beijing.[46] In Beijing, the detection of cases based on WHO case definitions had not been accurately and consistently performed, nor was hospital management and infection control. (34 p. 31) WHO also asked Chinese authorities to reexamine samples taken from victims killed by the SARS virus. (114) On April 23, schools were closed for two weeks, and on May 9, 2003, the State Council issued a new Regulation on Public Health Emergency Response to strengthen surveillance. (34 p. 84) Unlike other regions, in the Guangdong Province, infection control measures inside and outside hospitals had been implemented since February. Although the efficiency of masks has been questioned, people wore them in this province and, later in the outbreak, in other regions of China as well. Strict infection control measures have been applied, going even further than WHO's recommendations. This was reflected in the slowdown of new cases after the milestone of 5,000 cases was passed on May 12, 2003. After that date, the number of new cases increased less than 1% between May 14 and May 30, to reach 0% on May 31, 2003.

On the other hand, Vietnam and Hong Kong closely cooperated with WHO from the beginning of the outbreak. The fact that the outbreak was closely watched and documented by a WHO communicable disease specialist working in Vietnam, Dr. Carlo Urbani, helped make possible the early identification of the disease. Although the Vietnam outbreak involved a limited number of cases, the main increase in the number of cases occurred at the start of the outbreak, before the issuance of protection measures for members of health-care staff. Health-care staffers were particularly affected in Vietnam due to inappropriate case management actions that exposed personnel to the virus and contributed to a significant outbreak among this population. Due to the virulence of the outbreak in early March, a local team was assigned, with the approval of health authorities, to work with the GOARN experts who arrived on March 10 and 11. The next day, after investigating, these experts suspected that a new pathogen, not influenza, was the probable cause of the disease (34 p. 95).

Immediate implementation of control measures to prevent further transmission in hospitals, and surveillance for new cases, including contact tracing, was recommended. These measures were confirmed by the issuance of the global alert on March 12 after a teleconference with WHO Headquarters in Geneva to discuss urgent technical issues. These included case definition, case management and treatment guidelines, and the combining of information from the outbreaks in China, Hong Kong, and Vietnam. Vietnam agreed to cooperate with WHO's reference laboratories with respect to further testing related to the disease and to rely on international assistance in conducting research on the disease and the clinical management of hospitalized cases. It also assigned one hospital to the disease cases. On March 14, the Vietnamese government also established an interministerial steering committee and, following a WHO recommendation, a task force to manage the outbreak, which were privileged points for cooperation with the organization. The response to the SARS outbreak in Vietnam was an example of field cooperation, which on April 28, 2003, led to the removal of Vietnam from the list of areas with recent local transmission. Vietnam was among the first countries affected by SARS and the first to be removed from the list of affected areas.

The second trend shows outbreaks in waves that could still be brought under control in a relatively short time. Canada's health-care system has proven to be unprepared for such outbreaks, and the insufficient infection control measures taken at the beginning of the crisis failed to prevent the appearance of another cluster. While the first wave mainly concerned health-care workers, patients, and their visitors at four hospitals, the second wave primarily affected the workers and visitors of a single hospital ward. (85 pp. 66–67) Failure to provide information and contact tracing (with one patient not recognized as a SARS case) combined with inadequate case management (no isolation of the symptomatic case, which was then transferred to another hospital) was at the origin of this second cluster. With health infrastructures overwhelmed and patients being inadequately discharged, the communication problems and lack of human resources led on March 26, 2003, to the declaration of the provincial emergency in Ontario. The strict, if delayed, application of infection control measures helped contain SARS later than Singapore or Vietnam, which were also among the first countries to be affected by the disease.

Singapore suffered three intertwined waves of transmission, with peaks in the number of cases in mid-March and the beginning of April. It seemed that a few patients transmitted the disease among hospital staff and their community, creating clusters that accounted for the majority of SARS cases. Contact tracing and identification of index cases, as well as the application of stringent containment measures were key in containing the disease. The Singapore Ministry of Health formed a task force and cooperated with WHO from the beginning of the outbreak, accommodating the WHO field mission on March 21, 2003. Even before the issuance of the global alert, Singapore had already applied isolation measures and implemented quarantine at home for about 300 contacts who had been traced. (34 p. 105) Moreover, Singapore's containment measures went beyond WHO standard recommendations in both content and application. For example, certain community control measures involved contact tracing with the support of the army, mandatory quarantine at home and close surveillance, bans on hospital visits, and school closures, as well as measures affecting the management of health-care facilities that included the designation of dedicated SARS hospitals, isolation rooms, fever surveillance, and the use of complete protective equipment. Singapore even built a container with 130 wooden isolation rooms to accommodate SARS cases. To keep the population informed and disseminate measures that were to be respected, on May 21 Singapore also set up a "SARS Channel," a television station devoted exclusively to disseminating information about SARS. (34 p. 41) On May 31, Singapore was removed from the WHO list of affected areas.

Economic cost. Compared to the initial estimate of USD 30 billion, consumption of significant health-care resources and economic disruptions resulted in a total economic cost that was either lower (USD 18 billion) or higher (USD 59 billion), depending on the model applied. The total cost of SARS to Asian countries breaks down to over USD 2 million per person infected, (115 p. 39) a number derived from the total estimated cost of about USD 18 billion, using gross domestic product (GDP) as the measure of reference. The Asian Development Bank estimated total losses of USD 59 billion using total final expenditure (TFE) rather than GDP as the measure of reference, as TFE, which corresponds to the sum of domestic demand plus exports, was considered a more comprehensive measure of the impact.[47] In relative terms, Hong Kong and Singapore were the most heavily affected areas, while in absolute terms, China (except for Hong Kong) recorded the most important losses, representing about 30% of total losses, under both methods.

However, in 2008, a study of the economic impact of SARS revealed that its impact on affected economies was far smaller than had been suggested by contemporary media reports and model estimates. (116) In addition, current models used to assess the transmission potential of a disease and therefore to plan adequate intervention measures are not yet developed enough to include a cost comparison dimension of these measures. Finally, at the level of the organization, WHO's SARS budget and effective costs analyses were not made public, and therefore planned costs could not be compared with effective costs.

Although providing reliable and precise quantified estimates remains difficult, analysts agree that the costs of inaction (or of later or delayed action) would have been far greater both in terms of the ongoing health-care burden and the loss of human lives than the costs in economic disruption that countries did suffer from containment measures. One indication that the international response was appropriate in the case of SARS is arrived at by comparing the economic cost of the actions taken to contain the diseases to the estimated global cost of inaction. Preliminary estimates of the total economic costs were calculated during the SARS outbreak, and are provided in the section cost analysis above, as it constituted an important aspect in the risk assessment. In this section, the analysis pertains to final estimates computed on actual data once the outbreak was over, data that we treat as estimated effective costs of the outbreak for our analysis.

The total cost of SARS was considered to be lower than the total cost that would have been incurred had the outbreak lasted much longer, suggesting that the adequacy and timeliness of the measures undertaken shortened the duration of the outbreak. The fact that the longer duration might be caused either by delayed action or by a particularly high virulence of the disease that could resurge in waves was not discussed. If the outbreak had lasted more than one quarter, the cost would have been much larger, although estimates of the total impact varied. Rossi and Walker estimate that the economic impact of a similar outbreak lasting over two quarters of the year rather than one would probably be close to double the impact of SARS. (94 p. 21) But in the case of an extended outbreak, the economic impact should be larger than simply a multiplier of the SARS impact over one quarter, since it would have to include losses to nonessential trade and consumption, as well as secondary repercussions from the SARS impact that would increase the total estimated cost (94 p. 21).

In addition, the economic impact is related to the infection rate, suggesting that infectious diseases such as SARS, if not properly attended, could result in far more significant costs than what the effective costs of SARS actually were. *The World Health Report 2007* relied on Rossi and Walker's analysis to explain that, for infection rates of up to 1% of the world's population, one could expect a decrease in global GDP of 5%, with an additional loss of 1% per additional percentage increase in infection rate. (115 p. 39) Experts estimate that the resulting cumulative economic disruption would finally produce a shutdown of the global economy, (115 p. 39) which, fortunately, was avoided in the case of the SARS crisis.

Experts agree that SARS countermeasures had a cost (although they disagree on the final amount). But few analysts consider that inaction would have had a cost as well, and even fewer have tried to quantify it. In fact, inaction could have resulted in a new disease, SARS, becoming endemic (such as AIDS did, for example), or could have resulted in a pandemic of even larger scale. If SARS had proved the equivalent of the Spanish Influenza of 1918–1919, then losses would have been many times more than those seen in 2003, both in terms of human lives and economic impact. (94 p. 19) Rossi and Walker (94 pp. 21–23) established that pandemics infecting just 0.5%–1% of the world population (up to 65 million people) would probably see economic losses run from one to two trillion dollars per annum over a period of perhaps two to three years (based on 2005 GDP data). Such a small pandemic would represent a loss of 5%–6% of worldwide GDP, as compared to a Spanish influenza-like pandemic that could represent a loss of 30% of worldwide GDP (in 2005 terms) or over 10 trillion.

2.2.2 Cooperation and communication

WHO's four main recommendations were based on dialogue, were collegially decided, and were publicly communicated, as shown in Table 2.5.

From an internal point of view, the four above-mentioned decisions were the result of a dialogue among experts and not the deliberation of a single person. They were group decisions and were publicly communicated either by press conference or on the WHO website, or both. Consultation was internal with support groups of the task force such as infection control, clinical treatment, laboratory testing, public health measures, or travel measures, and was external to the networks of experts and national authorities in certain cases. The travel restrictions of April 2, 2003, were communicated to Chinese and Hong Kong authorities. Nevertheless, the travel restrictions were a bone of contention. Canada and the Philippines complained about the lack of transparency in the assessment of the level of local transmission that triggered the issuance of travel restrictions and about the fact that they were not consulted. They also questioned the lack of consideration of the economic impact of such travel restrictions entailed by the decision to issue such an advisory at a global level. As a result, the revised IHR 2005 included a consultation process between officials in the affected area and WHO as part of the formation of an appropriate international response to a public health emergency of international concern.

2.2.3 Response monitoring

WHO monitored the SARS response using the reporting of cases by national authorities. It ensured that WHO measures were put in place by following up on the number of cases and the observations made during field missions, issuing further recommendations if the original measures were not completely followed. Finally, WHO applied an incentive-based system to obtain cooperation and enforce recommendations.

2.2.3.1 *Reporting system: a key monitoring tool*

This SARS reporting system was a risk assessment and risk management tool. On the one hand, it allowed to follow-up on the development of an outbreak through the evolution of the increase of the number of cases, and assessment of the risk of further spread. On the other hand, it gathered information about SARS to follow up on the situation and take new or corrective action based on the analysis of this information. External and internal reporting, as well as information from both unofficial and

Table 2.5 WHO's four main recommendations about SARS

Recommendation	Consultation	Collegiality	Public communication
March 12, 2003: WHO issues a global alert about cases of atypical pneumonia.	Short consultation of experts and professionals in the field, WHO regional office, and Vietnam country office, as well as Vietnam and Hong Kong authorities.	Group decision[48] backed by Director-General (Dr. Heymann and members of his team; Dr. Ryan, head of GOARN; Dr. Rodier; and key personnel involved in the management of the outbreak in Vietnam and in Hong Kong).	Published on WHO website of Epidemic and Pandemic Alert and Response (EPR) within the media section.
March 15, 2003: WHO issues emergency travel advisory.	Short consultation of experts and professionals in the field, WHO regional office and Vietnam country office. No evidence of consultation of Vietnam and Hong Kong authorities at this stage.	Final decision by WHO Director-General based on group decision (Dr. Heymann, Dr. Rodier, and Dr. Ryan, together with Denis Aitken, senior adviser of the Director-General, and senior epidemiologists).	Published on WHO website of Epidemic and Pandemic Alert and Response (EPR) within the media section. Official and public message of the WHO Director-General: "This syndrome, SARS, is now a worldwide health threat. The world needs to work together to find its cause, cure the sick, and stop its spread." (80)
March 27, 2003: WHO recommends new measures to prevent travel-related spread of SARS.	Consultation of SARS task force, travel measures group and risk assessment group – Dr. Hardiman IHR Coordinator. Consultation of experts who are part of the collaborative virtual networks. No evidence of consultation of national authorities.	Group decision (Dr. Heymann, Dr. Rodier, and Dr. Ryan) and team members.	Published on WHO website of Epidemic and Pandemic Alert and Response (EPR).
April 2, 2003: WHO issues new travel advice for Hong Kong and Guangdong.	Consultation of experts who are part of the collaborative virtual networks. Consultation of SARS task force, travel measures group. Agreement of Hong Kong authorities during daily conference call with WHO team members of the SARS task force. No evidence of consultation of Chinese authorities.	Group decision (Dr. Heymann, Dr. Rodier and Dr. Ryan) and team members.	Published on WHO website of Epidemic and Pandemic Alert and Response (EPR).

official sources, was conveyed to the organization so that it could assess the risk and manage the outbreak. For example, the warning from unofficial sources initiated the verification and assessment processes. After issuance of the global alert, a formal reporting of SARS cases was put in place, and WHO published daily reports on the number of cases on its website. In parallel, reporting of epidemiological, clinical, and laboratory information occurred on a regular basis, mainly through the ground rounds (see discussion above on risk assessment mechanisms). These ground rounds were both a risk assessment and a risk management forum. New reports of information informed the risk assessment for reevaluation of the measures taken.

According to Greaves, (117 p. 288) a reporting system should be accurate enough to have a predictive value (a reported case should be a true case). It should be complete (with all or nearly all cases reported), timely (in that the reports are received by WHO in time for control measures to be effective), based on agreed case definitions, and electronic based. In practice, WHO's reporting system for SARS encountered problems in all these areas. The implementation of a reporting system facilitated the monitoring of the outbreak by providing epidemic trends and geographical maps, but the information was not fully reliable. It was a challenge for WHO to obtain accurate, complete, timely and case-definition-based information from the areas with local transmission of cases, as well as from areas encountering only imported cases, such as the United States. Some countries such as Thailand or Canada delayed the reporting of cases in order to avoid the impact on their tourism sector, but without major consequences for WHO analysis. Mistakes such as the reporting of cases that did not match the case definitions, as occurred in the United States, or that did not meet the laboratory requirements, as occurred in Taiwan, were subsequently corrected and final figures republished on the WHO website. While making our analysis of additional cases per day, we initially analyzed the data published under the *Cumulative Number of Reported Probable Cases of Severe Acute Respiratory Syndrome (SARS)* (104) on a daily basis and noted differences with the epidemic curves of affected areas that were published by WHO. We obtained negative values as a daily difference, which were corrected in the final epidemic curves for most of the affected countries, China being the most striking example. The completeness of the Chinese data was an issue, as indicated by the situation in Beijing. The WHO Beijing team estimated that Beijing might have as many as 200 cases of SARS, rather than the 37 officially reported cases, and requested improvement in the reporting and tracing system (118).

In addition, WHO needed SARS-related information to coordinate the global response, but had difficulty keeping up with the information flow. WHO was overwhelmed by the thousands of emails circulating in an uncoordinated way between country offices and headquarters, (36) and its website received up to ten million hits per day. The SARS task force was the central point of entry of information. The advantage was that it could centrally and consistently use the various internal sources of information (WHO mission reports, WHO regional and country offices communications, virtual networks sessions, teleconferences, phone conversations, email, etc.) to reassess the response to SARS. The disadvantage was that it failed to capture and manage every piece of relevant information in a timely and effective manner.

Although reporting was not perfect, countries generally participated in the reporting of cases. WHO launched the SARS reporting system on March 17, 2003, a few days after issuing the global alerts. Countries reported SARS cases in a standard format imposed by WHO on a daily basis, usually by email, and according to the case definitions provided by WHO. With the exception of China, which joined the network later, and the United States, which was reluctant to provide data to WHO, this reporting system was largely applied by areas with local chain of transmission. On March 24, 2003, 13 countries or regions (Canada, France, Germany, Hong Kong, Italy, Republic of Ireland, Singapore, Spain, Switzerland, Taiwan, United Kingdom, the United States, and Vietnam) reported the number of cases and deaths to WHO. China remained absent from the process until March 28, 2003, although Hong Kong and Taiwan reported their respective cases. The initial report format included the total number of cases, the number of deaths, and the local chain of transmission. On April 10, 2003, the number of new cases since the last WHO update and the number of cases who recovered were requested. On April 17, 2003, the last report was issued. This daily reporting constituted an important element of the evaluation of the evolution of the SARS outbreak in terms of local and international spread (presence of local chain transmission), severity of the disease (number of cases), and particular mortality (see discussion on case fatality ratio in the risk assessment mechanisms above).

2.2.3.2   Evaluating completion of measures

States generally complied with and applied WHO recommendations to contain SARS, sometimes after some delay, as in the case of China, or in an anticipatory manner, as in the cases of Vietnam, Singapore, and Hong Kong. Certain states, such as Singapore, even went beyond WHO recommendations, which were meant to set a minimal standard to respect. Anderson (72 p. 75) presented six categories of measures that can be undertaken to control a disease, which in fact correspond to the global recommendations issued by WHO, except for internal restrictions of population movements within a country. Table 2.6 summarizes the measures proposed by WHO and the measures applied by affected areas (except for the Philippines and Mongolia). The legal basis for action and the creation of a task force have been added to provide supplementary information, but are not part of the classification proposed by Anderson.

While social distancing measures were not prescribed by WHO, most affected areas applied them to control the disease. By doing so, they went beyond WHO recommendations. Isolation and quarantine were used with various degrees of coercion in different countries (e.g., surveillance of airline passengers' arrival in the United States, army surveillance in Singapore, a system of fines in Canada for failure to respect quarantine), but proved effective in reducing the mobility of the at-risk population, and therefore contributing to the containment of the disease. In addition, these affected areas set up a SARS-dedicated task force, which was not an explicit recommendation of WHO, but was contained as provision in the WHO influenza preparedness plan. Also, and not indicated in this table, it appeared that WHO recommendations in terms of case definitions and case management, and use of diagnostic tests, were largely followed by affected countries and other countries.

Field missions can contribute to the evaluation of the completion of measures, but the evaluation of completion remains voluntary. WHO lacks the authority to audit the activities of member states. WHO can neither review countries' measures for compliance with WHO's measures nor evaluate their effectiveness. WHO can act upon invitation or request for assistance from countries in order to provide support for disease containment (e.g., infection control, case management, etc.), but cannot act without the formal assent of the national authorities. In the case of SARS, WHO completed evaluation missions that drew conclusions about the adequacy of control measures taken in Guangdong, but not in Beijing. In Beijing, the underestimation of cases was reported even by health-care workers, contradicting the official position of the country. (58) However, these Chinese mission reports remained confidential and were not published. Because the evaluation of the completion of measures remains difficult, it has been proposed that the Communicable Diseases Department of WHO should include an operations and evaluation department to monitor the performance of member states and formally report their failures to adhere to established standards.

Table 2.6 WHO recommendations application by SARS affected countries

	China	Hong Kong	Singapore	Vietnam	Canada	Taiwan
Legal Basis						
No formal basis at the time of outbreak; generally accepted practice based on IHR revision project WHA resolutions (May 2003) 2002 Revision Project IHR	New Regulation on Public (May 9, 2003) Health Emergency Response	Quarantine and Prevention of Disease Ordinance	Diseases Act	Missing information	Code Orange alert	Revised Public Health Code
Creation of a task force						
SARS task force	Ad hoc SARS committee on April 20, 2003	Working group on Severe Community-Acquired Pneumonia (CAP), then HWBR task force (international and local experts)	Ministerial and bureaucratic task force	SARS task force Ministry of Health	SARS Scientific Advisory Committee	Emergency task force
Restrictions on entry to the country and screening at the point of arrival for fever						
Screening recommended from departure of affected areas	Missing information	Temperature checks of travelers departing from HK.	Temperature checks of travelers departing or arriving in Singapore.	SARS leaflets given to passengers departing from Vietnam	Screening of passengers departing from and arriving in Canada	Missing information

	China	Hong Kong	Singapore	Vietnam	Canada	Taiwan
Isolation of suspect cases						
Global alerts (detection and isolation of cases based on case definitions)	Done in Guangdong and in other Provinces; problems in Beijing where one hospital is designated SARS hospital	Done and SARS-designated hospital	Done and SARS-designated hospital, Tan Tock Seng	Done and SARS-designated hospital (French Hospital in Hanoi)	Done and Grace Hospital designated as SARS hospital and closed	Done and Hoping Hospital designated as SARS hospital
Encouragement of rapid reporting to a health-care setting following the onset of defined clinical symptoms						
Global alerts, WHO publicly requires a reporting of cases to WHO	Done after April 20, 2003 (War on SARS becomes a top priority)	Done	Done, plus education campaign	Done	Done	Done, plus education campaign
Rigorous infection control measures in health-care settings						
Hospital Infection Control Guidance, Discharge policy, Clinical description	Done in Guangdong and other Provinces, problems in Beijing	Done, but infection of health-care workers could not be prevented	Done, but infection of health-care workers could not be prevented	Done, but infection of health-care workers could not be prevented	Done, but infection of health-care workers could not be prevented	Done, but infection of health-care workers could not be prevented
Restrictions on movements within a country (restricting travel, mass gathering, etc.)						
No social distancing measures prescribed. Issuance of travel restrictions for countries and regions.	People's surveillance measures (quarantine, schools closing, temperature checks, etc.)	Quarantine of Amoy Gardens residents; evacuation of Amoy Gardens	Mandatory home quarantine, school closing Temperature checks in schools, offices...	None	Quarantine, temperature checks	Mandatory home quarantine
Contact tracing and isolation of contacts						
Management of SARS (guidelines)	Done	Done	Done	Done	Done	Done

2.2.3.3   Incentive-based enforcement

The implementation of the response did not depend on enforcement provisions. There were no enforcement provisions to ensure the application of WHO recommendations for SARS. Under IHR, member states were not obliged to notify WHO of SARS outbreaks and report cases nor to apply the measures recommended by WHO. Until the World Health Assembly resolution that authorized the use of unofficial sources of information, WHO member states did not delegate specific competences for the enforcement of these measures, rendering their respect or their implementation not mandatory for national authorities. However, WHO measures received a large audience and were largely followed by member countries, the media, and the medical profession, as well as by individuals with access to the Internet worldwide. The structure of the response, which included innovative and cooperative mechanisms fostering commitment, combined with fear of the consequences of the publicly communicated information, constituted the major enforcement mechanism of WHO.

The structure of the response and the use of an incentive-based strategy ensured cooperation. WHO compensated for the lack of enforcement tools by the use of a confidence incentive-based system to obtain cooperation. WHO produced and disseminated verified information about the SARS epidemic that was mutually beneficial to all who could be perceived as having an incentive to cooperate. WHO would also communicate about problems obtaining cooperation, which would be relayed in the media, raising international awareness (and pressure) from other member states to gain the cooperation of the reluctant states. WHO also argued that rumors could be more damaging than facts in terms of loss of reputation and economic impact. (115 p. 9) The consequences could be a loss of credibility that affected diplomatic relations and trade. The fact that countries did not want to be openly pointed to as the "bad player" helped in most cases to ensure accurate and timely reporting of outbreaks and cases. Attempting to conceal an outbreak in the age of global and instant electronic communication, as China did in the case of SARS, has become impossible, and the political, economic, and reputational price of such behavior is high. (119 pp. 140–141) WHO used a range of channels of communication, such as letters to Chinese authorities, to request access, issue travel restrictions, and publicly assign blame pronounced by the WHO Director-General. (54 p. 101) It remained unclear what weight the international pressure from WHO and other countries exerted on China's decision to cooperate as compared to the danger presented by the worldwide evolution of the outbreak and scientific evidence of a new virus probably originating in Guangdong. But for WHO, it was certain that Chinese cooperation was key to containing the outbreak worldwide.

In addition, governments reluctant to provide information about an outbreak for fear of the economic consequences of being on the list of SARS-affected countries could be pressured to do so through the process of verifying information coming from unofficial sources. This incentive-based system was officially included in the World Health Assembly Resolutions of 2003, as well as in the revised IHR in 2005. WHO used information and communication as a strategy to leverage cooperation from states, as it does not have and does not want the power to use coercion. Dr. Rodier from WHO concluded that "WHO cannot be both physician and police force. If we are perceived as the policeman, doors will be closed. ... Countries will comply because of a sense of global solidarity in the face of a common threat, but also they will comply because they prefer to maintain a good image and look responsible" (36).

Finally, the mandate of WHO is limited by the sovereignty of the country. WHO cannot decide to go into a country to proceed with on-site investigations unless it is invited to do so by that country. However, following the SARS outbreak in 2004, the idea was raised that the Security Council could intervene in such situations, although the modalities of such intervention have not been clearly set. If an outbreak of an overwhelming infectious disease cannot be verified and could represent an international security threat, the WHO Director-General can collaborate with the Security Council of the United Nations to establish effective quarantine measures. (120 p. 47 paragraph 144) The Security Council can support WHO in deploying investigators and experts, and in preparing to "mandate greater compliance." While it was clearly stated that the Security Council could assist in cordon operations, this mandate for greater compliance has not been clearly defined. In addition, to ensure compliance, certain authors propose that in cases of noncompliance, the United Nations Security Council be referred to the standards and absence of required corrective action. (121 p. 33) Such coercive action would contribute to the international securitization of public health issues and was not reflected in specific related rules of the revised IHR 2005.

2.3 Conclusion

WHO conducted a risk analysis that contributed to the reduction of the SARS pandemic risk. WHO organized multidisciplinary, internationally recognized, and geographically broad-based expertise to assess risk based on the latest scientific findings and the completion of innovative steering mechanisms relying on modern technologies. The quality of expertise and the innovative ways of organizing the experts in virtual networks significantly contributed to the risk analysis. WHO applied a risk analysis method, the legitimacy of which was action based rather than rule based given the nonapplicability of the IHR, while the cost analysis remained incomplete. WHO's response to SARS resulted in a decrease in casualties, was cooperation based, and was adequately monitored. The response resulted in the limitation of the international spread and the reduction of new cases, which led to the containment of the disease, and studies suggest that it was cost effective. In addition, the absence of consultation with countries before the issuance of travel restrictions reduced the level of cooperation, which remained otherwise significant. Finally, the reporting system provided useful information despite some problems with accuracy, completeness, and reliability. WHO recommendations were largely applied, despite the lack of enforcement provisions. The absence of coercive means of enforcement was compensated for by the structure of the response and the incentive-based system. These provided an alternative enforcement means that proved effective in helping rally China into the international partnership to fight the disease. Although cooperation and monitoring were impaired by minor deficiencies, on the whole they substantially improved the quality of the response. The quality of the relationship between risk analysis and the formation of an international appropriate response to SARS under WHO is illustrated in Figure 2.4.

The quality of risk analysis leaves some room for improvement. Risk analysis was impacted by the gap between WHO's need for global action and the competences that had been granted by member states, although WHO's direction was generally recognized and followed. Incomplete documentation of specific procedures regarding the management of health events, and the lack of experience with newly implemented structures such as GPHIN or GOARN, or with specially designed mechanisms such as the experts' collaborating networks and the ground rounds, may also explain some weaknesses in the process. The emergence of SARS was regarded as a real-life test of these structures and mechanisms. After the outbreak, WHO issued SARS-specific risk assessment guidelines to anticipate its possible resurgence and accelerated revisions of the IHR and the influenza preparedness plan in order to prepare for more significant outbreaks of infectious diseases. WHO rapidly coordinated a revision of the IHR in order to provide the organization and the countries with an adequate instrument for addressing outbreaks of infectious disease in a globalized world.

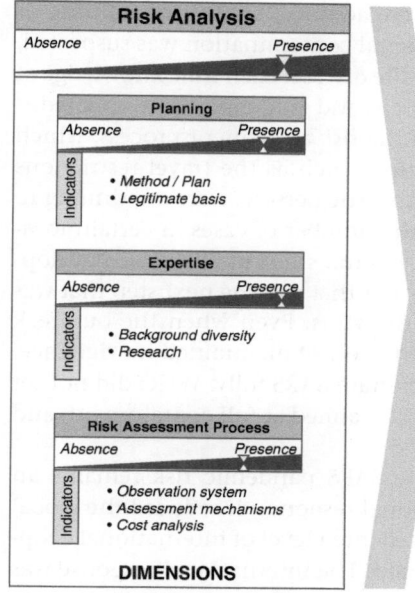
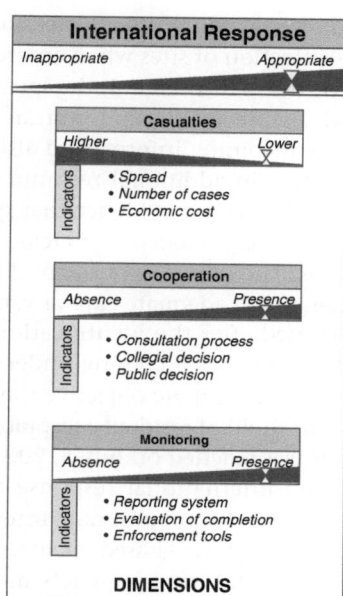

Figure 2.4 International response to SARS

Albeit challenged by the competition in a race to publish findings, WHO effectively led and coordinated collaborative scientific assessment of the risk of a SARS pandemic. It judged the risk of pandemic to be important and organized the international response in line with the results of its risk analysis. The initial high level of uncertainty about the disease led to the recommendation of control measures to ensure the maximum level of protection (i.e., early detection of cases, isolation, and barrier nursing), as well as the minimum disruption to travel and trade (the initial alerts did not include travel restrictions, but only indicated the affected areas). The establishment of virtual networks and the organization of ground rounds provided a platform of information sharing among virologists, epidemiologists, and clinicians in order to find the causative agent, establish the causal chain, evaluate the exposure and vulnerability of populations, and propose control measures to stop the spread of the disease. The virology network's results were instrumental in helping clinicians and epidemiologists more precisely tackle their research on transmission routes and case management, and more effectively plan their action in the field. Based on research progress, additional containment measures were adopted, such as quarantine or disinfection of sites when environmental contamination was suspected, in order to further limit the spread of the disease. Each time knowledge of the disease improved, recommendations and guidelines were updated.[49] New incoming information also fed the risk assessment process, which resulted in additional recommendations such as the travel restrictions issued based on evidence that symptomatic persons were continuing to travel and evidence of increases in the number of cases in certain locations. The duration of the outbreak was too short to allow the development of an adequate cure or vaccine, but that was the next step that was planned after the identification of the virus. Even when the outbreak showed signs of coming under control, WHO maintained its vigilance, since the ultimate objective was to contain SARS fully. WHO did not set a threshold of residual acceptable risk. It aimed at full containment, and this was reached on July 5, 2003.

The international response to the SARS pandemic risk remains an example of an appropriate international response: it reduced the global risk of SARS, was based on an unprecedented level of international cooperation, and was adequately monitored. The international response was mainly organized around containment strategies generated by the risk assessment and which included case and contact management, infection control in hospitals and other facilities, community-wide temperature screening, use of masks, isolation, and quarantine, and the monitoring of travelers and response at national borders. (122 p. 75) Interview-based screening at airports to detect symptoms was also conducted in affected most areas (although not the taking of passengers' temperatures, which was not explicitly indicated in WHO's recommendations). The implementation of infection control measures within hospital settings was particularly challenging, and required education campaigns. Healthcare staff had to be reminded and specifically trained to deal with SARS in accordance with its epidemiological and clinical characteristics.

Although risk analysis under WHO proved to be a determining factor in the formulation of an appropriate international response in the SARS outbreak, other factors also contributed to the containment of SARS, which is often referred to as a global public health success. First, political commitment supported the international response. In particular, Association of Southeast Asian Nations (ASEAN) countries met during the SARS crisis to agree upon intervention measures, which contributed to the achievement of the regional response. Also, China's eventual political commitment to fighting SARS was comparable in determination to its initial concealment and denial, showing how transparent reporting and communication, as well as international cooperation, can help contain a disease worldwide. Second, the availability of information and communication technologies, in particular electronic networking, allowed real-time performance of SARS risk analysis and the sharing of findings among scientists all over the world. This interconnectedness also benefited control efforts by allowing rapid and global dissemination of information and recommendations. (67 p. xxiii) Third, speed and leadership were key to ensuring control of an infectious disease such as SARS. At the global level, speed and leadership were ensured by WHO, with a new disease contained worldwide in a few months. At the national level, governments had enough power, willingness, and public health resources to participate in the international risk analysis and enact the containment measures. The initial delay in obtaining information about China and access to its territory could have been critical if the disease had been more infectious and measures to contain it had been taken less seriously by national authorities in Asia, Europe, and America. Finally, by fortune, virus characteristics such as its reproduction rate contributed to the containment of SARS.

The achievement of SARS containment revealed WHO's central role in the assessment and management of public health emergencies of international scope. WHO's leading role in the risk assessment and risk management of the SARS crisis was validated by the World Health Assembly in May 2003 by the approval of a SARS-specific resolution backed by a resolution on the IHR revision, solving the rules-based legitimacy issue of WHO in the face of SARS. This resolution increased the global role of WHO by requesting increased action regarding the update and dissemination of WHO guidelines, the strengthening of the activities of the Global Alert and Response team and of the collaborative networks, and development of the research and country assistance programs. One important novel point of the IHR resolution is the agreement about a more global active role for WHO in outbreak detection and verification, issuance of alerts, risk assessment, and evaluation of the adequacy of control measures. This resolution was influenced by the problems with communication, reporting, and access encountered with China during the SARS outbreak, but it also confirmed WHO's position as a leading actor in the assessment and management of infectious disease outbreaks at a global level.

3
Avian Influenza H5N1: International Preparedness against a Future Influenza Pandemic

"We had three pandemics in the last century – there is no reason to believe there won't be one in this century." (123 p. 404) These words of Dr. Klaus Stöhr, coordinator of the Global Influenza Programme (GIP) at WHO from 2001 to 2006, expressed the position of the organization's leaders regarding the risk of a human influenza pandemic. The poultry outbreaks in different Asian countries, the occurrence of human cases, and the international spread of the disease raised concerns in the worldwide health community from 2004 to 2005. Compared to the SARS disease, an influenza pandemic could multiply the casualties, as well as put pressure on health systems for a longer period of time and generate significant social disruptions and enormous economic costs.

The avian influenza virus A (H5N1) resurged in February 2003 in Hong Kong, raising the risk of a human influenza pandemic at the same time as the SARS outbreak began. It became of international concern when the zoonose spread from Asia to Europe, the Middle East and Africa in December 2004. In other words, this virus A (H5N1), which infects domestic animals such as poultry, ducks, and even pigs, is susceptible to evolving into a highly pathogenic human form that could easily contaminate humans and efficiently transmit among them. A human influenza pandemic originating from a virus against which populations are not immune could have a significant worldwide impact in terms of human lives lost and burdens on public health systems, as well as causing social disruptions and economic costs. The Spanish influenza of 1918–1919 that generated over 40 million deaths worldwide, (124 p. 39) as compared to the estimated 20 million deaths due to World War I, is often cited as the most striking example of a virulent influenza pandemic consequence.

This chapter focuses on the analysis of the avian influenza H5N1 from its resurgence in 2003 up to the end of 2008. Avian influenza H5N1 in humans remains rare, but is highly lethal. While the total number of human cases at the end of 2008 was limited to 393 in 15 countries, out of which 248 deaths occurred, (125) the case fatality ratio is high at approximately 63%.[1] For comparison purposes, after more than ten years, WHO registered 650 human cases, out of which were 386 deaths, resulting in a case fatality ratio of 59%. (126) Neither a vaccine nor effective drug treatments have been developed, although oseltamivir drugs (for example, Tamiflu) have shown some efficiency in certain circumstances. Between 2003 and 2009, a total of 63 areas and 15 countries reported H5N1 avian influenza in domestic poultry and wildlife to the OIE, out of which 50 countries have reported avian influenza only in domestic poultry. (127) From January through March 2004, more than 120 million poultry birds in Asia died of flu or were slaughtered to stop the avian influenza outbreak. (128 p. 406) Experts at the United Nations estimated that nearly 140 million domestic poultry either died or were destroyed. (129) In 2005, the losses of the affected countries were estimated at over USD 10 billion.[2]

In 2005, the international awareness of the risk of an influenza pandemic and the weaknesses in the countries', international organizations', and companies' preparedness to face this eventuality reached spheres beyond the international public health and scientific communities. The editors of *Nature* dedicated their May 26, 2005, issue to the avian influenza with this title: "Avian Flu: Ready for a Pandemic?" The *Nature* authors raised a red flag, and the information published was rapidly relayed in the media worldwide as well as on multiple websites, provoking debates and anxiety. The current H5N1 outbreak that originated in 1997 in Southern China, with a presumed interruption (no cases were reported during the interval 1997 to 2003) and resurgence in 2003, has been closely watched by health experts and members of the relevant national health institutions and international organizations as a potential source for an influenza pandemic. It finally reached an international public place, capturing the international audience's attention.

In 1997, Hong Kong authorities applied drastic measures to stop the epidemic. Within three days, Hong Kong's entire poultry population, estimated at around 1.5 million birds, was culled; (131) and sanitation and vaccination measures were implemented, such as hygienic measures for the cleaning and disinfection of market places, mandatory rest days, and the launch of a vaccination program for all local chicken farms.

Biosecurity and hygienic measures also were implemented on farms, as well as stricter import controls. This outbreak was considered to be the first alarm of an avian influenza with direct transmission to humans, causing severe illness with high mortality. The result was significant coverage in the Asian media, which increased the level of attention from influenza experts worldwide regarding the risk of an influenza pandemic. The swift reaction of Hong Kong authorities has been credited with reducing the risk of a human influenza pandemic, especially Director of the Hong Kong Department of Health, Dr. Margaret Chan.[3] After her appointment as Director, Communicable Diseases Surveillance and Response, as well as Representative of the Director-General for Pandemic Influenza, in June 2005, she was named Assistant Director-General for Communicable Diseases in September 2005 and will be coordinating WHO activities to face the risk of a human influenza pandemic of avian origin. No outbreak of the virus A (H5N1) occurred again until 2003; three incidents of human infection with other avian subtypes, namely H7N7 and H9N2, were documented in 1999 and 2003, but each only caused mild illness and resulted in only one death (131).

This alert reminded populations that twenty-first-century societies remain vulnerable to infectious disease epidemics, regardless of medicine's progress. The SARS outbreak was still present in people's memories and raised concern about the spread of infectious diseases worldwide. SARS, which had the potential to develop into a pandemic, probably originated in bats and then had to be transmitted to civet cats before infecting humans. The origin of the H5N1 influenza, like SARS, can be found in animals. Zoonoses have been watched and studied as they can develop into highly pathogenic human diseases and easily and rapidly spread worldwide. In particular, avian influenza viruses have the potential to mix with seasonal influenza viruses to result in pandemics. As the incubation period is longer for influenza, as compared to SARS, and is not associated with any visible symptoms (SARS could be detected during the incubation period as it was often associated with fever), early detection of the disease is compromised.

The influenza pandemic risk was largely debated in terms of the definition of an event, its likelihood of occurrence, and its potential impact. First, in order to result in a pandemic, an influenza virus must fulfill three conditions. A new virus emerges against which the population has little or no immunity. Then, this virus must be able to replicate in humans and cause disease, and, finally, it must be easily transmissible among humans. In summary, influenza pandemics arise when a "novel" influenza virus emerges, infects humans, and spreads efficiently

occurred currently as the three above-mentioned conditions have not been fulfilled yet. Some argue that the H5N1 virus is a novel virus that can create disease among humans, but that its sustainability and easy transmission from human to human have not yet occurred. Based on this approach, which is shared by WHO leaders, no pandemic exists, as the third condition is not met. In other words, WHO consider that "the emergence of an H5N1 strain that is readily transmitted among humans would mark the start of a pandemic." (132) Others insist that none of the three conditions are fulfilled at the present time since the human virus that would originate from the avian flu virus H5N1 and potentially cause a pandemic remains unknown. Based on this approach, none of the three conditions that give rise to a pandemic are currently fulfilled.

Since the resurgence of the virus A (H5N1), WHO has engaged in pandemic preparedness activities, cooperating with leaders of other organizations and member states. These activities are considered useful in preparation for the next pandemic, be it of an avian influenza H5N1 source or of another origin, as well as for new infectious diseases. The prepandemic phase 3[4] still allows for preparation and prevention, as the disease does not transmit easily from human to human. Dr. Margaret Chan,[5] Assistant Director-General for Communicable Diseases, emphasized that "for the first time in human history, we have a chance to prepare ourselves for a pandemic before it arrives." (134) In addition, these preparedness activities were declared useful as preparation for a microbiological attack. In an international post-September 11 and post-SARS context, this combination of arguments enhanced active international cooperation as well as national initiatives. Preparedness against this pandemic gave rise to unprecedented investments in surveillance of zoonotic diseases. According to the World Bank, donors contributed USD 3.9 billion to respond to H5N1 avian flu from 2005 to 2010 (135).

Finally, the risk of a human influenza pandemic moved to the top of the international agenda in 2005–2006 in relation to the significant sanitary, political, and economic consequences it may have worldwide. At WHO, pandemic issues were under the direct responsibility of the Director-General, who was directly involved in addressing this risk. In September 2005, President George W. Bush announced the International Partnership on Avian and Pandemic Influenza in New York. The two first objectives of this partnership consisted of fostering international cooperation to protect the lives and health of people and promoting timely and sustained high-level global political leadership to combat avian and pandemic influenza. (136) The avian influenza issue was also on the Group of 8 (G8) agenda in 2006, an organiza-

early detection and control of the H5N1 strain of avian influenza at its source, as well as on the prevention of and preparedness for a potential human influenza pandemic. The G8 leaders reaffirmed their support of the WHO-administered GOARN, to FAO and OIE, as well as the UN System Influenza Coordination Office (UNSIC) and international financial institutions in addressing this global threat (137).

The resurgence of the virus A (H5N1) in 2003 in Hong Kong and the subsequent outbreaks in Asia in 2004 have made this virus the strongest candidate for a human influenza pandemic during the period of time under study (2003–2008) and after. Therefore, describing how H5N1 avian influenza has emerged as a global risk and the way it has been addressed at the international level is important.

3.1   H5N1 avian influenza risk analysis

The two alerts that were raised regarding the resurgence of the H5N1 avian influenza virus among humans happened within the surveillance system of WHO. Human cases were reported by member state authorities, first by officials in Hong Kong in February 2003 and then by those in Vietnam and Thailand in January 2004. In parallel, poultry outbreaks were also reported in the Republic of Korea in December 2003 and in Vietnam, Thailand, Cambodia, and Laos in January 2004.

3.1.1   First alert: Hong Kong (February 2003)

In February 2003, two human cases of avian influenza A (H5N1), a father who would die from the disease, and his son, were reported in Hong Kong. This family had traveled to the Fujian Province in China, where their 8-year-old daughter died from an undiagnosed respiratory infection. The outbreak of a strange pneumonia in the Guangdong Province, combined with the confirmation of these two human cases of avian influenza H5N1 in Hong Kong, alerted WHO officials. At that time, researchers were not sure whether the two Hong Kong patients had the same illness as those in Guangdong (138 p. 1504), as the SARS outbreak was occurring simultaneously and was first believed to be influenza.

As of February 19, 2003, results from two laboratories confirmed the presence of an avian influenza virus in a boy who had hospitalized in Hong Kong since February 12. On February 19, WHO officials, believing that the world might be facing an avian influenza outbreak, went on alert and mobilized the Global Influenza Surveillance Network to investigate the source of infection, (139) only to discover later that a new disease had emerged, SARS. While the SARS outbreak put the world on alert and the disease was contained by July 2003, authorities in neither Hong Kong nor other Asian countries reported additional human cases of avian influenza H5N1 during 2003. However, outbreaks of H5N1 avian influenza in poultry hit the Republic of Korea beginning in December 2003, followed by outbreaks in Vietnam, Japan, Thailand, Cambodia, and Laos in January 2004.

3.1.2 Second alert: Asian regional outbreak (December 2003–January 2004)

The spectrum of an influenza pandemic resurged in January 2004, with human cases of avian influenza H5N1 that were reported in Vietnam and Thailand. On January 13, 2004, WHO published disease outbreak news regarding the avian influenza H5N1 in Vietnam, and on January 23, in Thailand, as well as an avian influenza fact sheet in the meantime. A travel advisory was issued on February 6, 2004, that did not impose travel restrictions but recommended that people limit contact with poultry when traveling in countries affected by animal and human outbreaks. (140) No global alert was issued, but WHO leaders sent investigation teams to study the transmission pattern of the disease in Vietnam and Thailand. According to WHO investigators, direct contact with infected poultry (or birds) was the primary source of infection, followed by exposure to an environment that may have been contaminated by feces from infected birds. However, the possibility of direct human-to-human transmission could not be completely eliminated. The WHO investigators' actions have continued since then, and they intensified in 2005 when people in Cambodia, Indonesia, and China were affected as well. From 1997 to 2004, the virus A (H5N1) had become more pathogenic, more lethal, and more resistant to drugs. Based on tests performed by WHO in Vietnam in 2004, the virus had become resistant to some antiviral drugs and could survive up to six days at 37°C, compared to two days in 1997 in the same test environment. (141 paragraph 3) Knowing the capacity of the influenza virus A to reassert itself or to mutate to infect humans probably in conjunction with seasonal influenza, WHO and its experts confirmed the risk of a worldwide A (H5N1) influenza pandemic.

Although the first two H5N1 human cases of the ongoing outbreak occurred in 2003, the analysis starts with the cases identified and reported in Vietnam in January 2004. These human cases, combined with avian influenza outbreaks in poultry in Japan and South Korea, initiated the risk analysis at WHO. These cases also corresponded to the end of the SARS outbreak that had mobilized most resources up until July 2003 and in the fall of 2003 to draw lessons from the SARS outbreak.

3.1.3   Method and legitimacy

WHO jointly applied four different layers of risk assessment methods for the avian influenza case. First, WHO used its risk assessment framework to assess the risk of an influenza pandemic based on the resurgence of the H5N1 virus in humans. Second, the avian influenza event was reported and evaluated under the EPR method using the "Guiding Principles for International Outbreak Alert and Response." (42) Third, it used the notification instrument that would become Annex 2 of the revised IHR for event detection, verification, and risk assessment. Finally, the influenza pandemic preparedness plan, in both the 1999 version and the revised version of 2005, prescribed the performance of a risk assessment to determine the level of alert ("pandemic phase").

WHO developed a two-way approach in order to assess the risk of a disease outbreak. On the one hand, it applies a "bottom-up approach" that relies on countries reporting, such as Hong Kong officials who reported human cases of avian influenza H5N1 in 2003, as well as officials in Vietnam and Thailand in January 2004. On the other hand, it can use a "top-down approach" based on the IHR resolution adopted by the World Health Assembly on May 28, 2003, that authorizes WHO to use nonofficial sources as a starting point for its outbreak verification process. (48) In the avian influenza case, WHO's risk analysis process in the first instance of the disease mainly consisted of a bottom-up approach that relied on the IHR identification and verification process for outbreaks of diseases.

3.1.3.1   *Annex 2 of the IHR (2005)*

Although the revised IHR was adopted in 2005 to come into force in 2007, WHO proceeded to a first analysis of the situation and a preliminary evaluation of the human influenza pandemic based on the IHR "Decision Instrument for the Assessment and Notification of Events That May Constitute a Public Health Emergency of International Concern" (46 pp. 45–48) that became part of Annex 2 of the revised IHR 2005. This method was documented as a process flowchart that is accompanied with explanations on how to apply this risk assessment process, and questions that need to be answered to evaluate the magnitude of the risk based on preestablished criteria. This document was meant to be a guideline for states' officials and WHO for the assessment and notification of events that might constitute a public health emergency of international concern. This notification instrument was available to WHO and state members since 2002, and the IHR working paper that was submitted for regional consultations in January 2004 included a preliminary version of

At that stage, the concept of "Events That May Constitute a Public Health Emergency of International Concern" (PHEIC) prevailed, while the final version also included a systematic notification for a predefined list of diseases (in the box on the left) and a list of events involving specific diseases for which the decision instrument should be used (in the box on the right). Figure 3.1 below, represents this risk assessment flow chart as stated in Annex 2 of the revised IHR.

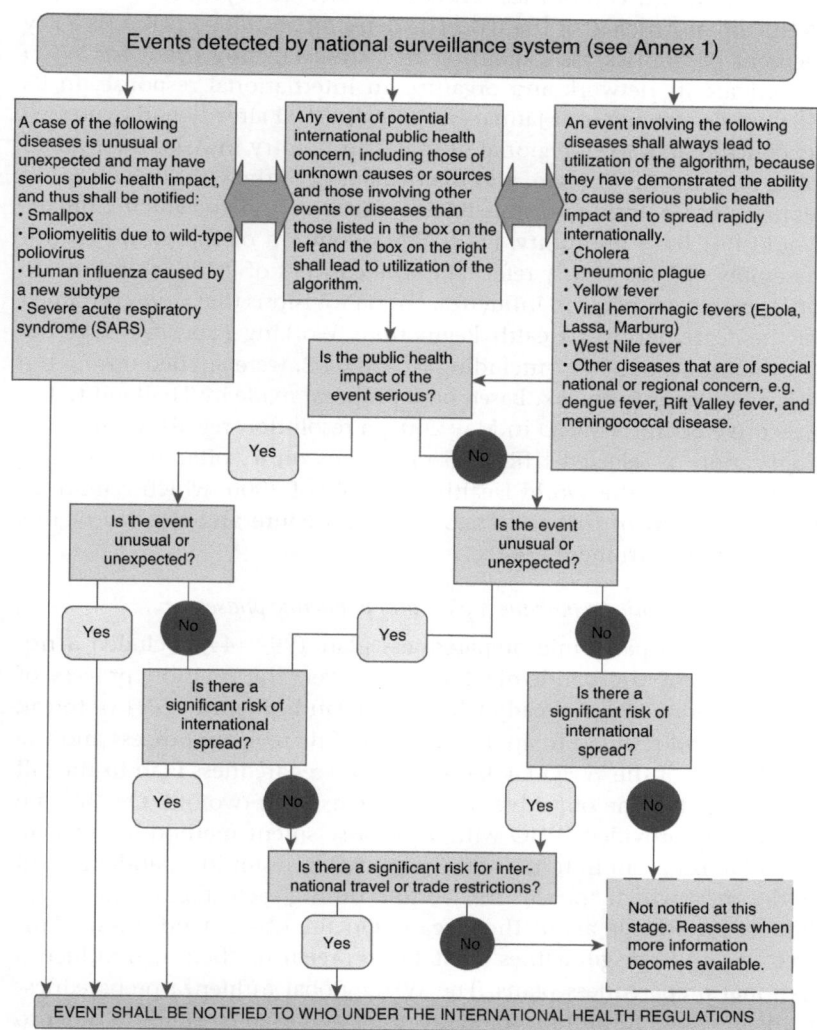

H5N1 avian influenza met the four criteria to be considered as a public health emergency of international concern: seriousness of the disease in terms of public health impact (high mortality); unexpectedness (unusual character of the disease that could result in an influenza pandemic); international spread (regional spread in 2004 and intercontinental spread in 2005); and risk of international travel and trade restrictions (travel precautions recommended and possible impact on poultry trade). If two of these criteria are met, state parties shall notify WHO under Article 6 of the IHR. The determination of a PHEIC is a key element of the risk assessment, as it is the triggering event for WHO to activate its network and organize an international response. In its first public statement of January 13, 2004, WHO already had expressed its concern about the regional outbreak in poultry in Asia, the human cases detected in Vietnam, and the instability of the virus, which could change into a form transmissible to humans and to which humans would not have immunity. (143) The resolution of the World Health Assembly of 2006 clearly referred to the concept of PHEIC to follow up on human cases of avian influenza. (144) Provisions that were contained in the "International Health Regulations Working Paper for Regional Consultations of 2004," including its Annex 2, were applied during the avian influenza outbreak. Based on a proposal made by Thailand to the Executive Board of WHO in May 2005, a resolution regarding the early application of selected IHR 2005 provisions on a voluntary basis was adopted during the World Health Assembly of 2006, which reinforced the application of this risk assessment procedure and the use of this notification instrument (144).

3.1.3.2   *Pandemic preparedness plan and pandemic phases*

The influenza pandemic preparedness plan 1999 (44) included a risk assessment of the pandemic level. However, the revision process of that plan was started already when the avian influenza H5N1 outbreak occurred and resulted in an acceleration of its revision process and the publication of the WHO Global Influenza Preparedness Plan in the fall of 2005. (145) The objectives of both plans were twofold. On the one hand, they provided WHO with a risk assessment method to evaluate an influenza event in terms of the potential to result in a pandemic and to decide at which "phase" the world is during each stage of the evolution of knowledge about the disease. On the other hand, these plans were meant to be guidelines for states in preparing their own influenza national preparedness plans. The WHO global influenza preparedness plans provided minimum standards to be achieved by states in order to ensure adequate control and protection measures in the case of a human influenza pandemic.

3.1.3.3   Legitimate basis for action

Until the early adoption of the IHR in May 2006 or the entry into force on June 15, 2007, the formal legal basis for action remained the IHR 1969, and the resolution on IHR of May 2003 that was limited in scope. During that period, the provisions of the draft of the revised IHR were used as the basis for action and were generally accepted by states.

The IHR 1969 did not apply to the H5N1 avian influenza for the same reasons it did not apply to SARS. The resolution on the revision of IHR, (48) adopted by the World Health Assembly in May 2003, provided a legal basis for WHO action, but did not cover the whole range of activities as prescribed in the revised IHR project in 2002. While states' officials are urged to establish focal points and ensure collaboration with agencies involved in animal care, they do not have the obligation to notify WHO of the avian influenza disease. Under this resolution, WHO can use nonofficial sources of information that report outbreaks, issue alerts in the case of a serious threat after having informed the government(s) officials concerned, collaborate with national authorities in assessing the severity of the threat and adequacy of control measures, and conduct on-the-spot studies to ensure that appropriate control measures are being employed. This resolution provided a limited formal legal basis for action until April 2006, when the World Health Assembly adopted a resolution (144) on the early and voluntary application of the IHR (2005) to strengthen pandemic preparedness and response, in particular in surveillance, reporting, information sharing, and the setting up a National IHR Focal Point. The revised IHR were adopted in May 2005 (IHR 2005) to come into force on June 15, 2007. Early adoption was applied by states willing to do so, and on June 15, 2007, the IHR 2005 came into force and provided the formal legal basis for WHO actions.

In practice, the provisions included in the draft of the revised IHR that was submitted to the WHO Executive Board in January 2004 and that circulated during the year to result in a final draft in the fall of 2004 were applied in regard to the outbreak of avian influenza. Although the final version of IHR included some changes in scope and procedure, such as the joint use of a list of diseases and the concept of an event that can consist of a PHEIC, the provisions remained essentially similar. While the revised IHR 2005 did not contain the possibility of on-the-spot studies, as mentioned in the resolution on IHR, authors of the IHR 2005 linked the notification with the possibility of seeking assistance from

WHO as an incentive for states to report an outbreak. Annex 2 in its generic form, which pertained to a concept and not a list of diseases, was available to state officials for assessment and notification.[6] In fact, in the case of the avian influenza, national authorities of affected areas spontaneously reported the outbreaks and the number of cases to WHO, which initiated the verification and assessment process in return. The importance of timely and transparent reporting might have been influenced by the SARS experience. For Vietnam, it was also a way to seek assistance and have investigations on-site about the transmission of the disease in 2004.

In addition, avian influenza required more cooperation among institutions than did the SARS outbreak, due to the important impact on animal health. WHO's cooperation, mainly with FAO, OIE, and the World Bank, found its legitimate basis in Article 2 of the WHO Constitution, which grants competence to WHO "to establish and maintain effective collaboration with the United Nations, specialized agencies, governmental health administrations, professional groups and such other organizations as may be deemed appropriate." (146) The health mandate provided to WHO from its member states, therefore, allows the organization to cooperate and develop partnerships in order to address health issues efficiently at an international level.

3.1.4   Expertise organization

The diversity of the background and the international track record of the experts who were involved in the risk assessment and their capacity to apply the latest research into WHO protection measures characterize the pandemic preparedness activities.

3.1.4.1   *Background diversity*

WHO organized its expertise around three poles: the institutional expertise organized through the "traditional" consultation procedure in place at the WHO (member states consultation and international meetings); the combination of field experts internal and external to WHO – a new procedure implemented especially to address the risk of an H5N1 influenza pandemic; and the creation of a specific "task force" within the WHO that was fully dedicated to the avian influenza issue. The diversity of background of the expertise will be evaluated in terms of multidisciplinarity, geography, and institutional representation.

Member states' consultation.   The first pole of expertise relies on the regular consultation procedure that was in place at WHO. Each text that was prepared by WHO experts internally was reviewed by official representatives of governments of WHO member states. For example, the *WHO Global Influenza Preparedness Plan* that was reviewed and published in 2005 was developed according to this procedure. A group of experts tasked by WHO and consisting of approximately 15 persons, in consultation with WHO regional and country offices prepared the *WHO Global Influenza Preparedness Plan*. This plan had been in preparation for about ten years (a first version had been published in 1999) and was reviewed by regional offices of WHO and representatives designated by the ministries of health of member states. Similarly, the "WHO Checklist for Influenza Pandemic Preparedness Planning" was developed during a meeting of approximately 15 experts called by WHO. Finally, the measures found in "Responding to the Avian Influenza Pandemic Threat: Recommended Strategic Actions" were elaborated by WHO experts and reviewed by WHO regional offices. The WHO risk analysis and measures to be taken to reduce a risk were contained in these documents that were prepared by a combination of operational, strategic, and review dedicated persons. Dr. Klaus Stöhr and his team played a critical role in initiating the documentation preparation process and coordinating the review and the issuance of these documents that formalized the position of the organization regarding the risk of an influenza pandemic. We found no evidence regarding the diversity of backgrounds of the experts involved in that process.

International meeting (November 7 to 9, 2005). From November 7 to 9, 2005, WHO jointly convened an international meeting on avian influenza and human pandemic with FAO, OIE, and the World Bank that was held at WHO headquarters in Geneva to assess the risk to human health. The meeting was unprecedented in its design, attendance, and the scope of the work. More than 600 experts from over 100 countries gathered, agreed on the importance of the risk, and designed priority actions to prevent the emergence of a pandemic virus (or to delay its initial international spread) and to prepare countries to cope more effectively with a pandemic (147 p. 2).

During these two days, representatives exchanged information about avian influenza and discussed the latest research findings and countries' challenges in dealing with the outbreak or implementing pandemic coping capacities. The commitment of the organizations was evidenced by the presence of top-level managers and the decision to follow up with another conference in Beijing in January to address the financial needs for carrying out the proposed actions.

The meeting resulted in an action plan in six major areas: control at the source in birds; surveillance; rapid containment; pandemic preparedness; integrated country plans; communications. (148) These actions were summarized in the "WHO Strategic Action Plan for Pandemic Influenza 2006–2007," which serves as a reference for the international response in four categories of actions: reducing exposure to the H5N1 virus; strengthening of the early warning system; intensifying rapid containment operations and building the capacity to cope with a pandemic; and coordinating research. (149) An additional point raised in the meeting was included in the research section and relates to the timely and sufficient availability of vaccines and drugs.

Experts Consultation: Containment protocol.   The second pole of expertise was organized in a multistakeholder consultation. The preparation of the "WHO Interim Protocol: Rapid Operations to Contain the Initial Emergence of Pandemic Influenza" in March 2006 was the first application of this new procedure. The meeting's aim was for participants to design the bases for responding to avian influenza outbreaks and containing them to avoid a pandemic, and organization leaders gathered experts from different backgrounds in order to work on a document that was drafted by WHO internal experts. The participants were selected based on their field of expertise, professional background, activity, and organization in order to address as many aspects of the issue as possible and propose the most appropriate and comprehensive response. These working groups included international subject matter experts who were recognized for their contributions to the field of infectious diseases and work for various institutions (such as research institutes, universities, laboratories, and centers for disease control), independent experts, WHO internal experts, WHO regional representatives, officers of other international organizations (such as the International Migration Organization) or UN agencies (such as FAO), and representatives from the private sector (such as the Roche Group).

The formation of this protocol followed a completely different process than the influenza preparedness plan. It was prepared and reviewed through technical meetings and focused on technical issues and operations. This protocol was prepared by subject matter experts more than country representatives and was associated with a clinical meeting on how to use drugs and treat human cases. It was also based on a review of the literature that was performed by three specialists, who analyzed the relevancy and soundness as well as reliability of the material to be used in the drafting process. A first draft of the "WHO Pandemic Influenza Draft

Protocol for Rapid Response and Containment" was ready on January 27, 2006. (150) This draft was updated to serve as the basis for the work of the Global Technical Meeting on Early Containment Protocol for Pandemic Influenza that was held in Geneva from March 6 to 8, 2006 to discuss a influenza pandemic containment strategy.[7]

The purpose of that meeting was to reach a technical consensus on rapid detection, assessment, and response to the signs that were showing a development of the avian influenza virus toward more transmissibility among humans. (151) The meeting gathered 72 participants, of whom 19 were external experts. The participants were dispatched into three working groups: Operations; Surveillance and Epidemiology; Public Health Measures for Containment and Control. Experts in these groups reviewed and modified the entire draft to ensure the relevance and completeness of the measures proposed. The meeting resulted in the publication of the "WHO Pandemic Influenza Draft Protocol for Rapid Response and Containment" on the WHO website on March 17, 2006.[8] At the end of March 2006, and to complement the work that was being done, WHO organized two additional technical meetings on preparedness for the impact of pandemic influenza on refugee and displaced populations and on social mobilization to reduce the risk of avian influenza.

The composition of the expertise was intended to cover most of the technical and institutional aspects in the containment of an influenza pandemic. Information was missing about the area of expertise for eight participants who were all working for WHO. Table 3.1 shows the breakdown of participants by area of expertise.

Table 3.1 also shows that areas of work were largely diversified (more than 25 different areas of expertise) among external experts and WHO participants. It also indicates a predominance of epidemiology (25%), followed by public health (8%), emergency action, and surveillance (4%). This meeting included experienced staff from WHO headquarters, regional, and country offices who specialized in operational planning, outbreak response, logistics, epidemiology, laboratory diagnosis, infection control, ethics, social mobilization, and public and media communications.

Figure 3.2 concentrates on the 19 external experts (representing 26% of the participants) who attended this global technical meeting. It also shows a predominance of epidemiology (26%), followed by logistics, occupational health, immunology and vaccines, and public health (all at 11%). These external experts came from 17 different institutions, including universities, state agencies, agencies or programs of the United

Table 3.1   Breakdown of participants by fields of expertise, WHO global technical meeting on early containment protocol for pandemic influenza, March 6–8, 2006

Field of expertise	Number of experts	Percentage
Epidemiology	18	25.0%
Not available	8	11.1%
Public Health	6	8.3%
Surveillance	3	4.2%
Communication	2	2.7%
Infection Control	2	2.7%
Logistics	2	2.7%
Virology	2	2.7%
Biosafety	1	1.4%
Emergency Aid	1	1.4%
Emergency Aid, Food Assistance	1	1.4%
Emergency Disease Control	1	1.4%
Epidemiology and Public Health	1	1.4%
Epidemiology & Clinical Research	1	1.4%
Ethics	1	1.4%
Expert Adviser	1	1.4%
Global Migration and Quarantine	1	1.4%
Health Action in Crisis	1	1.4%
Health Technologies	1	1.4%
Human Resources	1	1.4%
Immunology	1	1.4%
Interagency Coordination	1	1.4%
International Health Regulations	1	1.4%
Medicines Policy	1	1.4%
Microbiology and Laboratory Systems	1	1.4%
Microbiology and Vaccines	1	1.4%
Nursing	1	1.4%
Occupational Hygiene	1	1.4%
Pandemic Contingency Planning	1	1.4%
Partners Network	1	1.4%
Procurement	1	1.4%
Research on Influenza	1	1.4%
Training	1	1.4%
Vaccines	1	1.4%
Veterinary	1	1.4%
Virology and Vaccines	1	1.4%
Virology and Zoonotic Diseases	1	1.4%
Grand Total	**72**	**100%**

Nations (FAO, United Nations Children's Fund [UNICEF], World Food Programme [WFP], and United Nations System Influenza Coordination [UNSIC]), the International Federation of Red Cross and Red Crescent

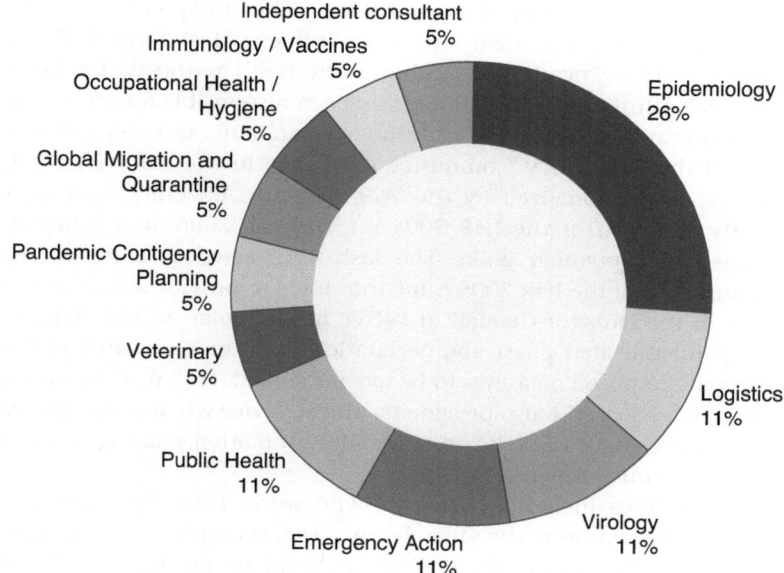

Figure 3.2 Breakdown of fields of expertise for external experts, WHO global technical meeting on early containment protocol for pandemic influenza, March 6–8, 2006

and Europe), one independent consultant, and one logistics experts from the Roche Group. The presence of a representative of the Roche Group was a completely new occurrence in such consultations. He was there to discuss drug stockpiling and distribution aspects after the Roche Group donated a stockpile of 3 million courses of oseltamivir (Tamiflu) (150 p. 13) to WHO to carry out the containment plan and dispatch these drugs at the source cluster. In addition, these experts had previous experience in containing infectious diseases, such as SARS or Ebola.

The expertise for the preparation of this protocol was broad-based geographically, with a multidisciplinary background in terms of the large variety of disciplines represented, as well as a diverse and international institutional representation. The experts from organizations both outside of WHO and within WHO represented institutions located in 12 countries from all continents. The financial, logistics, and legal fields were also represented, but were not numerous, and all came from WHO. While more social science aspects were included in the governance of avian influenza compared to the analysis of SARS, expertise remained

Avian influenza task force and decision-making.   The third pole of expertise was composed of a fully dedicated avian influenza task force that was formed at WHO. Since the beginning of the H5N1 outbreak, Dr. Klaus Stöhr, Global Influenza Programme, had been responsible for setting up and coordinating the work of an influenza pandemic task force on the model of the Emergency Committee prescribed in the IHR.[9] This task force was institutionalized by the World Health Assembly resolution on early adoption of the IHR 2005 on May 26, 2006, and officially organized in September 2006. The task force acted as a temporary mechanism until the IHR 2005 came into force to provide advice at the request of the Director-General of WHO, in particular on key changes to the pandemic alert phase and declaration of a pandemic, and on the appropriate response measures to be recommended. (153 p. 1) Members of the task force might also provide technical advice when requested by the Director-General of WHO on other relevant matters relating to avian and/or pandemic influenza (153 p. 2).

This task force included personnel who worked on SARS, and the leading individuals were the same. From a legal standpoint, its activities relied first on the draft of the revised IHR and later on the revised IHR that went into force on June 15, 2007. The draft of the "WHO Pandemic Influenza Draft Protocol for Rapid Response and Containment" that was submitted to the Global Technical Meeting of March 6 to 8, 2006, as described in the previous sections, details the composition and the activation of this task force. This task force is an independent multi-disciplinary advisory body to the Director-General of WHO that will be convened upon receipt of a signal of emergent pandemic influenza. (150 p. 11) The document also described the activities and responsibilities of the task force as well as its relationship to the Director-General of WHO. The use of this task force was retrieved from the protocol by the experts during the meeting of 2006.

However, the task force was active before its formal approval by the adoption of the resolution for the immediate application of the IHR (2005) on a voluntary basis by the World Health Assembly on May 26, 2006. This resolution, considering the risk posed by avian influenza and pandemic influenza, requested that the Director-General of WHO "use the influenza pandemic task force as a temporary mechanism until entry into force of the International Health Regulations (2005) in order to advise the Organization on the response to avian influenza, the appropriate phase of pandemic alert and the corresponding recommended response measures, the declaration of an influenza pandemic, and the international response to a pandemic." (144 p. 4) This Influenza Pandemic Task

Force (IPTF or "the Task Force") met for the first time on September 25, 2006, in Geneva in order to organize the Task Force and appoint its members and to plan for any emergency and other relevant advice that may be required of it. (153 p. 1) It was constituted and acted as the future emergency committee prescribed in Article 48 of the IHR 2005, its role and activities were comparable.[10] The WHO Director-General selects experts who provide advice on whether an event constitutes a PHEIC and its termination, as well as recommendations to address the risk. The IHR "emergency committee" (the committee of experts or the influenza pandemic task force in the case of the avian influenza) provides advice, but does not create policies, which is the responsibility of the World Health Assembly and the Director-General. The task force was composed of a group of experts who worked on the avian influenza and provided advice to the WHO about measures to be taken. Experts are selected for their discipline expertise and excellence. They should have different relevant backgrounds such as clinical expertise, epidemiology, virology, or anthropology and constitute a geographically representative group of experts available and able to work under tight time constraints.

Field missions. Mission teams of investigators were sent to probe outbreaks, assess risk, and provide assistance to affected areas. In January 2007, WHO recorded nine missions with the GOARN and 30 joint assessment missions of WHO officers and national authorities. (154) The missions, run jointly by WHO and the GOARN, also included representatives of FAO and of OIE when infection control measures and the culling of animals were required, and with other institutions, such as the joint mission with the Asian Development Bank to Vietnam. Field missions were not only diverse in terms of backgrounds of experts but also in terms of organizations represented. WHO sent team missions to areas affected by the H5N1 avian influenza, among which were Vietnam, Thailand, Turkey, Azerbaijan, Indonesia, and Egypt. Based on the list of participants published in Annex 3 of the Turkey mission report (155) issued by WHO, we built Table 3.2, overleaf, which illustrates the multidisciplinary aspect of the expertise involved. The area of work was not indicated for one expert, but this has a negligible impact on our analysis.

The mission was divided into coordination and field teams, which partly explains the majority of WHO officers in the mission, with a representation of 41%. The WHO officers came mainly from the WHO Regional Office for Europe and headquarters and included high-level officers. Veterinary experts (15%) included three representatives of FAO,

Table 3.2   Breakdown of fields of expertise for WHO avian influenza H5N1 field mission in Turkey, 2007

Field of expertise	Number of experts	Percentage
WHO officers	16	41%
Veterinary experts	6	15%
EU Representatives	5	13%
Epidemiology	3	8%
Technical Officers	3	8%
Medical Officers	2	5%
Public Health Specialists	2	5%
Laboratory Specialists	1	2.5%
Not Available	1	2.5%
Total	39	100%

which shows the interagency collaboration between human health and animal health institutions. The European Union representatives (13%) also provided personnel in agriculture and public health. The mission was also broad based, with 14 different institutions, including the European Commission, United Nations bodies (such as FAO or UNICEF), centers for disease control, research institutes, and state public health agencies located in nine countries. While a communications officer was available to lead interviews in the field, no economic and legal officers to address the financial aspects of the outbreak or the compliance with the IHR and local rules were part of the group.

International track record.   Both experts from WHO and external experts in charge of the risk assessment of the outbreak presented an international track record in their areas of expertise. Most of them also had practical experience in the field in managing infectious disease outbreaks, including the SARS outbreak in 2003. International track records were assessed mainly using publications in peer-reviewed journals such as *The Lancet* or the *New England Journal of Medicine*. The research of references was enlarged to the Medline database available through the *Lancet* search engine, (156) in which evidence was found of international track records for the members of the WHO Influenza Pandemic Task Force and the participants in the Global Technical Meeting on Early Containment Protocol for Pandemic Influenza held at WHO headquarters in Geneva from March 6 to 8, 2006.

The Influenza Pandemic Task Force was composed of 11 WHO officers and 20 external experts. The WHO officers group included Dr. Heymann (Acting Assistant Director-General), Dr. Ryan (Director Epidemic and

Pandemic Response), Dr. Rodier, and Dr. Fukuda[11] (Coordinator Global Influenza Program), who also worked on SARS, and who had written approximately 90 publications, while the group of external experts had written approximately 600 publications. The 19 external experts of the containment protocol meeting had written over 150 publications, out of which approximately 20 were from the international organizations' experts. The 72 members of the WHO staff had over 550 publications.

3.1.4.2 Research

The coordination of international research and the quality and transparency of this research are essential to enhancing the risk analysis in order to shape the most adapted measures to address the risk. The prolific research activity and production of scientific articles about virology, clinical management, epidemiology, and economic and social aspects of the avian influenza and the pandemic risk have been undertaken during the period under analysis and still continue. Global coordination of research by WHO essentially covers two situations: research during the preparation phase and research during the pandemic itself. (149 pp. 17–19) Research during the pandemic itself will be organized in the same manner as for SARS in virtual networks of experts to gather epidemiological data in real time. (157 p. 20) These data will be used in predictive models in order to adjust the measures to be taken. Studies of the virus and, in particular, the tracking of its changes in virulence will be used to predict the severity of the disease in the next waves. Studies about drugs' effectiveness will also have to be performed to detect resistance or alternative treatments. We primarily focused our analysis on research about virology and epidemiology during the preparedness phase as the pandemic was not declared during the period under study.

WHO had as an objective to coordinate international research on avian influenza and organized it around the following structures: international conferences to share information; technical meetings to work on specific issues and produce guidance (such as the containment protocol described in the previous section); telephone conferences when necessary. WHO formed its group of experts based mainly on the influenza network (as in the case of SARS), which resulted in the involvement of similarly renowned experts in the management of the avian influenza. The influenza network that includes national centers and collaborating centers has a long history and experience in analyzing viruses due to its yearly work on seasonal viruses. This network was also a major provider for laboratory expertise in the H5N1 avian influenza case. Article 47 of the revised IHR 2005 prescribed the creation of a roster of experts in all relevant fields of expertise. The WHO Director-General appoints the members of this roster in accordance with WHO Regulations for Expert Advisory Panels and Committees and shall appoint one member at the request of each state and one for relevant intergovernmental and regional economic integration organizations. This roster of experts could reach 300 to 400 people and should be multidisciplinary and international, but in December 2008, 56 experts (158) were designated by states (not even 30% of state parties participated). In addition, an informal preliminary version of the emergency committee that was provided for in the revised IHR 2005 was set up to advise WHO leaders in decision-making. The exact composition of this committee was not disclosed, but it included experts who are internationally recognized in the field.

Research on changes in the virus and its ability to cross barrier species has been key to the development of recommendations in clinical management and in preparedness activities. The virus has been known since 1997, and its resurgence in 2003 and 2004 has been closely watched, in particular, to determine if it had the ability to easily infect humans and become transmittable among humans. A first study performed on ten human cases in Vietnam showed that human transmission could not be excluded. (159) This gave rise to the inclusion of additional precautions to protect health-care workers in the clinical management of patients. Hygiene campaigns were carried out during field missions to prescribe how to handle dead poultry and how to limit possibilities for infection in households among members of a family. In addition, researchers in the WHO Global Influenza Surveillance Network studies found some genetic similarities between the 1918 virus and the H5N1 virus circulating in 2005, which raised the level of alert within WHO. One field of investigation was also the possible transmission from human to human. Research conducted in Thailand evidenced that transmission from a girl to her mother and her aunt probably occurred during close contact without protection in September 2004 and established that the virus was not a new variant, but did not confirm the mode of transmission as the index seemed not have been in contact with poultry. (160 p. 338) These results were reflected in the WHO document "Avian Influenza: Assessing the Pandemic Threat" (161) that synthesized the state of knowledge and assessed the risk of a human influenza pandemic. This risk assessment included as a temporarily reassuring element the fact that human-to-human transmission was rare, and an element of concern was the fact that the H5N1 virus presented similarities to the Spanish influenza virus. (161 pp. 8–18) These elements gave rise to further surveillance recommendations and the pursuit of studies about the virus's evolution, as well as research to develop new methods for detecting the virus in environmental samples to better understand the relationship between animal and human disease (130 p. 7).

Another example of how virology and laboratory research provided valuable input into the risk assessment to issue recommendations is the "Influenza Research at the Human and Animal Interface: Report of a WHO Working Group," (162) which was published based on the work done by a group of 22 laboratory directors and senior scientists gathered in Geneva on September 21 to 22, 2006. This report integrated the results of the latest studies that showed that virus shedding patterns were changing and that the virus had acquired the capacity to transmit back to wild birds from poultry, which explained certain spread trends and which was an additional source of concern for a pandemic. Culling infected poultry remained the strategy based on Japan and Korea successes in containing the animal outbreaks and in avoiding infection in humans. However, culling is costly and disruptive; therefore, the experts recommended to countries with fewer resources to vaccinate poultry, such as Vietnam did. This approach is not without risk and should be watched carefully, as Hong Kong did in 1997, as it can disseminate the virus.

The early containment strategy that was developed for avian influenza H5N1 was primarily based on research results and included past experience with avian influenza in Hong Kong in 1997 and the Netherlands in 2003 (H7N7 virus), and with SARS in 2003. According to two mathematical modeling studies by Ferguson et al. (163) and Longini et al., (164) published in 2005, the combination of public health measures in the region where the pandemic virus emerged, along with the administration of antivirals, could possibly contain the outbreak before it spreads internationally. Ferguson et al. showed that prophylactic and social-distancing measures, combined with antiviral treatment, would be effective if the reproduction number is below 1.8. (163 p. 213) Longini et al. came up with similar conclusions for a reproduction number below 1.6 by using a model for rural Southeast Asia. Targeted antiviral prophylactic, quarantines, and prevaccination would be essential to contain the new virus at its source. (164) They also envisaged that WHO's stockpiling of 120,000 treatment courses in 2005 could possibly be sufficient to contain the disease, while they advised a stockpile between 100,000 to 1 million. (164 p. 1087) Ferguson et al. suggested stockpiling 3 million or more courses of oseltamivir. (163 p. 213) Detection, rapid identification of the cluster to deliver the cures, availability of sufficient stockpiles, population cooperation for social distancing measures, and international cooperation would be essential in order to succeed. (163 p. 213) If the containment strategy cannot prevent the pandemic, it is expected the development of the pandemic would slow for a few weeks or months, which would allow for some time to develop vaccines. Officials from the Roche Group committed to giving WHO 3 million courses of oseltamivir (Tamiflu) (165) for one of the main measures of pandemic containment.

Professor Ferguson was one of the advising experts to WHO regarding avian influenza, and he also published papers on the transmission dynamics of SARS. (73) His two studies were used as the basis for developing the containment protocol and were quoted on page 8 of the March 3, 2006, draft of the "WHO Pandemic Influenza Draft Protocol for Rapid Response and Containment." (150) Professor Ferguson participated as one of the experts in the technical meeting of March 6 to 8, 2006. The updated containment protocol published ten days later clearly refers to the stockpiling of 3 million courses of oseltamivir that Roche donated to WHO in 2005, half of which will be stored in the United States and half in Switzerland. (150 p. 13) Further research will be done on effectiveness of different measures and on Tamiflu as well due to resistance arising in certain patients in different countries such as Egypt.

3.1.5   Risk assessment process

The avian influenza risk assessment process consists of a series of steps that should lead to the adoption of risk management measures that are issued by WHO. Demonstrating that WHO experts proceeded to a risk analysis, showing that a risk assessment process was in place in the avian influenza case, is important. The presence of an observation system and risk assessment mechanisms and the realization of a cost benefit analysis constitute the three major components of the risk assessment process.

3.1.5.1   *Observation system*

Avian influenza surveillance is mainly based on the Global Influenza Surveillance Network, which is described in the section on observation systems in Chapter 2. Previously in this chapter, the successive alerts and activation of the Global Influenza Surveillance Network in 2003 for the Hong Kong cases and in January 2004 for the Vietnam cases were mentioned. Officials in affected countries notified WHO of outbreaks through this network. While accuracy and completeness were questioned in the Egyptian reporting, Indonesian officials openly opposed WHO in not reporting outbreaks and not sharing viruses (166).

Virus analysis and development of vaccines was a central point of the preparedness activities. In response to the risk of H5N1 pandemic, in 2004, WHO established the WHO H5 Reference Laboratory Network as an ad hoc component of the WHO Global Influenza Surveillance Network (GISN). (167) The four WHO Collaborating Centers for Reference and Research on Influenza, the WHO Collaborating Centre for Studies on the Ecology of Influenza in Animals, and other laboratories with internationally recognized expertise in avian influenza are part of this network. Major tasks of this WHO H5 Reference Laboratory Network are to collect virus specimens that are made freely available to WHO laboratories working on the development of vaccines, perform antigenic analyses, participate in the WHO process to select, develop, and distribute candidate vaccine viruses of H5N1, and provide WHO with surveillance data.

3.1.5.2   Risk assessment mechanisms

Risk assessment mechanisms included the completion of the risk assessment method, evaluation of the pandemic phase with the support of the task force, and uncertainty reduction. The determination that the H5N1 avian influenza outbreak qualified as a PHEIC based on Annex 2 of the IHR was a key driver in launching an international response. Due to the high level of uncertainty, estimates of the risk vary significantly in regard to the epidemiological assumptions, which are reflected in the evaluation of the cost of a pandemic.

The WHO risk assessment process was based on the Global Influenza Surveillance Program as the main observation system, and the risk assessment mechanisms included the application of the overall risk assessment framework jointly with Annex 2 of the revised IHR 2005 and the "Guiding Principles for International Outbreak Alert." In addition, the risk assessment mechanism contained in the 2005 global influenza preparedness plan was applied in making a decision about the pandemic phase. WHO carried out risk assessment activities regarding the risk to human health and made joint recommendations with OIE and FAO to reduce the avian influenza spread among animals. WHO officials cooperated closely with both organizations in order to remain informed about the evolution of the disease in the animal population, as the control of the disease among animals was represented as a precondition to the reduction of the risk to humans.

Pandemic phases risk assessment.   WHO initially activated the "Influenza Pandemic Preparedness Plan of 1999" in January 2004 to assess the risk and declare the corresponding pandemic phase. The revision process of the influenza pandemic preparedness plan was accelerated, and its draft served as the basis for the reassessment of the phases until 2005. The "WHO Global Influenza Preparedness Plan" (145 p. 2) of 2005 provided a classification of an influenza pandemic in six phases that was summarized and published on the WHO website, as shown in Table 3.3 below:

Table 3.3   Classification of influenza pandemic phases, WHO global influenza preparedness plan of 2005

Inter-pandemic phase	Low risk of human cases	1
New virus in animals, no human cases	Higher risk of human cases	2
Pandemic alert	No or very limited human-to-human transmission	③
	Evidence of increased human-to human transmission	4
New virus causes human cases	Evidence of significant human-to-human transmission	5
Pandemic	Efficient and sustained human-to-human transmission	6

The distinction between the phases depends on risk assessments based on the latest current knowledge about the risk. (145 p. 6) The adoption of one phase triggers a series of measures to be undertaken by WHO and member states in order to prevent an influenza pandemic from arising or to handle it once it occurs. Inter-pandemic Phases 1 and 2 correspond to the suspicion or the evidence of a new virus strain in animals that could result in human infection. The assessment evaluates the risk of human infection and includes factors such as pathogenicity in animals and humans, occurrence in domesticated animals and livestock or only in wildlife, geographic spread, and virus characteristics. Preparedness measures (promoting global surveillance and contingency planning) and public health measures to protect persons at risk (measures to reduce risk of infection, vaccine development, availability of antiviral drugs) should be put into place.

For phases 3, 4, and 5, the risk of a pandemic is assessed by evaluating the rate of transmission, geographical location and spread, severity of illness, presence of genes from human strains (if derived from an animal strain), and other scientific parameters. For Phase 3, measures are needed to detect, notify, characterize, and prevent the spread of disease, but the disease remains essentially not transmissible from human to human. These measures include states' guidance and laboratory confirmations, information and communication actions, and recommendation of measures for affected and nonaffected areas, such as infection control measures (wearing face masks) and social distancing measures (confinement). Phase 4 is characterized by limited human-to-human transmission and triggers measures to contain the disease within limited foci or to delay its spread to avert a pandemic and to gain time to implement measures. Phase 5 corresponds to a substantial risk of pandemic with larger clusters of localized human-to-human transmission that would lead to an intensification of the measures in Phase 4. Finally, Phase 6 would be the pandemic, which is characterized by increased and sustained transmission in the general population. WHO's actions would aim to minimize the impact by closely monitoring epidemiological, virology, and clinical features of the disease and its global impact and assessment of the effectiveness of measures. These actions would also include mitigating the impact in affected countries by promoting increased production of vaccines and antivirals, and optimizing patient care.

Based on the assessment of the risk of an H5N1 influenza pandemic, WHO declared the world to be in Phase 3. (133) Phase 3 is characterized by human infection(s) with a new subtype, but no human-to-human spread or, in most rare instances, of spread via a close contact. (145 p. 7) WHO provided guidance to national authorities regarding risk assessment and risk response, country assistance, and laboratory testing. It fostered collaboration to collect strains, established case definitions, and published avian flu-related information. WHO officials also promoted vaccine development and antiviral stockpiles.

The world remained in Phase 3 during the period under study (it is currently in the "alert" phase (168), according to the Pandemic Influenza Risk Management – WHO Interim Guidance published in 2013), which implied the continuous assessment of the risk to change phases, the adoption of preparedness measures, and risk communication activities. The level of risk and the measures to be taken are reevaluated on a regular basis regarding the evolution capacity of the virus to transmit among humans. Phase 4 would be declared based on a risk assessment performed once a new human virus appears and transmits easily among humans. Although transmission among humans was recognized in specific clusters (e.g., in Vietnam and Thailand), WHO officials considered that these sporadic cases in different countries did not constitute an increased human-to-human transmission. As a consequence, the pandemic alert was not upgraded to Phase 4. However, as the H5N1 virus is still circulating among animals and humans and causing illness and deaths, and the risk of an influenza pandemic remains present, Phase 3 was not downgraded to Phase 2.

The WHO Director-General is ultimately in charge of declaring that the world is in a specific pandemic phase and of deciding on a change of phase. The Director-General's decision was based on a written recommendation that was issued by a committee composed, at the time of the outbreak, of the Assistant Director-General for the Communicable Diseases cluster (Dr. Margaret Chan), the Director of the EPR team (Dr. Mike Ryan),[12] the Global Influenza Programme leader (Dr. Klaus Stöhr), their regional equivalents, and selected experts. A teleconference was organized to discuss the avian influenza evolution, and before or during this conference, the participants could ask for epidemiologic complements of information in order to give their opinion on the current situation. Such teleconferences usually result in recommendations that are drafted by the reporting person and take the form of a "Note for the Record" that is transmitted to the Director-General as support for the group's decision.

Risk assessment method implementation. The "Guiding Principles for International Outbreak Alert" (see risk assessment mechanisms in Chapter 2) was applied with the general risk assessment framework and in the general frame of the global influenza surveillance program. The implementation methods included detection, verification, and communication of the avian influenza cases, as well as risk assessment steps. Detection followed the specific procedures established within the Global Influenza Surveillance Program. In this risk assessment, WHO considered elements such as context, the fact that the disease was known, its regional and then intercontinental spread, its potential serious health impact (high mortality rate), its transmission capacity (from animal to human), its potential impact on travel and trade (impact on poultry trade), and the capacities of infrastructures and health care to handle the disease, in order to make a first decision on how the event should be handled (in pandemic Phase 3, the number of cases is limited).

The alert regarding the resurgence of the H5N1 virus in February 2003 was given through the normal routine surveillance activities of the WHO Global Influenza Surveillance Network. Influenza surveillance follows preestablished procedures that have a long history of practice. The first human case of avian influenza H5N1 was reported in Hong

Kong in February 2003. This case, as well as a second case identified in Hong Kong, followed the general routine procedure established for the surveillance of influenza. The first examination of the patient at the hospital detected a flu virus of type A, generating the performance of further laboratory analysis to determine the virus identity and whether it was of A (H5N1) type. A representative in one of the WHO reference centers located in Hong Kong confirmed the presence of the influenza virus A subtype H5N1 in the first sample analyzed. The usual influenza surveillance procedure prescribes that a hospital representative should communicate the results of the analysis to an official in the ministry of health, who will transmit them to the WHO regional office. The WHO regional office will then inform the WHO headquarters in Geneva, which is what happed in that case. Simultaneously, officials in the ministry of health of the concerned country can also inform WHO headquarters, which was also the case for these two avian influenza cases. The same procedure will apply for other cases reported in other countries later in the process. Once the cases are verified, WHO will publish a report on its website.

The identification of these two human cases coincided with and was related to the strange pneumonia cases (later known as SARS cases) that were reported in China, Hong Kong, and Vietnam during the same period of time and led to the publication of a disease outbreak report. This report explained that avian influenza H5N1 had been detected among a family that had traveled to South China and that the WHO Global Influenza Surveillance Network was put on alert. (139) Even after the risk of an avian influenza pandemic was ruled out in order to focus on the new disease, SARS, these two cases of avian influenza H5N1 remained a concern for Hong Kong authorities, based on the precedent of 1997. The H5N1 virus was a strong candidate for a human influenza pandemic due to its virulence and its capacity to mutate or to reassort. The WHO officials follow up on infectious disease outbreaks during regular technical meetings held every morning at the WHO headquarters while avian influenza officers meet weekly or on an ad hoc basis, specifically, or more frequently if deemed necessary. Past experience with the Spanish flu, the flu of 1957, and the flu of 1968 also raised concern among experts. A pandemic was expected to be more devastating due to the intensification of international trade and travel, but the capacities to respond to such diseases have also improved worldwide.

In terms of application of the overall risk assessment framework, the situation is different from SARS due to the fact that H5N1 avian influenza is a known disease for which the causative agent is identified and characterized. On February 19, 2003, the results from two laboratories confirmed the presence of the influenza virus A subtype H5N1 in one of the two patients reported by Hong Kong authorities. The causative agent was identified and was similar to an influenza outbreak in Hong Kong in 1997 that had been detected in 18 patients, causing 6 deaths. The high pathogenicity of the virus A (H5N1) already was established in 1997. At that time, the systematic culling of the entire poultry population in Hong Kong and the closing and disinfection of animal markets, as well as the implementation of sanitary days was the key to eradicating the virus in Hong Kong and are considered to have averted a pandemic.

Animals are the principal vector of the disease. The disease probably found its source in waterfowl and has propagated among chicken and ducks. The virus has crossed the species barrier, infecting pigs and feline animals. As animals, in particular poultry – and in some cases pigs – are the main vectors of the disease to humans, the reduction of the risk to human health is conditioned by the reduction of the risk to animal health.

In 2003, further investigations were performed, as other members of the family were sick, and one daughter had died on February 4, 2003, in Fujian Province, China. Hong Kong authorities pursued laboratory and epidemiologic investigations to determine the source of infection as no outbreaks of avian influenza had been reported in Hong Kong, but the investigations were put on hold due to the SARS outbreak and the absence of other cases reported. Outbreaks in Korea and Vietnam could be traced back to the same agent, and on August 8, 2004, epidemiological research traced the first human case in China to November 25, 2003, which was misidentified as a SARS case in Beijing. This case became the first confirmed case of the avian influenza outbreak of 2003–2004.

In addition, the cause-effect relationship became known, as well as the lethal capacity of the virus. The exposure assessment consisted of estimating how humans could become exposed to the virus and with what effect. If the H5N1 virus origin was clearly identified in all Asian countries that were affected in the first months of 2004, the exposure conditions and the populations at risk were more difficult to estimate. Investigation missions were led in Vietnam and Thailand to learn more about the modes of transmission of the disease from poultry to humans. These studies led to the conclusion that the disease was transmitted through close contact with infected poultry and that in Thailand, the disease may have had other symptoms than those initially observed. Initial research done on ten patients in Vietnam identified close contact (holding, killing, or preparing food) with infected poultry as the probable source of infection in eight out of nine patients for whom a clear history could be taken, but could not completely rule out human-to-human transmission within two family clusters. (159) This study also referred to previous research done based on the 1997 outbreak of H5N1 influenza in Hong Kong, where limited human-to-human transmission was evidenced, but could not be sustained. The authors also reminded readers that previous evidence has been found that this virus has the ability to jump and cause devastating illness in humans.

The circulation of the avian influenza virus H5N1 within East Asian countries, and later in the Middle East, Europe, and Africa, has increased the risk of an influenza pandemic by multiplying the sources of a potential outbreak of human influenza originating in the H5N1 avian influenza animal reservoir. The sources of the risk have been identified as wild birds that have traveled along the migration roads, contaminating ducks and poultry, as well as pigs in certain circumstances. The different virus strains have been identified and analyzed in order to produce vaccines and watch the evolution of the virus, so as to anticipate a mutation or a reassortment that could affect humans more easily and intensively. The risk of a human influenza pandemic mainly relies on the capacity of the virus A (H5N1) to reassort or mutate into a new virus more – or equally as – pathogenic than the virus A (H5N1) that would transmit easily and efficiently among humans. A human pandemic may also originate in another virus, but the H5N1 represents a potential source for a human pandemic. First, the virus is highly pathogenic and lethal both for animals and humans. Second, the virus probably is of Chinese origin, has spread internationally, and has developed among domestic poultry that live closely with humans and therefore constitute a risk for humans to catch the disease. Third, the disease has been present for a certain period of time among animals and has become endemic in some parts of the world, affecting poultry and other animals such as pigs. This is a reason why experts have been evaluating the risk of human influenza derived from avian influenza H5N1 as likely and, in particular, in a mutated or reasserted strain of virus A (H5N1).

The dose-response or cause-effect assessment relates to the amount of exposure necessary to cause the disease. The virus also became more lethal in 2004 and could survive longer in the environment, (169) but direct contact with infected poultry, or surfaces and objects contaminated by their feces, is considered as the main source of infection. The groups at risk are rural populations that keep small poultry flocks around their house and poultry farm workers. Cooked food is without risk, but consuming raw poultry or eggs in affected areas should be avoided. In

1997, as in 2003 and early 2004, the identified human cases were linked to close contacts with animals and, in some cases, to ingestion of raw poultry food or blood, but the disease has not been easily transmitted from human to human. Isolated cases of human transmission have occurred, but have not resulted in easy and effective transmission from human to human. Finally, risk characterization should result in the calculation of a risk, such as the number of people who could catch the avian influenza in a particular population. This phase can give rise to a quantitative result mostly in the form of a probability or a qualitative result expressed by scenarios. Modeling studies were used as a basis to produce different scenarios, usually a mild and severe scenario (sometimes with a middle-range scenario). The results varied significantly based on the method applied, the data used, and the assumptions made.

Controversies arose about the probability of the occurrence of a human influenza pandemic and the severity of its consequences. The position of WHO is that a human influenza pandemic is certain and will occur in the twenty-first century. Therefore, its probability of occurrence is 1, and compared to previous pandemics, its impact is expected to be significant worldwide. WHO worked on only this scenario, acknowledging as uncertain the timing of this pandemic and the virus (the source of the novel virus could be H5N1 or another virus). Professor Robert Webster, a world-renowned and influential virologist at St. Jude Hospital and an expert at WHO, has constantly warned the world about the occurrence of an influenza pandemic for approximately 30 years. More nuanced opinions, such as that of Professor Edwin D. Kilbourne, who retired from New York Medical in 2003, considers it "possible" that a virulent virus such as the agent of the Spanish influenza of 1918–1919 could confront the world again, and that "probably" medical technology and competence (including vaccines, antivirals, and antibiotics) could control it. He insists that no one knows whether there will be another Spanish influenza. (170 pp. 38–39) No definitive consensus exists among scientists about the certainty and the timing of an influenza pandemic of virus A (H5N1).

However, the risk of an avian influenza pandemic or another pandemic that may find its source in animal diseases is considered as real by a majority of scientists. Professor Robert Webster, borrowing the terms from Dr. Malik Peiris,[13] has qualified the risk of an influenza pandemic of H5N1 origin as "low probability, high impact." (171 p. slide 83) If the H5N1 becomes easily transmissible among humans and its case fatality ratio stays above 50%, the world would face a catastrophe. Although other influenza viruses have the potential to evolve into a pandemic virus, the H5N1 virus has particularly worried WHO and its experts. First, there is the existence of an H5N1 panzootic (a pandemic among animals), which constitutes a significant reservoir for infecting humans. Since the resurgence of the virus in the beginning of 2003, it has spread westward to affect Russia, Kazakhstan, Turkey, certain parts of Europe, and even Africa. It has also become endemic in parts of Asia and, more recently, in Africa. Second, the virus is highly lethal among animals and humans. Its case fatality ratio, both in birds and humans, is over 50%. Once an influenza outbreak starts and reaches a certain level of local or regional spread, continued worldwide spread of the virus is considered inevitable. Therefore, this pandemic could be particularly harmful, considering the fact that little or no immune protection has been developed against this H5N1 virus in the human population. Third, the H5N1 virus has the capacity to change in unpredictable ways, which would allow the new virus to spread efficiently and sustainably among people.

While experts mostly agree that the risk of a human influenza pandemic exists, the severity of its impact in terms of human lives is debated. This debate and its outputs were critical, as the estimated number of deaths is a central element for preparedness activities. An influenza pandemic could affect 20% to 50% of the population, with an unknown mortality rate, offering a wide range of possibilities for estimating the risk. Based on past pandemics, WHO communicated that up to 25% of the worldwide population, which represents about 1.5 billion people, may be affected by an influenza pandemic. (115 p. 47) During the meeting of November 25 to 26, 2004, held in Bangkok, that gathered representatives from WHO, ASEAN, and three countries, Dr. Klaus Stöhr, project leader of the GIP, publicly communicated WHO's first estimate of 2 to 7.4 million deaths due to an influenza pandemic. The WHO experts based their estimate on the model used by data produced by Martin Meltzer,[14] a health economist from the US CDC in Atlanta, whose model was based on the "mild" pandemic in 1968 (172).

The number of deaths has remained a controversial issue, due to the high level of uncertainty around the characteristics of the future influenza pandemic, including the novel virus's pathogenicity and virulence. Dr. Klaus Stöhr, project leader of the GIP from 2001 to 2006, estimated in the fall of 2004 that in a few months, a human flu pandemic could cause 20% of the world's population to become ill, about 28 million people to be hospitalized (if enough beds are available), and 7 million to die. (173 p. 2195) In comparison, the Spanish influenza pandemic of 1918–1919, against which all modern pandemics are measured, resulted in approximately 20% to 40% of the worldwide population's becoming ill and over 20 million deaths.[15] The WHO experts considered that the Spanish influenza was such an exceptional event that it should not be used as a benchmark for modeling the spread, morbidity, and mortality of the potential H5N1 human influenza pandemic. In addition, WHO argued that better nutrition and health conditions in 2004 compared to the period in which the Spanish influenza occurred, are positive factors to include in an analysis. (175) The WHO officials' announcement of a possible pandemic was controversial and put the organization in a difficult position. In the past, WHO had announced pandemics that did not occur. WHO may have used this cautious approach in order to safeguard the organization's credibility in the face of skeptical governments (176 p. 124).

However, experts such as Dr. Michael Osterholm, director of the Center for Infectious Disease Research and Policy at the University of Minnesota, considered the estimate of 2 million to 7.4 million deaths too cautious and responded to this estimate on November 25, 2004, saying that a 1918-like pandemic could kill at least 72 million. (172) In 2005, he published his conclusions about possible higher casualties, ranging from 180 million to 360 million deaths globally, based on the rate of death of the Spanish influenza. (177 p. 1842) On November 29, 2004, Dr. Shigeru Omi, director of WHO's Western Pacific Region Office in Manila, in response to this contestation of WHO's estimate, publicly said that the number of deaths could be as high as 20 million, 50 million, or "in the worst case," 100 million. (172) On December 8, 2004, WHO published a statement recognizing the scientific grounds of the different estimates and providing a range of 2 to 50 million deaths, in which the 7 million deaths were presented as a best-case scenario. (175) WHO justified the significant differences in estimates by the high level of uncertainty about the characteristics of the disease and the difficulties in making extrapolations from past pandemics. First, the proportion and the categories of the population that would be affected by the disease as well as the pathogenicity of the virus remain unknown. Second, the pandemics that were used as references for extrapolations presented different characteristics and incomplete or disputed data. Finally, extrapolations from past pandemics should take into account changes in the environment and the level of preparedness. While certain experts, such as Dr. Osterholm, still considered WHO's revised estimate as insufficient and lacking in leadership, others considered it an improvement and a recognition of the uncertainty surrounding this issue. (172) Various estimates were produced by different experts, including a worst-case scenario based on extrapolation on the lethality of GenZ of the 2004 H5N1 virus that reached an estimate of 1 billion deaths (176 p. 126).

Beyond the fight over numbers, this debate shows the difficulty experts may face in reaching a consensus in situations involving a high level of uncertainty and how the measures proposed could vary as a function of these estimates, such as contingency planning for health infrastructures and drug stockpiling. The WHO experts' assessment presented the risk of an influenza pandemic as certain and realistic, and emphasized the unprecedented opportunity to prepare for it. (178 p. 478) This risk assessment was associated with two unknowns: the time frame, and the virulence of a subsequent pandemic virus. (178 p. 478) The WHO experts justified their estimates by the fact that pandemic viruses present great variations in mortality, severity of illness, and patterns of transmission. In the fall of 2005, having considered the potential and the evolution of the H5N1 virus among animals and humans worldwide, WHO declared the world in Phase 3 of the pandemic classification: "a new influenza virus subtype is causing disease in humans but is not yet spreading efficiently and sustainably among humans." (133) Since that date, WHO has regularly confirmed that the world remains in the prepandemic Phase 3. In the fall of 2008, during the 2008 Wright Colloquium, Professor Webster underlined the fact that the H5N1 virus may not become the next pandemic virus due to its evolution so far, but that preparedness remains essential in facing the next virus that will come within the next 10 to 15 years and is useful in fighting seasonal influenza, as well (171).

Uncertainty reduction.   Uncertainties essentially are related to the pandemic timing and its severity. The virulence of the pandemic virus cannot be known in advance, although comparisons can be made with previous pandemic viruses or the H5N1 2004 strain. No one can predict with certainty when a pandemic will start, although an increase in the number of animal cases and human cases, combined with the appearance of seasonal influenza virus periods, increases the possibility of a pandemic occurring during these periods. The severity remains a highly debated issue, as explained in the section above. Scenario-building provides the possibility of reducing uncertainty, but the sensitivity to changes in parameters, such as the reference event (e.g., Spanish influenza or 1957 flu) or the infection rate, produces very different results that complicate the preparedness activities. Experts in the United States established a moderate scenario based on the 1958–1968 pandemic and a severe scenario based on the Spanish influenza. (179 p. 18) While in both scenarios they assume that 30% of the population would get sick (90 million), out of which 50% would need medical care (45 million), hospitalization (including intensive care and mechanical ventilation) as well as the number of deaths varies significantly. In the moderate scenario, they predict 865,000 hospitalizations and 209,000 deaths, compared to 9,900,000 and 1,903,000 in the severe scenario. Planning for these extreme scenarios is difficult, as even an event such as the moderate scenario involves significant loss of human life and a high burden on health care. As a comparison, worldwide seasonal influenza epidemics result in about 3 to 5 million cases of severe illness, and about 250,000 to 500,000 deaths (180) each year. European Union officials' summary of the main national plans considered that in the absence of any intervention, during a period of 9 to 15 weeks, 30% of the population would get sick, with an average of 0.37% deaths among infected people, (181 p. 4) which would result in about 150 million persons infected and 550,000 deaths. Based on these figures, case fatality ratios – understood as the proportion of deaths among ill persons – are respectively 0.23% and 2.1% for the American moderate- and severe scenarios and 0.37% for Europe, compared to the WHO conservative scenario of 0.49% (182 p. 71).

During 2004 to 2005, due to uncertainties regarding the disease's evolution among animals and its transmission to humans, and in rare cases among humans, precise computations of the risk remained difficult. However, experts agreed that a risk of a human influenza pandemic of H5N1 origin existed. In particular, the capacity of the H5N1 virus to cause severe outbreaks in humans was evidenced in Hong Kong in 1997. At this stage, WHO believed that the outbreak could be controlled through the elimination of the animal reservoir (mostly poultry) to reduce the risk of human infections by the current virus and prevent it from having opportunities to transform into a human influenza pandemic virus. Later, it will be shown that if specific culling helps reduce the spread of the disease in one localized context, it appears to be ineffective in the longer term to reduce the risk of pandemic. Table 3.4 summarizes the elements that were known during this initial period.

As the level of uncertainty remains significant in regard to the risk of a human influenza pandemic, the risk assessment has been a continuous process based on global surveillance and the work of experts who have relied on the latest experimental and empirical studies to increase their knowledge about the current avian influenza virus H5N1 and, in particular, about the different virus strains that circulated in the different

Table 3.4   Balance between known and unknown facts about an H5N1 influenza pandemic

Known	Unknown
Severe disease in humans caused by avian influenza virus A subtype H5N1	Pathogenicity and virulence of novel pandemic virus
Highly lethal – Case fatality ratio above 50% for animals and humans	Case fatality of influenza issued from pandemic novel virus
International spread of avian influenza H5N1	Rapidity and scope of international spread
Not easily transmittable – close contact needed with infected animals	Transmission modes – expected to be similar to those of regular influenza
Symptoms	Symptoms
Global impact	Magnitude of global impact
Drugs' effectiveness	Drugs' effectiveness

countries, transmission modes, symptoms, clinical management, and effective treatments. However, all this knowledge was accumulated regarding the avian influenza virus H5N1, while experts recognized that the disease that may ultimately result from it may present different features. Increasing knowledge about the H5N1 virus may not necessarily result in expanded knowledge about the novel virus, requiring that the process start again from a situation of a higher level of uncertainty. However, as the H5N1 is virulent in its current form, studying it and preparing for its sustainable transmissible version in humans appeared to the experts as a rational approach with which to start.

Although progress has been made on the knowledge spectrum since the virus subtype H5N1 appeared in 1997 in Hong Kong, uncertainty remains about the final virus that could come from the virus H5N1. One may consider the H5N1 disease in humans as a potential risk in 2004, and as the causative agent, the causal chain is known, as well as evidence about transmission by close contact. The H5N1 virus was clearly identified as provoking severe disease for humans. Knowledge about the avian influenza H5N1 in humans has progressed during the period considered here, mainly regarding the transmissibility of the disease, clinical features, and analysis and sequencing of the virus strains, but the risk is not completely known. Studies have shown that the virus develops in different strains – and these should be closely watched as one could give rise to a pandemic – and also that transmissibility among humans may occur in rare cases. Different models based on expert judgments to formulate probabilities and potential damage in order to estimate the number of human deaths, as well as the social and economic costs, have been proposed and serve as a basis for discussion and analysis both at the international and the national levels.

Task force role in risk assessment.   The Avian Influenza Task Force functioned as the emergency committee prescribed in the IHR 2005. In the case of the avian flu, the WHO collaboration with outside experts relied on the influenza network of laboratories and experts. For existing diseases referred to as "known risks," such as regular influenza, WHO was already working with a network of external experts. WHO officers already knew the personnel of focal points who were involved in the management of infectious diseases, but this information was not centrally documented and accessible within the organization. Dr. Stöhr, who was instrumental in setting up the multicollaboration center during the SARS outbreak, benefitted from his experience and contacts to organize this task force internally (WHO personnel) and externally (experts). Members of this task force provided advice to the Director-General, but did not constitute the only source of information for the Director-General. The Director-General also received information from other organizations, governments (and not only through their ministries of health), and personnel in other internal WHO programs.

The Director-General was directly involved in the management of the H5N1 avian influenza issue, with the support of senior experienced staff from WHO's headquarters in Geneva (in particular from the GIP and the Epidemic and Pandemic Alert and Response team) and from the regional offices. The advice of experts, including risk assessment results, was an essential aspect of the decision-making process. The Director-General had to balance expert advice with other information that came from ministries of health, for example, or other organizations (governmental or nongovernmental) or internally from WHO-related programs.

For example, in the case of the avian influenza, vaccination recommendations from experts were considered in light of the opinion of experts in the WHO vaccine programs that proved to work well and be effective over the past 40 years. The Director-General also relied on internal experience and skills to ensure the feasibility of a recommendation and to adjust it, if necessary. Lessons from the SARS outbreak could be used to improve action, in particular, in dealing with affected areas. Finally, political considerations also played a role, such as governments that expressed their worries about the impact of the avian influenza on their economies (e.g., tourism) or international trade (e.g., trade of poultry or related food products). The Director-General had the final word on the measures to be adopted and communicated, such as the decision of the pandemic phase (see above). Any change in phase has to be decided by the Director-General of WHO, based on the risk assessment that is prepared within the organization and with the contribution of external experts.

3.1.5.3   Cost analysis

WHO included a cost analysis within the risk assessment, both with regard to human lives and in monetary terms. WHO's evaluation of human life losses was based on modeling studies, and the estimate initially used was largely debated. In summary, human life losses could range from 2 million to 1 billion. WHO undertook preparedness actions in any case, but the estimation of drugs and vaccine needed, for example, has to be based on an estimate. This estimate could be effective (matching the needs) or ineffective (excess of stockpiling or lack of drugs), both of which would generate costs to be compared to the initial estimates. We did not find evidence of such analysis.

Another critical aspect for the emergence of the avian influenza as an international issue is its impact on the economic system, in particular on trade and travel. Different studies were performed on the risks of the infectious diseases and their impact on the economies. While the US CDC estimated the loss from USD 71 billion to USD 166 billion for the US economy only, (183 p. 114) the global impact of an influenza pandemic ranges from USD 200 billion to USD 4 trillion, depending on the duration of the pandemic, its attack rate, and mortality. The epidemiological uncertainty is reflected in the uncertainty of the global economic impact.

Table 3.5 overleaf provides an overview of different estimates.

During the international "Meeting on Avian Influenza and Human Pandemic Influenza" (188) that gathered 600 delegates from over 100 countries, held on November 7 to 9, 2005, in Geneva by WHO, Milan Brahmbhatt presented the World Bank perspective on the economic impact of an influenza pandemic and the estimated cost of a human pandemic of USD 800 billion per year, (189) which corresponds to a 2% loss in the worldwide GDP. This estimate was higher than the cost of SARS, as World Bank experts considered the duration of an influenza pandemic would be longer than the SARS outbreak of 2003. In comparison, SARS resulted in a loss of 2% in the East Asian GDP over three months in 2003. WHO used the World Bank estimate as a reference already in 2005 in its summary report (147) of the November

Table 3.5   Estimates of global economic impact of an influenza pandemic

Source	Model	Mild scenario (GDP loss)	Ultra scenario (GDP loss)	Comment
Warwick McKibbin, Alexandra Sidorenko (2006). (184)	APG-Cubed Model	0.8% USD $330 billion	12.6% USD $4.4 trillion	Model applied to 20 countries
World Bank (2005). (185)	Oxford Economic Forecasting model (OEF)	2% GDP USD $800 billion per year	4%–5% USD $1.5–2 trillion. (186)	Mild scenario used by WHO as reference
Vanessa Rossi, John Walker, (94 p. 18) Oxford Economic Group (2005)	Oxford Economic Forecasting model (OEF)	USD $150–$200 billion	5%–6% USD $1–2 trillion	Extrapolation of SARS
Erik Bloom, Vincent De Wit. (187) (2005)	Oxford Economic Forecasting model (OEF)	2.3% USD $14.2 billion	6.5% USD $282.7 billion	Impact on Asian Economies

international conference and continued to use it repeatedly during the period under study (190).

The International Pledging Conference on Avian and Human Influenza that was held in Beijing, on January 17 to 18, 2006, for the purpose of addressing the financial needs expressed during the WHO meeting of November 2005, resulted in funds pledged of USD 1.9 billion. These funds aimed to cover WHO, FAO, and OIE strategies to reduce the risk of a pandemic. The FAO and OIE strategy aimed to control avian influenza in terrestrial poultry in Asia to reduce the risk of human infection and the risk of a pandemic virus arising. These funds do not include the funds allocated directly by the organizations in their regular budget. For example, in the risk assessment, WHO included a budget for pandemic preparedness, which constituted an improvement as compared to the SARS preparedness. Officials at WHO established a strategic two-year action plan covering 2006 and 2007 that described their strategy regarding an influenza pandemic, goals, actions to be undertaken and the expected results, as well as the estimated costs for these strategies. They presented an evaluation of the funding requirements to complete the two-year strategy and reach the expected results in terms of reducing human exposure to the H5N1 virus, strengthening the early warning system, intensifying rapid containment operations, building the capacity to cope with a pandemic, and implementing global coordination of scientific research and development (157 p. 22).

In total, as illustrated in the Table 3.6, WHO needed a budget of USD 100 million to carry out this action plan, of which about one-third was allocated to the work that took place at WHO headquarters. These costs of USD 100 million should be added to the USD 1.9 billion pledge from donors, as well as costs from regular budgets of other organizations, and preparedness costs related to national investments requested to upgrade health infrastructures, to establish emergency plans, and to improve surveillance activities.

In the risk assessment, WHO experts referred to the World Bank mild scenario estimate of USD 800 billion per year as a justification to undertake costly actions for preparedness that could save future higher costs. Based on the SARS experience and modeling studies, WHO experts considered that the social and economic disruptions generated by an influenza pandemic will be more significant due to the interconnectedness and

Table 3.6   WHO strategic action plan budget, 2006–2007

Strategic action plan goals	2006–2007 WHO Funding Requirements in USD Million							
	HQ	AFRO	AMRO	EMRO	EURO	SEARO	WPRO	TOTAL
Reduce human exposure to H5N1	3.0	0.5	0.6	0.5	0.6	0.5	0.5	6.2
Strengthen the early warning system	5.0	3.0	2.0	2.0	3.0	3.5	3.5	22.0
Intensify rapid containment operations	10.0	3.0	1.1	3.0	3.0	3.0	3.0	26.1
Build capacity to cope with a pandemic	4.0	4.0	4.0	4.0	4.0	4.0	4.0	28.0
Coordinate national and international science & research	13.0	0.5	0.6	0.5	0.5	1.0	1.0	17.1
Total funding requirements	35.0	11.0	8.3	10.0	11.1	12.0	12.0	99.4

interdependency of trade and economic systems and the nature of the disease. (149 p. 3) In this context, the approximate USD 2 billion costs appear to be highly accurate. When referring to the World Bank estimate and the funds needed to carry out preparedness activities, WHO implicitly carried out the message that these costly actions would be inferior compared to the current estimated costs of a pandemic and that these investments to reduce the panzootic risk, to improve surveillance, and to reinforce coping capacities could possibly result in lower costs than estimated in the event that a pandemic arises.

3.2   Avian influenza H5N1 international response

The determination of whether a PHEIC exists was a key driver for the initiation of an international response. It generated early communication about the public health risk and, in particular, the risk of international spread. WHO issued statements of information and recommendations to guide states in their risk reduction activities.

The WHO response to reduce the risk of an influenza pandemic is articulated around six cornerstones that are addressed: (1) reducing the opportunities for human infection; (2) strengthening early warning systems; (3) building the capacity to cope with a pandemic; (4) containing or delaying the spread at the source; (5) reducing morbidity, mortality, and social disruptions; (6) coordinating scientific research. The first three activities are preparedness actions that take place prepandemic, while containment and reduction of the impact are launched when the virus emerges. While research activities are conducted in prepandemic periods to increase the level of knowledge about the risk of an influenza pandemic, during the pandemic phases, guiding the response and providing for corrective action are crucial. Scientific assessment of the epidemiological characteristics of an emerging pandemic, evaluation of the effectiveness of health interventions, and evaluation of medical and economic consequences of the pandemic will influence the allocation of resources. The main recommendations in relation to the six cornerstones mentioned above are described in the document "Responding to the Avian Influenza Pandemic Threat: Recommended Strategic Actions," (130) and were further developed in the "WHO Strategic Action Plan for Pandemic Influenza 2006–2007." (149) These two documents were used as the basis for our analysis as they synthesized the measures taken by WHO since 2004.

Between January 2004 and December 2008, WHO issued more than 50 guidelines, recommendations, and descriptions regarding the avian influenza H5N1 (191) in the areas of diagnosis and treatment, food safety, infections control, vaccines and antivirals, and surveillance to address the outbreak and to prepare for an influenza pandemic. We analyzed how the risk assessment was completed once the H5N1 resurgence occurred as a general activity and focused on particular aspects to show how each aspect contributed to the issuance of these strategic actions. For more details about these actions, we referred to specific recommendations that were issued, as the study of all recommendations would not have been feasible due to time and scope constraints linked to this research. The global strategy for the progressive control of highly pathogenic avian influenza published in collaboration with United Nations' FAO and the OIE underlined human health and animal sector preventive measures that could be jointly implemented, such as surveillance of human cases and poultry outbreaks, which were used as an indication of the measures necessary to reduce the exposure of humans to the H5N1 virus. While WHO's preparedness activities for facing an influenza pandemic started before 2004 with the issuance of an influenza pandemic preparedness plan in 1999, they have intensified since the resurgence of the H5N1 virus in 2004. WHO accelerated the revision of this plan, which was made available in the spring of 2005 to serve as a guide for countries' authorities to organize their preparedness and contingency actions. This release contributed to building countries' response capacities. As containment is a key concept in use since 2002, we also analyzed the preparation of the containment protocol that will be a key instrument in delaying or containing the disease at its source. Research activities were addressed as an inherent part of the scientific risk assessment in order to determine how research results were included in the measures recommended by WHO.

The measures proposed were essentially preparedness measures, such as the reduction of possibilities of infection arising from animals, development of preparedness plans, reinforcement of health infrastructures and surveillance systems, development of vaccines, and the stockpiling of drugs. The WHO experts' strategy regarding avian influenza aims at reducing human exposure to the H5N1 virus, strengthening the surveillance system and early warning, containing the disease at its source or limiting its spread, building the capacity to cope with the pandemic, and coordinating international scientific research and development. (149) WHO coordinated a cooperative response and used adequate channels of communication in regard to the avian influenza H5N1. Coordination with other organizations, such as the United Nations and the World Bank, was necessary as one organization could not ensure the totality of actions at the global level, and additional funds were required. Animal health being intertwined with human health, cooperative action with OIE and FAO was essential to ensure risk reduction in both areas. Cooperation was also achieved with the private sector in regard to the production and stockpiling of drugs. Finally, cooperation with other initiatives and institutions, such as the World Bank for the financing of the activities, was ensured.

3.2.1 Reduction of casualties

Casualties in terms of animal and human cases increased and peaked in 2006, but have decreased since then up to 2008. However, the avian influenza is endemic in certain countries, and the situation remains preoccupying as the virus could mutate and spread among populations.

WHO took measures to limit the exposure of humans to infection by issuing infection control measures and food safety recommendations and proceeding to information campaigns during field missions. In parallel (and jointly with WHO in certain field missions), FAO and OIE carried out culling operations to reduce the number of infected animals, therefore limiting the opportunities for human contagion. These measures contributed to the preservation of the collective interest by reducing the risk of an H5N1 pandemic, limiting the geographical spread of the disease among animals and humans, and reducing the number of cases. These measures were carried out during the entire period under study following the outbreaks in animals.

Table 3.7 shows an overview of the outbreaks in animals up to February 2009, the status of each area in terms of avian influenza among animals, and the correspondence with human outbreaks.

This table shows that in 2009, out of the 63 areas that reported avian influenza outbreaks among animals (domestic poultry and wild animals), only 8 reported new outbreaks in animals and 3 in humans. This illustrates a trend that the disease was coming under control, except in certain countries such as Vietnam, China, and Egypt, where it has become endemic. It also shows that officials in approximately one-third of the countries declared them to be H5N1 free, and one-fourth declared their outbreaks resolved. However, information about animal cases was not available for countries such as Indonesia, where the disease is entrenched, and for other developing countries. No evidence shows that these countries are H5N1 free or that the outbreaks have been resolved. Similarly, human cases may not be reported due to insufficient detection capacities or lack of resources to do the reporting.

Table 3.7 Outbreaks of avian influenza H5N1 among animals and humans by affected area

H5N1 Avian influenza Affected areas	Status at Feb 2009 of animal outbreaks	Animal cases reported			Human cases reported			Reported cases 2009
		month	day	year	month	day	year	
Republic of Korea	free	Dec	12	2003	None			No cases reported
Vietnam	*notified 2009*	*Jan*	*8*	*2004*	*Jan*	*11*	*2004*	*outbreak*
Japan	free	Jan	12	2004	None			No cases reported
Hong Kong	notified 2009	Jan	19	2004	None			No cases reported
Thailand	free	Jan	23	2004	Jan	23	2004	No cases reported
Cambodia	resolved	Jan	24	2004	Feb	2	2005	No cases reported
Lao PDR	notified 2009	Jan	27	2004	Feb	26	2007	No cases reported
Indonesia	not available	Feb	2	2004	Jul	21	2005	No cases reported
*China**	*notified 2009*	*Feb*	*4*	*2004*	*Nov*	*25*	*2003*	*outbreak*
Malaysia	free	Aug	19	2004	None			No cases reported
Russia	free	Jul	23	2005	None			No cases reported
Kazakhstan	not available	Jul	29	2005	None			No cases reported
Mongolia	not available	Aug	10	2005	None			No cases reported
Turkey	free, resolved	Oct	6	2005	Jan	5	2006	No cases reported
Romania	free	Oct	7	2005	None			No cases reported
Taiwan	not available	Oct	20	2005	None			No cases reported
Croatia	not available	Oct	21	2005	None			No cases reported

Continued

Table 3.7 Continued

H5N1 Avian influenza Affected areas	Status at Feb 2009 of animal outbreaks	Animal cases reported			Human cases reported			Reported cases 2009
		month	day	year	month	day	year	
United Kingdom	resolved	Oct	23	2005	None			No cases reported
Kuwait	free	Nov	11	2005	None			No cases reported
Ukraine	free	Dec	2	2005	None			No cases reported
Iraq	not available	Feb	1	2006	Jan	30	2006	No cases reported
Bulgaria	not available	Feb	3	2006	None			No cases reported
Nigeria	resolved	Feb	8	2006	Jan	31	2007	No cases reported
Greece	not available	Feb	9	2006	None			No cases reported
Italy	not available	Feb	11	2006	None			No cases reported
Slovenia	not available	Feb	12	2006	None			No cases reported
Iran	free	Feb	13	2006	None			No cases reported
Germany	notified 2009	Feb	14	2006	None			No cases reported
Egypt	*not available*	*Feb*	*17*	*2006*	*Mar*	*20*	*2006*	*outbreak*
France	free	Feb	17	2006	None			No cases reported
India	notified 2009	Feb	18	2006	None			No cases reported
Austria	not available	Feb	18	2006	None			No cases reported
Bosnia-Herzegovina	not available	Feb	20	2006	None			No cases reported

Slovakia	not available	Feb	20	2006	None			No cases reported
Hungary	free	Feb	21	2006	None			No cases reported
Azerbaijan	resolved	Feb	24	2006	Mar	14	2006	No cases reported
Georgia	not available	Feb	24	2006	None			No cases reported
Niger	not available	Feb	27	2006	None			No cases reported
Pakistan	free	Feb	27	2006	Dec	15	2007	No cases reported
Serbia-Montenegro	resolved	Mar	1	2006	None			No cases reported
Switzerland	not available	Mar	1	2006	None			No cases reported
Poland	free, resolved	Mar	6	2006	None			No cases reported
Albania	free	Mar	7	2006	None			No cases reported
Myanmar	free	Mar	9	2006	Dec	14	2007	No cases reported
Cameroon	not available	Mar	11	2006	None			No cases reported
Denmark	resolved	Mar	14	2006	None			No cases reported
Afghanistan	not available	Mar	15	2006	None			No cases reported
Israel	free, resolved	Mar	16	2006	None			No cases reported
Sweden	resolved	Mar	16	2006	None			No cases reported
Jordan	free	Mar	23	2006	None			No cases reported

Continued

Table 3.7 Continued

H5N1 Avian influenza Affected areas	Status at Feb 2009 of animal outbreaks	Animal cases reported			Human cases reported			Reported cases 2009
		month	day	year	month	day	year	
West Bank/Gaza Strip	free	Mar	23	2006	None			No cases reported
Czech Republic	not available	Mar	27	2006	None			No cases reported
Burkina Faso	not available	Apr	3	2006	None			No cases reported
Sudan	free	Apr	17	2006	None			No cases reported
Côte d'Ivoire	resolved	Apr	19	2006	None			No cases reported
Djibouti	resolved	Apr	24	2006	May	12		No cases reported
USA	not available	Aug	14	2006		None	2006	No cases reported
Bangladesh	notified 2009	Mar	30	2007	May	28	2008	No cases reported
Saudi Arabia	free	Apr	2	2007	None			No cases reported
Ghana	resolved	Apr	12	2007	None			No cases reported
Togo	resolved	Jun	22	2007	None			No cases reported
Benin	resolved	Dec	5	2007	None			No cases reported
Nepal	notified 2009	Jan	16	2009	None			No cases reported

* Outbreaks in poultry announced on January 27, 2004. First case retrospectively dated November 25, 2003, confirmed in August 2006 as wrongly attributed to SARS.

Table 3.7 is based on data through February 2009 reported by countries to WHO (192) and OIE. (193) The sections below are based on data reported by countries to WHO (192) and to OIE up to December 2008. Two OIE databases were used: the WAHID database (194) for data since 2005 and the HANDISTATUS II (195) for data prior to 2005.

3.2.1.1   Spread limitation

International spread continues but to a lesser extent. Risk reduction can be expressed by the number of affected countries remaining stable or decreasing during the period. The risk of an influenza pandemic is linked to the avian panzootic. Therefore, and although WHO focused on measures to protect humans, WHO, FAO, and OIE assisted countries in decreasing the risk of a human influenza pandemic by reducing the presence of the H5N1 virus among animals. Massive culling campaigns took place in Asia, and carcasses were destroyed, which should result in outbreaks being stopped or even resolved. One limitation of this approach is the completeness and reliability of data, as reporting is essentially based on spontaneous notifications of H5N1 outbreaks to OEI as well as an indication of the number of cases, the number of deaths, and the number of animals destroyed. We have considered the cases of avian influenza (and not the suspected cases that are also reported to OIE) to remain closer to the approach used for human cases, which are confirmed laboratory cases. The total number of deaths refers to the birds that died from the avian influenza, while the total number of animals destroyed is the result of the killing and destruction of carcasses. These data were gathered by country[16] and aggregated for the purpose of this analysis.

Spread in humans.   Between 2003 and 2008, 393 human cases of avian were reported to WHO by officials in 15 countries. Table 3.8 overleaf, illustrates the chronological progression of the avian influenza disease in humans worldwide and provides the number of cases by country and by year with an indication of the first reporting date for each onset.

This table shows that avian influenza among humans has spread as of 2008, recording one new country affected by the disease, Bangladesh, during that year. It also highlights the fact that from 2003 to 2005, the disease remained regional and mostly affected East Asian countries (China, Vietnam, Thailand, Cambodia, and Indonesia). It moved to the Middle East and Africa in 2006, and continued to affect countries in Asian and African continents into 2008. If Europe has been affected by avian influenza among animals, no human cases have been reported.

Table 3.8   Number of human cases of avian influenza H5N1 per country and per year of onset

Reported	Country	2003	2004	2005	2006	2007	2008	Total cases
Nov-25-03	China	1		8	13	5	4	31
Jan-11-04	Viet Nam	3	29	61		8	6	107
Jan-23-04	Thailand		17	5	3			25
Feb-02-05	Cambodia			4	2	1	1	8
Jul-21-05	Indonesia			20	55	42	22	139
Jan-05-06	Turkey				12			12
Jan-30-06	Iraq				3			3
Mar-14-06	Azerbaijan				8			8
Mar-20-06	Egypt				18	25	8	51
May-12-06	Djibouti				1			1
Jan-31-07	Nigeria					1		1
Feb-26-07	Lao PDR					2		2
Dec-14-07	Myanmar					1		1
Dec-15-07	Pakistan					3		3
May-28-08	Bangladesh						1	1
Total of cases		4	46	98	115	88	42	393

Note: China's first case retrospectively confirmed in 2006. Vietnam's first cases occur in December 2003 and are reported in January 2004.

In addition, North and South America, as well as Australia, have been spared, both from animal and human cases.

Thailand, Turkey, Iraq, Azerbaijan, and Djibouti did not record any avian influenza cases among humans in 2007 and 2008. Although it may be too early to declare these areas free of avian influenza, this reflects the effects of the measures that were implemented. In other countries, avian influenza became endemic, such as in China, Cambodia, Vietnam, Indonesia, and Egypt. In Egypt and Indonesia, the situation remains seriously preoccupying. Indonesia is the most affected country, and officials in that country did not succeed in controlling the disease. The quality of the surveillance system and the reliability of the reporting system in Egypt were questioned, as well as the absence of measures taken by government officials.

In fact, the incidence of the disease among humans depended on the level of the avian influenza outbreak among animals, in particular in poultry, and the presence of backyard flocks in households. Massive culling was one effective measure in controlling the outbreak among poultry in 1997 in Hong Kong, as well as improved sanitary measures in markets. Hong Kong officials have not reported any other human cases since 2003, although some infected wild birds were found and an outbreak in commercial poultry occurred in December 2008. The next section provides information about the spread in animals.

Spread in animals. The avian influenza H5N1 outbreak that started in China has affected 63 areas in total, reaching a peak of 54 areas affected in 2006. Table 3.9 shows the areas affected in the years from 2004 up to February 2009. The "1" indicates that the H5N1 avian influenza has been found in that country but not the numbers of outbreaks, as some countries have experienced numerous outbreaks. This table shows that a peak occurred in 2006 in a number of affected countries, which is also reflected in the number of reported human cases. This trend reflects the risk of infection of humans in dealing with sick poultry. In general, outbreaks in animals precede human cases. If outbreaks can be detected immediately and destruction measures taken rapidly, a chance exists to reduce the risk of human contamination.

3.2.1.2 Human life impact

The threat to human life on a worldwide basis can be measured through the evolution of the number of human cases of avian influenza per year worldwide and in the most affected countries. Between 2003 and 2008, a total of 393 human cases of avian influenza resulted in 248 deaths, with a case fatality ratio of about 63%.[17]

Avian influenza cases among humans. Figure 3.3 overleaf shows the yearly evolution of the total number of the human cases of H5N1 avian influenza in the world from 2003 to 2008.[18]

The number of avian influenza cases increased up to 2006, with a peak of 115 cases, and then decreased steadily up to 2008. This decrease occurred after the increased surveillance, protection, and infection control measures were put into place, including massive culling of birds in affected areas. Officials of WHO started communicating these measures in 2004 and 2005, and have continuously updated the guidelines and recommendations. A major set of measures was issued in 2005 and early 2006. These measures were associated with funds delivered in different key areas for the surveillance and control of an influenza pandemic and produced effects in the years up to February 2009. However, this positive trend of the reduction of human cases of avian influenza worldwide should be considered with caution.

First, the situation remains of concern in developing countries where efforts have been made to improve surveillance and the detection of

Table 3.9 H5N1 avian influenza affected areas as reported to OIE

Countries	2004	2005	2006	2007	2008
Cambodia	1	1	1	1	1
China	1	1	1	1	1
Hong Kong SAR	1	1	1	1	1
Indonesia	1	1	1		
Japan*	1			1	1
Korea Rep. of*	1		1	1	1
Laos	1		1	1	1
Malaysia*	1		1	1	
Thailand	1	1	1	1	1
Vietnam	1	1	1	1	1
Croatia		1	1		
Kazakhstan		1	1		
Mongolia		1	1		
Romania*		1	1	1	
Russia*		1	1	1	1
Turkey*		1	1	1	1
Ukraine*		1	1		1
Afghanistan			1	1	
Albania*			1		
Austria			1		
Azerbaijan			1		
Bosnia Herz.			1		
Bulgaria			1		
Burkina Faso			1		
Cameroon			1		
Czech Rep.			1	1	
Denmark			1		
Djibouti			1		
Egypt			1		1
France*			1	1	
Georgia			1		
Germany*			1	1	1
Greece			1		
Hungary*			1	1	
India*			1	1	1
Iran*			1		1
Iraq			1		
Israel*			1		1
Italy			1		
Ivory Coast			1		
Jordan*			1		
Myanmar*			1	1	
Niger			1		
Nigeria			1		1
Pakistan*			1	1	1

Table 3.9 Continued

Countries	2004	2005	2006	2007	2008
Palestinian Aut. Terr.*			1		
Poland*			1	1	
Serbia & Montenegro			1		
Slovakia			1		
Slovenia			1		
Spain			1		
Sudan*			1		
Sweden			1		
Switzerland			1		1
United Kingdom			1	1	1
Bangladesh				1	1
Benin				1	
Ghana				1	
Kuwait*				1	
Saudi Arabia*				1	1
Togo				1	1
Nepal					
Number of affected areas by year	**10**	**13**	**54**	**28**	**23**

Notes: Hong Kong and Palestine are considered as separate reporting entities by OIE. Data were not available for Taiwan and Nepal outbreak occurred in January 2009.

* Countries self-declaring freedom from highly pathogenic avian influenza (HPAI) after outbreaks of H5N1 avian influenza in domestic poultry.

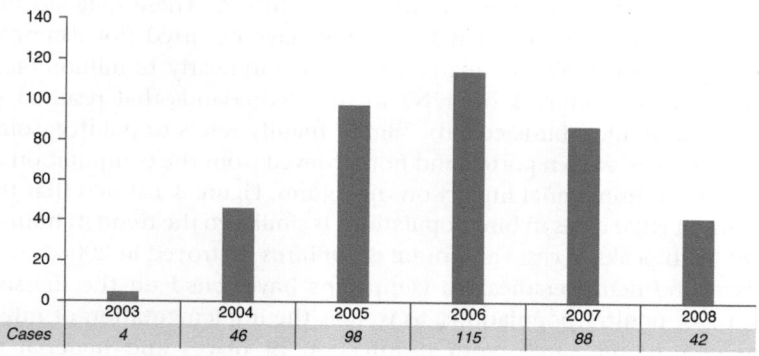

Figure 3.3 Human cases of avian influenza H5N1, 2003–2008

cases. Experts find it difficult to estimate the influence of the implementation and improvement of an avian influenza surveillance system, as well as the introduction of detection tests in poultry in a number of cases. Improvement in the detection and reporting of cases may contribute to an increase in the number of cases, while insufficiently developed or absent systems will result in underestimating the data. For developing countries, on the one hand, surveillance systems are costly and difficult to implement, and on the other hand, the reporting of human cases of avian influenza may constitute a lower priority level for these countries that are affected by other recurring and more lethal diseases.

Second, H5N1 avian influenza symptoms can be attributed to other diseases such as regular influenza or pulmonary infectious diseases. If suspected cases are not confirmed with further laboratory analyses, the identification and reporting can be impacted.

Third, not only is the number of cases an important indicator, but also the capacity of the virus to transmit easily from human to human is a key factor in the generation of a pandemic. Although the number of human cases has decreased and remains limited, a pandemic can still emerge if the virus becomes easily contagious among humans. Studies have confirmed that transmission of H5N1 avian influenza from human to human has occurred in rare situations, among family members, for example. However, the virus has not yet acquired the ability to transmit easily and efficiently among humans.

Avian influenza cases among animals. Up to February 2009,[19] avian influenza among animals affected 63 areas, with about 27 million bird cases, resulting in 9 million deaths and 112 million birds destroyed. The data are based on reports to OIE of the number of cases, the number of deaths, and the number of animals destroyed. These data do not include outbreaks other than H5N1 that have occurred (for example, the outbreak of H7N3 in Canada that resulted in nearly 14 million birds culled and the outbreak of H7N7 in the Netherlands that resulted in around 30 million birds culled). "Birds" mainly refers to poultry; some wild bird cases were reported and not retrieved from the computation as they had an immaterial impact on the figures. Figure 3.4 shows that the pattern of HPAI cases in bird populations is similar to the trend in human cases, with peaks of cases and numbers of birds destroyed in 2006.

Avian influenza eradication campaigns have relied on the massive culling of poultry populations, as well as the implementation of infection control measures, from disinfection of places and material to hygiene measures for individuals who come into contact with poultry.

In certain cases, biosecurity measures have been implemented, as well. As shown by Figure 3.5, significant eradication campaigns were undertaken in 2004, although their success depended on the compensation scheme that is offered to poultry owners. Most of the cases occurred in small poultry flocks, and inciting the populations to identify (if possible) and to report the disease was difficult, especially when it constituted the poultry farmers' main subsistence source.

3.2.1.3 Economic cost

One element that shows that the international response was appropriate in the case of avian influenza consists in comparing the effective economic cost of the actions taken in the case of avian influenza to the estimated global cost. In terms of costs, expenses for actions undertaken

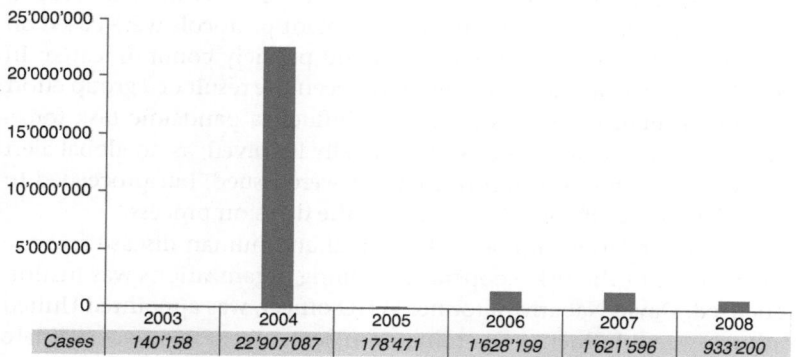

	2003	2004	2005	2006	2007	2008
Cases	140'158	22'907'087	178'471	1'628'199	1'621'596	933'200

Figure 3.4 Numbers of avian influenza H5N1 cases in birds, 2003–2008

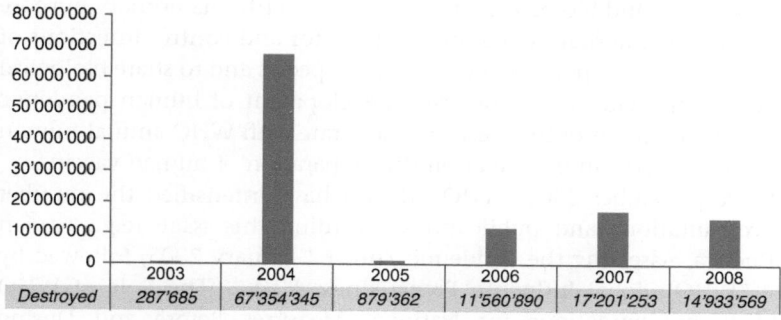

	2003	2004	2005	2006	2007	2008
Destroyed	287'685	67'354'345	879'362	11'560'890	17'201'253	14'933'569

Figure 3.5 Numbers of animals destroyed, 2003–2008

remain lower than total estimated economic costs if a pandemic occurs. The international response to avian influenza was costly, in particular culling activities, vaccination campaigns, surveillance, and implementation of infection control measures. The cost was estimated at USD 10 billion in agricultural losses in 2005 alone (130 p. 4).

During the Sixth International Ministerial Conference on Avian and Pandemic Influenza held Sharm El-Sheikh, Egypt, on October 24 to 26, 2008, officials from FAO presented estimates showing that H5N1 avian influenza has cost over USD 20 billion in economic losses. (196 p. 9) According to FAO, if an influenza pandemic occurs, the cost to the global economy could be around USD 2 trillion, and investments in preventive and control strategies are likely to be highly cost effective (196 p. 9).

3.2.2   Cooperation and communication

The elaboration and the decisions of WHO officials in their recommended strategic actions and the containment protocols were based on dialogue, and were collegially decided and publicly communicated. In the avian influenza case, guidelines have been the result of a group effort after a consultation process led by the influenza pandemic task force. The Director-General was not systematically involved, as no global alert was published and no travel restrictions were issued, but proceeded to the declaration of Phase 3, according to the decision process.

Due to the relationship between animal and human disease and the global nature of the risk, cooperation among organizations was institutionalized. David Nabarro, a former WHO officer, was appointed United Nations System Influenza Coordinator in September 2005 to coordinate the action between the various bodies related to the United Nations. In addition, the OFFLU is a joint network of OIE and FAO experts on influenza that was established in 2005 to cooperate in infection control, data sharing, and biological material sharing. (197) Its primary purpose is to support international efforts to monitor and control infections of avian influenza in poultry and other bird species and to share biological material and data to support early development of human pandemic vaccines. Members of this network cooperate with WHO animal-human interface experts, in particular on the preparation of human vaccine.

Since December 2004, WHO officials have intensified the number of consultations and publications regarding this issue (e.g., "Avian Influenza: Assessing the Pandemic Threat," January 2005, followed by the "WHO Global Influenza Preparedness Plan," "The Role of WHO and Recommendations for National Measures Before and During Pandemics," the "Checklist for Influenza Pandemic Preparedness

Planning as Well as Recommendations for Strategic Actions," and in 2006, the "WHO Pandemic Influenza Draft Protocol for Rapid Response and Containment"). The avian influenza issue was discussed at the World Health Assembly in May 2005, and participants decided to continue the preparedness activities and to increase support for affected countries. In addition, WHO jointly organized with FAO and OIE a three-day conference from November 7 to 9, 2005, at its headquarters in Geneva, gathering professionals from the organization, representatives of member countries, and representatives of international organizations and civil society, as well as health experts or consultants to discuss the situation of the avian influenza, to agree upon actions to be taken, and to estimate financial needs to achieve these protection objectives.

This conference was followed by the donors' pledging conference in Beijing in January 2006, sponsored by the Chinese government, the European Commission, and the World Bank in order to raise funds according to the needs and priorities defined in Geneva in November 2005. Funds amounting to USD 1.9 billion were pledged during that conference. (198) The participants also took this opportunity to set an agenda for the coming months in terms of the preparation of a protocol for rapid response and containment, as well as standard operating procedures in case of the occurrence of an influenza pandemic. Government officials' awareness had increased; from fewer than 50 countries that had a pandemic preparedness plan in spring 2005, the proportion grew to approximately 120, representing about 60% of the 194 member states of WHO (199).

Finally, the influenza pandemic risk has been a concern at the highest levels nationally and internationally and has resulted in new cooperation initiatives to address the issue globally. At WHO, pandemic issues are under the direct competence of the WHO Director-General. The international meeting of November 2005 in Geneva gathered the leading officials of OIE, FAO, WHO, and the World Bank to discuss risk assessment and produce recommendations. The avian influenza issue has also been put on the 2006 G8 agenda. Members of the G8 recognized that priority efforts should focus on the early detection and control of the H5N1 strain of avian influenza at its source, as well as on the prevention of and preparedness for a potential human influenza pandemic. Members of the G8 reaffirmed their support of the WHO-administered GOARN, of FAO and OIE, as well as of the UN System Influenza Coordination Office (UNSIC) and international financial institutions in addressing these global threats. (137) In addition, President George W. Bush announced the International Partnership on Avian and Pandemic Influenza in

September 2005 in New York. The first two objectives of this partnership consist of fostering international cooperation to protect the lives and health of people and promoting timely and sustained high-level global political leadership to combat avian and pandemic influenza (136).

In terms of communication, WHO created a specific website dedicated to avian influenza as part of the general WHO website. On its website, WHO clearly positioned itself as the coordinator of the global response to human cases of H5N1 avian influenza (200).

3.2.3   Response monitoring

WHO monitored the H5N1 avian influenza response based on national authorities' reporting of cases database. It ensured that WHO measures were put in place by following up on the completion of preparedness activities, such as elaboration of preparedness plans, antiviral stockpiling, and virus sharing for vaccine production. Finally, WHO applied an incentive-based system to obtain cooperation and enforce recommendations.

3.2.3.1   *Reporting system*

This WHO reporting system for avian influenza H5N1 was essentially based on voluntary notifications from states. A formal reporting mechanism was already in place in the influenza network, and state officials notify the network of outbreaks. However, as explained in Chapter 2, a challenge remains for WHO to obtain complete, timely, and accurate information. Since June 15, 2007, when the IHR came into force, state officials have been required to notify WHO of diseases that are on the list of Annex 2 or of events that qualify as PHEICs, which is the case for avian influenza H5N1. In the first two months of 2009, only China, Vietnam, and Egypt reported outbreaks, while avian influenza is known to be endemic in Indonesia. WHO will follow up on the number of cases and the number of deaths. On the one side, they are allowed to follow up on the development of an outbreak through the evolution of the increase in the number of cases and assess the risk of further spread. On the other side, they gather information about avian influenza from different sources that can be combined into useful information made available to states on the WHO website. After June 2007, while the outbreaks in poultry continued generating sporadic infections in humans, the reporting of cases stopped. (115 p. 49) WHO still obtained information about the outbreaks using nonofficial sources. The pandemic risk was considered as exaggerated, although for WHO experts, the risk still persisted, although they were not able to assess the level of its risk without complete and accurate reporting. Reporting plays a role in both assessing and managing the risk. Without any data, WHO experts cannot accurately evaluate the risk.

WHO also administers FluNet, an Internet-based geographical information system of which time data on any country can be accessed in real time. In the avian influenza case, it could be used to learn more about circulating virus trends and epidemiological trends. The network should be able to capture a virus with pandemic potential or any outbreak of severe illness or rapid spread (115 p. 46).

3.2.3.2   Evaluating completion of measures

The evaluation of completion should be done at different levels. WHO has issued measures to help countries become prepared for a human influenza pandemic, providing them with guidance in preparedness planning. In addition, WHO and OIE have recommended containment measures that include the achievement of culling programs and the implementation of hygiene protection measures in farms and markets. Finally, in regard to human risk, information campaigns have been made to inform people about how to handle live and dead animals that are susceptible to the disease and how to protect themselves from getting the disease from these animals.

Build capacities to cope with a pandemic.   WHO recommended that state officials elaborate and test an influenza preparedness plan and that they institute an antiviral stockpile. In 2006, 23 countries ordered an oseltamivir national stockpile, (130 p. 2) which continued to increase after that date. The WHO stockpile of 3 million courses of treatment was upgraded to 5 million. Countries such as the United States, Switzerland, and other countries in Europe stockpiled Tamiflu.

WHO issued a preliminary version of the preparedness plan in March 2005 and the final version in November 2005. This document is entitled *WHO Global Influenza Preparedness Plan: The Role of WHO and Recommendations for National Measures before and during Pandemics,* and aims at assisting WHO member states in responding to a pandemic influenza. This WHO guide was the result of a consultation on WHO-recommended national and international measures before and during influenza pandemics that took place at WHO headquarters in Geneva on December 13 to 15, 2004. The WHO guide on preparedness planning was applied to this situation, and is often publicly mentioned as a reference. For example, members of the European Union adopted an EU Influenza Pandemic Preparedness Plan in March 2004 based on previous recommendations of WHO experts, following the 1999 plan, and indicated on the organization's website that they had completely reviewed their plan in order to ensure better coherence with WHO recommendations and the revised plan that was issued in 2005. The Federal Office of Public Health (FOPH) in Switzerland also based its plan on the WHO program.

This WHO preparedness plan has been one of the WHO recommendations that has been largely followed by national authorities, as evidenced by the number of plans submitted to WHO increasing regularly after some initial reluctance following the controversial announcement of a pandemic risk. Governments initially were not inclined to invest in pandemic preparedness activities, and WHO encountered difficulties in convincing countries such as the United States and certain Asian countries to elaborate their preparedness plans. Another issue was the content of the plans and the test of their operating procedures. As of November 2005, approximately 120 countries had developed a preparedness plan, compared to only 50 (201) a few months before. By August 1, 2006, over 176 countries had drafts or completed national plans, (202) although the quality was often inadequate. By 2007, the objective was that all member states would have national preparedness plans devised, implemented, and tested to provide the backbone of the response to a potential pandemic. As this objective was not met and the quality of certain plans remained poor, WHO revaluated the situation in the midterm strategic plan 2008–2013 and set further objectives. WHO reported that 90 countries have funded preparedness plans and standard operating procedures in place for major epidemic-prone diseases, such as an influenza pandemic, and that 70 countries that have the basic capacity in place for safe laboratory handling of pathogens and safe isolation of patients. (203 p. 22) The targets for 2009 are 135 countries with plans and 100 with laboratory and isolation capacities, and for 2013, 193 countries in both areas.

WHO has also communicated on a regular basis on any matter related to the human influenza pandemic risk and the status of the disease. WHO is an institution in which knowledge of the disease has been gathered, the risk analysis performed, and solutions proposed.

Coordinate research – vaccine development.　One objective of WHO was to promote research to find a vaccine and increase manufacturing capacity in order to accommodate demand during a pandemic. The virus-sharing network collected, analyzed, and diffused H5N1 virus specimens in accordance with WHO's commitment to promote vaccine development and production. Between 2003 and 2007, WHO member states shared 8,815 human and animal specimens from avian influenza A (H5N1) suspected and/or confirmed cases with WHO laboratories, where 788 viruses were isolated and maintained in WHO laboratories and 14 viruses selected for further development into A (H5N1) vaccine viruses. (204) Until January 2008, eight reverse-engineered genetics vaccine viruses, suitable for vaccine development and production, were available for distribution, and 292 institutions received one or more of these samples and developed vaccine viruses, while 47 institutions received wild-type vaccine viruses (204).

Sharing viruses is essential in order to be able to watch the evolution of the virus and to develop vaccines. However, since 2005, Indonesian authorities have shared only two virus samples with WHO (166 p. BO7), although it is the country most affected by H5N1. The Indonesian officials also stopped notifying OIE and WHO about bird flu outbreaks or human cases starting in 2007, not complying with the IHR (166 p. BO7). WHO had other sources to confirm human outbreaks, but the lack of cooperation in virus sharing was more problematic. The Indonesian Ministry of Health developed the concept of "viral sovereignty," according to which viruses should remain the property of individual states. Indonesian authorities did not see any benefit in sharing their viruses, when their country is unlikely to benefit from a vaccine in the case of a pandemic. In 2003, 62% of the world's influenza vaccines were used by nine developed countries. (123 p. 406) While 90% of the global capacity of vaccine production is located in developed countries, essentially in Europe and North America in 2009, six manufacturers in developing countries have started to acquire the technology to produce influenza vaccines and have received technical and financial support from WHO. (205) By the end of March 2007, Indonesian authorities resumed sharing vaccines after an international meeting held in Indonesia, during which new terms were issued regarding the sharing of vaccines and a commitment was received from WHO in favor of negotiating with vaccine producers to transfer technology and make vaccines available to developing countries. The Indonesia case illustrates how maintaining cooperation to reduce risk can be difficult, in particular when the burden of efforts and the sharing of benefits are not perceived as fair.

WHO also encouraged the use of vaccines for regular influenza in order to increase the demand and therefore the production capacity to satisfy this demand. Although the worldwide influenza vaccine manufacturing capacity has increased from 300 million to 420 million doses, it has remained below the demand in the case of a pandemic during

2006–2007.[20] Production of cell cultures rather than eggs or of recombinant technologies was researched, as well as ways to reduce the lead time of vaccines. In the spring of 2007, the first H5N1 vaccine was approved in the United States. Both objectives of the manufacturing capacity of a vaccine and the development of a vaccine were partially achieved in 2007.

Panzootic reduction.   The panzootic has been reduced, although sporadic outbreaks still arise in certain countries, and in others, the situation is endemic, as in Indonesia or Egypt. Countries carried out massive and costly culling campaigns, but they have not succeeded in eradicating the virus so far. A compensation scheme was established, which planned for a rate of compensation compared to the market price of the animal (15% to 20%). Notifications do not occur due to economic costs to animal farmers; therefore, the compensation plan should provide an incentive to cooperate.

3.2.3.3   Incentive-based enforcement

The IHR 2005 is the only legally binding instrument that provides reporting guidelines, and it does not include enforcement mechanisms, such as sanctions for noncompliance with the rules or verification controls. As explained in Chapter 2, WHO established an incentive-based system that leverages different aspects, such as credibility, pressure from peers, and influence of the organization. The IHR 2005 added a positive incentive by linking notification to assistance and confidentiality. A country whose authorities notify WHO about an outbreak can seek assistance, and during the consultation phase, the information is not publicly disclosed. For example, this incentive was already used by Vietnamese officials in 2004. An additional benefit that can be seen from cooperating in the notification and the handling of outbreaks such as avian influenza is that information is collected from different sources by the organization and can be disseminated to state members in order to improve their response capacities. However, these guidelines do not solve the economic issue. Notification of an outbreak leads to economic losses in terms of consumption, tourism, and travel, but also can trigger trade sanctions that could remain in place for a long time. Furthermore, adequate and effective compensatory systems are not in place to promote citizens' notifying their authorities of disease, and then to WHO, OIE, or FAO. Compensation for losses incurred due to the disease itself, the massive culling of poultry, the isolation of animals, or the imposition of stricter and costly infection control measures could be another tool to ensure adequate reporting of diseases and application of control measures.

3.3 Conclusion

Our analysis showed that WHO conducted a risk analysis that resulted in the reduction of the H5N1 avian influenza pandemic risk. Officials of WHO organized a multidisciplinary, internationally recognized, and geographically broad-based group of experts to assess risk based on the latest scientific findings and the completion of innovative steering mechanisms that relied on multistakeholders' assessments, such as the design of the protocol of containment. WHO applied risk analysis methods to determine the notification of an event, the pandemic phase, and the risk of a pandemic. The process legitimacy was first action based and then became rule based once the early and final adoptions of the IHR had taken place. WHO performed a cost analysis for internal purposes and used the World Bank estimate as a benchmark for the cost estimation of a pandemic.

In turn, WHO's response to the avian influenza risk resulted in a decrease in casualties, was cooperation based, and was adequately monitored. The response resulted in limitation of the international spread and reduction of the number of cases, both in humans and animals. In addition, based on World Bank experts' estimate of USD 800 billion in costs, the measures carried out were cost effective. Finally, the reporting system provided useful information at the beginning that faded once the risk decreased. Some accuracy, completeness, and reliability issues jeopardized the quality of information. WHO recommendations were largely applied, although they included no enforcement provisions. The absence of coercive enforcement means was compensated by the structure of the response, and by the incentive-based system that contributed to the reaching of an agreement on vaccines.

Although not all indicators were present at 100%, the present analysis showed that the three constitutive aspects of the risk analysis and appropriate international response to avian influenza were evidenced. The quality of expertise and the innovative ways of organizing the experts and other stakeholders gathered in a risk assessment process, including cost analysis, significantly contributed to the risk analysis, while planning encountered some legal issues until the enactment of the revised IHR. The decrease in casualties contributed to reducing the risk, but the incomplete evaluation of the cost prevented it from reaching the maximum level. Some deficiencies in reporting did not lead to questioning about the overall presence of monitoring. The existence and the quality of the relationship between risk analysis and the formation of an internationally appropriate response to the risk of an H5N1 avian influenza pandemic under WHO is illustrated in Figure 3.6.

An influenza pandemic has the potential to significantly disrupt social and economic structures, as well as international trade and travel. WHO actions essentially focus on sanitary issues that are at stake, and WHO leaders based their analysis on expertise and the evolution of knowledge about the disease: its gravity (capacity of the health infrastructures to face a significant outbreak and even a pandemic); its morbidity and mortality (number of cases, number of deaths); and the populations concerned. A high level of uncertainty remains regarding the timing and the severity of a pandemic. Modeling studies provide a basis on which to start, but the outcomes vary significantly. Activities of WHO experts aim at reducing the pandemic risk by acting to reduce human exposure to the virus, strengthening the surveillance and early warning system, establishing containment operations (vaccine, medication, and social distancing measures), building capacity (through preparedness planning), and coordinating international research. WHO mobilized its state

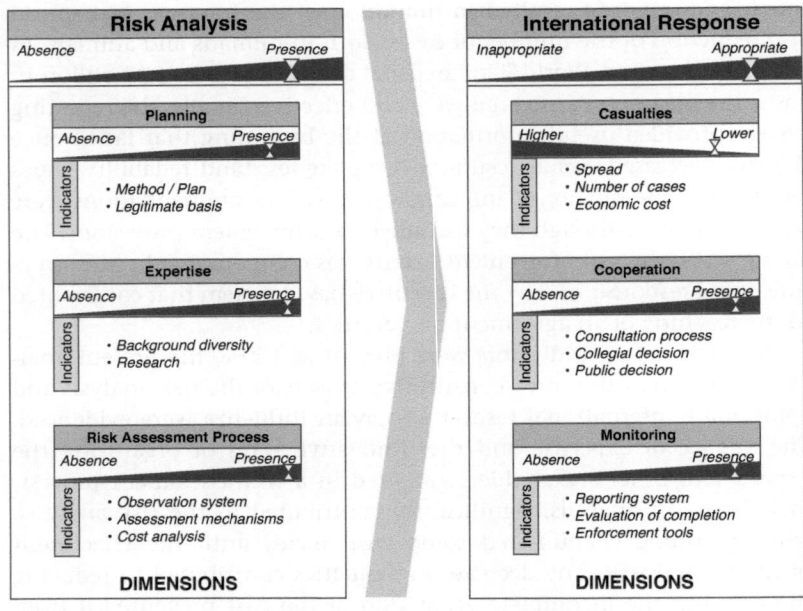

Figure 3.6   International response to avian Influenza H5N1

members, governmental agencies or organizations, NGOs, the scientific community (research centers, laboratories, and universities), the private sector, and the media. Experts at WHO have performed a pandemic risk assessment and created a pandemic preparedness plan meant to serve as a reference on a worldwide basis for government officials to develop their own plans. Officials at WHO reached an agreement with Roche managers, who decided to provide the organization with an international stockpile of Tamiflu, the only medicine proven to have some (but not systematic) efficiency in treating patients affected by the avian flu. This stockpile is aimed at treating the first zones affected, in hopes of stopping the propagation of the disease and, therefore, the development of a pandemic. In addition, the three-day international conference in November 2005 in Geneva pursued three objectives: providing a global status on the avian flu and the related human pandemic risk in the world; proposing measures to go forward; and estimating funding needs. The conference of the donors held in January 2006 was the next step in securing funding that was necessary to undertake pandemic preparedness activities.

WHO played a key role in the public health surveillance, risk analysis, and recommendations for action in the case of the avian flu. On one side, this role directly resulted from the competencies attributed by the member states to the organization through founding documents; in particular, its constitution and the IHR established the governance role of WHO. On the other side, WHO can rely on competency networks, capacities, and infrastructures, as well as the experience it has acquired in managing different critical public health issues around the world since its creation in 1947. Actions of WHO are limited by national sovereignty in the case of notifications and field investigations, but in the case in which officials of a country such as Indonesia discontinue their reporting of cases and refuse to share their viruses, leaders of WHO can provide a forum for addressing these concerns, as they did for Indonesia when they exposed Indonesian officials' concerns and became committed to helping them find satisfactory solutions regarding access to vaccine production for developing countries.

The response of WHO was considered appropriate for the following reasons. The WHO activities were recognized not only by its member states but also by other intergovernmental organizations, public and private research institutes, universities, pharmaceutical companies, and other actors from the private sectors as well as NGOs. In addition, WHO's new method of organizing expertise guaranteed a more diverse background of participants to assess the risk and make recommendations.

The fact that this expertise can be mobilized rapidly to intervene in countries is also a factor of success. Moreover, officials of WHO positioned the organization as a worldwide coordinator of efforts to prepare for a pandemic. While WHO was leading the governance process at early stages, OIE and FAO claimed their legitimacy for action to control the disease at its animal source. (206 p. 217) OIE competed with WHO to have the avian influenza put on top of the animal health and respectively human health agenda, to be recognized as the leading organization in global risk governance, widen their scope of action and obtain more funding resources. (207) Despite tensions and disagreement due to their own logic, interests, and practices, these organizations cooperated. WHO had to collaborate with leaders of other UN bodies such as OIE and FAO, funding institutions, governments, the private sector, research institutes, laboratories, and universities to keep the pandemic preparedness activities in process. Also, the worldwide institutional structure and involvement of WHO officers who were committed at all levels of the organization allowed them to carry out the response.

Finally, the adoption of the IHR provided WHO with an adequate instrument for addressing global risk. By December 2008, authorities in 193 countries designated focal points, in 152 countries accessed the event information management site, and in 56 countries nominated national experts for the roster of experts. (158) By June 2009, the capacities have been upgraded based on WHO assistance. Although it was not yet approved when the H5N1 outbreak started, the IHR revision draft was applied until its anticipatory entry into force in 2006 or its regular entry into force in 2007. The functioning of a task force acting as an emergency committee, as planned under the IHR, ensured direct communication between subject matter experts and top management of WHO in addressing the risk.

The international response was impacted primarily by cooperation issues with countries' authorities who refused to report or reported unreliable information. This action was not only the source of incorrect or nonavailable data, but it also prevented WHO experts from further carrying out the risk assessment in good conditions and, therefore, making the best targeted recommendations. Sovereignty arguments were used by Indonesian authorities to obtain some guarantees about the availability of vaccines to developing countries. Indonesian officials balanced their country's sovereignty rights and shared commitments, and finally decided to cooperate in virus sharing. The IHR does not include sanctions in such cases of noncompliance with the rules. The potential consequences of noncompliance are considered as a compliance tool, as well as pressure from other states' leaders, WHO officials, and public outcry.

Another issue was the duration of the outbreaks. After the initial measures generated a decrease in the number of outbreaks in animals and humans cases, some governments began to believe that the risk was exaggerated. The question of the effectiveness of measures taken to reduce the probability of occurrence of the pandemic risk remained open. Finally, the cost of these measures played a role, as well. Costly measures were requested over a long period of time, stretching the resources of certain countries, while international compensatory mechanisms and national mechanisms operated slowly – for a pandemic that has not come.

Despite these weaknesses in monitoring and cooperation, empirical evidence showed that WHO's risk analysis process integrated more actors, included cost analysis and funding needs evaluation, and contributed to improving pandemic preparedness worldwide and reducing the risk of an avian influenza pandemic. The H5N1 avian influenza remains an example of an appropriate international response, reinforcing the leading role of WHO in dealing with infectious diseases at the global level.

4
Cases Comparison: Outlook on H1N1 Influenza Pandemic and Conclusions

As globalization continues to blur borders and increase interdependence, risk transcends national borders, causing major challenges in risk governance. While risk interdependence and the increased complexity of the international environment require the formulation of global responses to global risks, risk governance processes to cope with them are emerging. (2, 4) The effects of globalization render the question of risk governance and the role of international organizations in this emerging process particularly relevant. This is well illustrated in the health sector. Epidemics and pandemics know no borders and are often characterized by a high level of uncertainty regarding the causality of risk and its potential social and economic consequences.

Our main argument in this book was that WHO has positioned itself as a leading organization in the governance of pandemic risks and we aimed to shed light on the essential organizational features of these emerging global risk governance processes as expressed in the analytical framework presented in Chapter 1. Within the constraints and limits expressed in the introduction and previous chapters, we can conclude that WHO has positioned itself as a leading organization in the governance of pandemics, thanks to the setup and deployment of strategies, processes and instruments that have been developed over the past 15 years. In particular, we have explained how WHO gained the capacity and legitimacy for action in pandemic management and how it conducted a science-based risk assessment that set the basis for the formation of the international responses to the SARS and avian influenza H5N1.

The following sections relate the case studies to this main argument and provide an outlook on the H1N1 pandemic. The first section provides a summary of the two case studies. Then the common features and differences between the case studies and their implications for our argument are highlighted. Finally, some of the findings in the case studies are related to issues in the management of the H1N1 influenza pandemic, and comments are presented on its impact on the role of WHO in future pandemics.

4.1 Cases comparison

Risk analysis refers to a science-based participative process that results in an estimation of a risk and leads to proposed measures to control it. WHO mainly positioned itself as a leading organization in the risk governance process with the performance of this risk analysis and the formation of international responses to the SARS and avian influenza risks, in a reactionary manner once the risk started to materialize for SARS, as well as in an anticipatory manner for the risk of a human influenza pandemic, thus contributing to risk reduction in the cases of SARS and avian influenza H5N1. SARS was a situation in which a new disease emerged, while the H5N1 avian influenza virus was a known illness. In the case of SARS, risk analysis and response had to be formed simultaneously from a situation in which the institution was close to complete ignorance, while risk analysis in the case of avian influenza started from preestablished knowledge about the virus and its characteristics, thus allowing for more room to prepare the response.

4.1.1 Reduction of the risk of a SARS pandemic

The performance of risk analysis conducted by WHO reduced the risk of a SARS pandemic by producing preparedness measures for unaffected areas, along with containment measures in affected areas, in a short period of time. Although the SARS risk materialized by a multiple-country outbreak of an infectious disease, its development into a major pandemic was avoided. The international spread was limited, and the number of human cases minimized. Although the overall cost was estimated to be USD 20 billion it was, nevertheless, lower than the expected cost of inaction. The response was organized in a cooperative manner and adequate monitoring was carried out, which provided the information that fed the risk assessment and led to the containment of SARS by early July 2003. A credibility-based incentive system was used to enforce measures.

The SARS risk assessment was aimed at responding to an emergency situation that was provoked by the emergence of an unknown infectious disease that was spreading worldwide. It was, therefore, not a complete anticipatory exercise as the risk started to materialize, but the magnitude of its consequences remained unknown. A high level of uncertainty surrounded the emergence of SARS as its hazard (the causative agent of the disease) was unknown. Additionally, the risk (the potential effect that this unknown hazard might cause) and the consequences (real effects if the risk comes true) were also unknown. It was extremely difficult to estimate the risk of a pandemic from this multiple-country outbreak of a new infectious disease. Therefore, based on the limited available information, risk analysis activities consisted of estimating the risk of a worldwide pandemic in order to take precautionary measures, while working simultaneously to discover the causative agent in order to be able to target the infection control measures and clinical treatment. In a sense, in the preliminary stages of the outbreak, risk analysis prescribed measures that were aimed at stopping the progression of the disease within affected countries, as well as preventing its spread beyond the affected countries, while not knowing the risk source. WHO issued its first global alert, followed by a series of recommendations and information that were made public and accessible on its website and organized the expertise in parallel to continue the assessment of the disease based on ongoing events in order to reduce uncertainty and adjust measures.

One new and key feature of the SARS risk analysis was the constitution, the organization, and the role of expertise. For the first time in its history, WHO set up and coordinated virtual networks of virology, clinical, and epidemiology experts in a continuous real-time cooperative risk assessment. This science-based risk assessment process was meant to be a privileged interface for the exchange of information, research findings, and ideas in order to design and implement the most easily adapted measures. This innovative risk governance mechanism was instrumental in discovering the causal agent, monitoring the clinical course of the disease, and providing epidemiological information to refine the recommended measures. This cooperation was overall a success, which should not minimize the challenge it represented in terms of managing different agendas, priorities, and competition in a race to publish findings, as well as the characteristics of the virus itself.

With SARS, WHO took the lead and the responsibility in assessing and managing risk in an emergency situation of global scope. During the few years preceding the SARS outbreak, WHO had been increasingly involved in managing outbreaks in different parts of the world, suggesting that its role was changing toward the coordination of global risk governance processes in addition to the conduct of long-term public health programs. The SARS outbreak consisted of the first real test of this new global role. It was a learning experience in global risk governance that was followed by the integration of the lessons learned into the strengthening of the risk-based approach to prepare for future outbreaks. WHO's legitimacy to conduct that risk governance process was recognized by states and other actors. From a state perspective, implementation of new practices preceded the formal approval of the rules and the documentation of risk assessment plans and mechanisms, resulting in an action-based legitimacy rather than a rule-based legitimacy. The revision of the International Health Regulations had already been launched, and if WHO's actions were inspired by the 2002 project, these measures had not been approved by member states prior to their application. States could have opposed WHO by refusing to cooperate and report cases, by trying to form coalitions to block the resolution that was proposed at the World Health Assembly, or by launching a media campaign that denied the legitimacy of the organization to act. The situation was not without issues, such as the initial reluctance of the Chinese to cooperate or the reaction of Canada against travel restrictions, but overall, the recommendations of WHO were applied. However, in response to WHO's increased role, states included a consultation phase before the issuance of an alert as part of the revised IHR 2005, revealing the willingness of states to keep a hand on the management of health issues.

In the midst of the SARS outbreak, cases of avian influenza among humans were confirmed in Hong Kong in February 2003. This announcement caused WHO to suspect that the outbreak that the Asian countries and Canada were facing might be of an avian influenza origin. This assumption would eventually be ruled out, and WHO would have to deal with two different risks in parallel: SARS and a human influenza pandemic, the latter benefiting from the lessons learned in dealing with the former.

4.1.2 Reduction of the risk of an H5N1 human influenza pandemic

WHO carried out a risk analysis in order to anticipate and prepare for a human influenza pandemic. The risk of a pandemic that could originate in the H5N1 avian virus has not materialized, as the current H5N1 human virus does not transmit easily among humans. This virus, which caused the death of numerous animals and of a limited number of humans, was known from a previous outbreak in Hong Kong in 1997 to be a virulent and highly lethal virus. Experts feared that it could transform into a malignant form easily transmissible between humans, causing a pandemic resulting in a high rate of death and significant economic and social costs worldwide. The characteristics of the virus and the fact that humans caught the animal disease were the first indicators of a pandemic risk, and led to the declaration of phase 3 in the pandemic scale established by WHO. In 2005, the predictions were alarmist as this pandemic was compared to the Spanish influenza, initiating a dispute among experts about its potential significant consequences in human losses ranging from 2 million deaths to more than 300 million on a worldwide basis, with cost estimates ranging from USD 200 billion to USD 4 trillion depending on the parameters and assumptions used in the models. WHO led a risk analysis to estimate the risk of such a pandemic, its potential impact, and the measures that could be taken in terms of one scenario. If the H5N1 virus did not cause the pandemic, another virus would; therefore, preparedness was key and would serve in any type of pandemic or a biological accident. While experts disagreed about the probability of occurrence of a pandemic, they agreed about the severity of its consequences. The risk analysis led by WHO was aimed at reducing uncertainty by carrying out research in virology, epidemiology, and clinical aspects of the disease to prepare for the next pandemic.

Risk analysis led to a response that included two types of measures: preparedness measures (pre-pandemic) and containment measures (pandemic). The first set of measures consisted of reducing the opportunities for infection in humans and increasing the preparedness level of member states and WHO by strengthening early warning systems and building up capacities to cope with a pandemic. WHO provided guidance on preparedness plans and public health measures, granted technical and financial support to less-developed countries, and worked on measures to contain any outbreak at its roots. WHO also promoted the development of vaccines and the extension of vaccine manufacturing capacity as well as antiviral stockpiling. The second set of measures aimed at containing the disease at its roots or delaying its international spread, and reducing its casualties once a pandemic started. The containment protocol consisted of a roadmap to prepare WHO and its partners to intervene quickly once the pandemic risk materialized. Finally, research is key in prepandemic and pandemic activities. WHO organized an international, multidisciplinary, and institutionally broad-based expertise to plan, carry out, and integrate research results into the risk assessment. WHO organized multistakeholder technical meetings and international conferences about the animal and human sides of the disease, as well as funding operations to be assessed comprehensively to target the responses, gather the competencies, and secure commitments to achieve the response.

WHO's cooperative-based response resulted in a risk reduction characterized by a decrease in casualties in animals and humans with a cost remaining below the expected total cost of a pandemic. Indonesia's resistance to virus sharing and concerns regarding vaccine accessibility to developing countries was taken into account and an agreement was reached. The transfer of the manufacturing capacity of vaccines has begun, but is a long-term process, raising concerns about the availability and cost of vaccines in developing countries. WHO has, for the most part, addressed this issue with manufacturing companies. Despite some quality issues in the reporting of cases, the response was adequately monitored. WHO's strategy was based both on an action-based and a rule-based legitimacy as the adoption and the entry into force of the revised IHR 2005 occurred during the formation of the response. The IHR 2005 was a compromise between WHO's practice in the SARS case and states' concerns about their sovereignty, which resulted in the integration of a consultation phase with the affected state or states before the raising of a global alert. The concept of public health emergencies of international concern was validated and coexists with a list of diseases that require notification. The IHR 2005 provided WHO and states with a more appropriate international instrument with which to handle infectious diseases, including a notification instrument that appears as a standard risk assessment plan in its Annex 2, focal points to ensure coordination, and an emergency committee consisting of multidisciplinary and internationally recognized experts. The IHR 2005 does not plan for coercive sanctions, but rather operates on a credibility-based and notification-assistance incentive system.

WHO learned from the SARS experience in terms of organization of expertise, conduct of operations, and communication, and consolidated its global coordinating role of risk assessment and risk management at the international level. Cooperation was challenging as it involved more partners due to the multiple facets of the issue and the different initiatives launched in the fields of animal and human health. WHO moved toward a multistakeholder process both for the risk assessment and the completion of the response. For example, preparedness activities could essentially be funded by the pledges administered by the World Bank. The time factor played a role, however, as the disease in animals could be detected and its opportunities to infect humans reduced by animal-culling campaigns and implementation of infection control measures. As time passed, the commitment to preparedness actions declined and questions were raised about the cost-effectiveness of pandemic preparation as the risk of a pandemic of avian influenza origin did not materialize. Within the limits of the availability of sources and scope constraints of this research, the evidence gathered for risk reduction in Hong Kong, Japan, and Korea that did not encounter human cases, as well as the reduction of animal and human cases in other affected areas, suggests that the risk was effectively reduced.

4.1.3   Common features and differences

Empirical studies of SARS and avian influenza present common features. First, these two risks relate to risk governance in the field of health and find their origin in animals. Second, the development and the international spread of these animal diseases and their human disease counterparts are essentially due to human practices (ways of living, production processes, and travel and trade activities). Third, these risks were addressed by an international organization, WHO for the SARS and avian influenza (for its human health aspect). These risks have a potential global impact and consequences that go beyond the organization addressing them. Finally, these risks gave rise to significant economic costs and enormous media coverage in regard to the thus far limited number of human fatal cases.

The first conclusion that can be drawn is that the performance of risk analysis under a multilateral institution influences the quality of the international response. In the cases of SARS and avian influenza, it suggests that risk analysis contributes to better preparedness and increased capacity to handle risk during its occurrence, thereby resulting in risk reduction. The steps and characteristics of the risk analysis process also matter in the formation of the response, in particular the constitution and the organization of expertise, the integration of the latest research results, and the presence of a risk assessment framework. These cases have the following in common: they show the importance of the presence of a risk framework and of the constitution and work modalities of a diverse and internationally recognized body of expertise, as well as the integration of these results into the risk estimation to better target the response so as to reduce the risk.

First, the type of expertise involved in risk analysis is a driving element of the quality of the risk analysis. The constitution of a body of expertise that presents a diverse background and scientific excellence played an important role in the successful containment of SARS and in the evaluation of the risk of a human influenza pandemic. Its organization in virtual networks on secure websites with regular teleconferences was an unprecedented venue in which to share information about multiple facets of an issue and integrate them into an estimation of the risk. The same mode of operation was planned for a human influenza pandemic, but as the pandemic did not arise, expertise was gathered in technical meetings and consultation meetings. Avian influenza expertise was also internationally recognized, and included experts who were involved in the SARS outbreak as well. Moreover, WHO moved toward a multi-stakeholder process involving experts from other international organizations and NGOs, as well as representatives from the private sector. While scientific expertise is not free of biases, the position of WHO is that the diversity in terms of field of expertise, institutional experience and cultural origin seems to reduce independence issues and result in a more comprehensive appraisal of the risk based on the confrontation of different points of view, and, therefore, a more appropriate response.

Second, the integration of the latest research results into the appraisal contributes to the adjustment of the measures proposed. SARS and avian influenza have in common an animal component, a potential global impact, and a significant level of uncertainty. While in the SARS cases the level of uncertainty was essentially linked to the fact that the disease was new and its causative agent unknown, in the case of avian influenza, the virus H5N1 had been known since 1997, but the human pandemic virus remains unknown. These situations render the estimation of the probability of occurrence, timing, and severity of an avian influenza pandemic difficult, and moreover render the estimation of the severity of the consequences for SARS difficult. The integration of research results, such as the discovery of the SARS virus or limited transmission of avian influenza among humans, allowed for the issuance of more precise case definitions, clinical treatment recommendations, and infection control measures.

Finally, the presence of a risk assessment framework creates a common language and culture regarding risk and sets the criteria for its assessment. A risk assessment framework complemented by specific methods was available at WHO. The SARS outbreak and the avian influenza were addressed based on the overall risk framework of WHO and the alert and response plan, giving rise to specific SARS guidelines in case of its resurgence and specific influenza pandemic guidelines. However, the method remains the same and was consolidated by the adoption of the IHR 2005, which included a risk assessment plan for notification as its Annex 2.

In terms of the response, these cases illustrate the importance of the structure of the response, underlining in particular the role of cooperation in providing risk reduction. Dialogue, integration of dissenting views, and collegiality in decision-making, as well as transparency were essential elements of an appropriate response. The SARS case showed how cooperation was a critical factor in the containment of SARS. In particular, it suggests that successfully bringing China into the network of experts and establishing a reporting system that overcame its initial reluctance to participate was critical to the containment of SARS. In an influenza pandemic, cooperation would be even more critical as influenza viruses are more malignant than SARS. Cooperation between WHO and authorities of affected areas in the risk assessment process as well as in the implementation of the response is essential to contain an infectious disease at its roots or in its early stages in order to prevent its spread throughout the world and reduce casualties. Public health infrastructures have shown their limits in the SARS case and may not be able to face a more virulent, more easily, and faster-spreading disease such as influenza. Focusing on building capacities and cooperation in gathering the necessary funds to improve these capacities worldwide, in particular in developing countries, which are more vulnerable, was one key aspect of WHO's preparedness activities for an influenza pandemic. WHO's decisions in the SARS and avian influenza outbreaks involved the highest levels of the organization after consultation with the task force and experts, reaching a consensus on the decisions to be made. Although there was dissent regarding travel recommendations in the SARS case and sovereignty issues in sharing avian influenza viruses to produce vaccines, the mode of action was essentially based on cooperation and more transparent communication, resulting in the publication of decisions, recommendations, and guidelines on the organization's website. This way, the same level of information was available not only to professionals but also to individuals independently of their affiliation or location.

In addition, WHO, which is an internal organization with the IHR that did not apply to SARS and avian influenza H5N1 (until its entry into force in 2007) and disposed of through nonexistent enforcement mechanisms, encountered difficulties in policy making and the enforcement of decisions, particularly in the case of avian influenza H5N1. WHO relied on its incentive-based mechanism and cooperation to promote its recommendations and follow up on their implementation. WHO faced less resistance during the SARS crisis and consolidated its mechanism during the avian influenza H5N1. However, WHO's activities were significantly impaired by the fact that the avian influenza H5N1 did not result in a human pandemic, thus rendering cooperation and negotiation initiatives more difficult in the longer term, and by the fact that competing organizations such as OIE invested in the governance field.

Finally, a learning curve appears in these two cases that should be put into historical perspective. The BSE crisis had a significant impact; it led to the creation of the European Food Safety Agency in 2002 and of food safety agencies in other European countries, and fostered the development and use of risk analysis frameworks, such as the Red Book risk analysis framework. In addition, the development and implementation of an integrated risk framework, as well as the constitution of an international, multidisciplinary, and qualified expertise to inform decision-making provided the EU with the capacities for action in health and food safety risks. The BSE case was the first animal-origin food safety crisis of such magnitude. At the time, the EU was not structured nor equipped to deal with such risks in a context of globalization and interdependence. The situation and its evolution constituted a real learning process for the EU and, after that, for other organizations, among which was WHO.

Although WHO started to build its risk approach in the 1990s, the development of an overall risk framework for the organization and member states was published in 2002, coinciding with the setup of new structures such as the GPHIN for information purposes and the GOARN for assessing outbreaks and providing field support. SARS and avian influenza, which occurred after the BSE crisis, benefited from the development and institutionalization of risk approaches. SARS was a real-life test of this new model, as well as the field of innovative experience in organizing the work of experts. WHO debriefed the SARS case with the principal partners to draw lessons from this experience, retain best practices, and define areas for improvement. Risk analysis of avian influenza, as well as the design of the response, was more complete than in the case of SARS. WHO has learned from the SARS experience to improve its structures and processes, as well as to enhance its role as a privileged and unavoidable actor of risk governance at the global level. This learning curve is reflected in the enlargement of the cooperative process to other stakeholders, increased coordination activities, issuance of guidelines to assess and manage events that may become public health emergencies of international concern, definition of strategic actions, and cost analysis. WHO further developed and reinforced its risk governance structures and processes through the management of SARS and avian influenza H5N1.

Our analysis also underlines some differences between the two cases, particularly in relation to their context as well as the role and capacity of the multilateral institution. First, the two situations happened almost simultaneously but in different contexts, which had an impact on the multilateral institution's risk-related activities. The response to the risk of a SARS pandemic was designed in an emergency context. SARS was addressed under greater pressure as this disease was new; it presented a significant risk to humans for which no cure existed; and it was rapidly spreading worldwide, while avian influenza H5N1 was already known, thus permitting more room for analysis, which may have contributed to the more comprehensive, systematic, and timely completion of the avian influenza risk analysis steps by WHO. In the avian influenza case, there was the feeling that time remained to get prepared and put into place measures that would reduce its consequences. For example, our analysis did not find evidence of cost considerations in dealing with SARS, while some sort of cost-benefit analysis pertained to avian influenza H5N1. While SARS was being transmitted directly from human to human, avian influenza H5N1 remained essentially transmissible among animals, and from animals to humans. The emergence of SARS and the reemergence of avian influenza H5N1 occurred in the context of growing concern about infectious diseases and increasing expectations of the role of WHO, which may have facilitated its action during the SARS outbreak and laid the groundwork for WHO's course of action during the avian influenza outbreak.

Second, these cases reflect a difference regarding the capacity of WHO to perform the risk analysis and to decide and implement the response. During the SARS outbreak, WHO was active on all fronts, playing a key – and almost unchallenged – role in assessing risk and coordinating the response and being listened to and followed in its actions by member states (sometimes not without protest) and other actors during a short period of time. On the opposite end, WHO, which had benefited from the precedent of SARS, encountered difficulties in imposing and maintaining its leadership over time. From a human health issue and presented as such by WHO in the early stages of its action, the avian influenza H5N1 reintegrated the animal health preoccupations as advocated by OIE. Funds and activities (such as culling operations, information campaigns, etc.) were the fact of OIE.

The institutional capacity of an organization can be evaluated based on three elements: assets, skills, and capabilities. (208 pp. 183–215 cited in 2 p. 53) *Assets* represent the foundations of the institution capacity and include rights and obligations that are expressed in rules, norms, and regulations; resources (financial resources and infrastructures); competencies and knowledge (pool of experience and expertise);

and organizational integration, which is the capacity to mobilize and combine these assets. (2 p. 53) *Skills* refer to the quality of institutional and human performance. In dealing with risk, institutions should be flexible and adapt to changing contexts or parameters of activities, have a vision and innovate by introducing new practices, and show steering capability, that is, driving changes that have impacts on the outside world. (2 p. 54) *Capabilities* provide the framework to transform assets and skills into successful responses to risk: capabilities are layers of relations, networks (defined here as close cooperative structures that go beyond relations), and regimes (rules that actors should comply with) (2 p. 54).

In terms of assets, rules have traditionally been a contentious issue in the field of risk, (2) which was the case with WHO's travel restrictions, which gave rise to protest, but to a lesser extent than Indonesia's refusal to share H5N1 viruses. In terms of resources, WHO remained constrained by its budget (209) (USD 3,977 million in 2014–2015, USD 3,959 million in 2012–2013, 4,540 in 2010–2011 and 4,227 in 2008–2009[1]), while in terms of competencies and knowledge, WHO could mobilize a larger pool of experience and expertise. Organizational integration varies from one institution to another. WHO can mobilize its expert network quickly and organize the logistics to send teams rapidly into the field, which individual governments may not be able to do. WHO managed to access and retrieve the organization's assets in order to channel them toward risk reduction, in both the SARS and avian influenza H5N1 cases.

The analysis of the skills that express the capacity of organizations and institutions to deal with evolving and emergency external conditions (2) suggests that WHO had a vision and brought new practices into its risk analysis, showed flexibility in adapting to the evolution of the outbreak and incoming information, and provided leadership and direction in driving the risk analysis and response processes, while ensuring flat and integrative communication processes in teleconferences and meetings. For example, WHO introduced new cooperation practices to assess the SARS disease, while developing relations with member states and other actors, such as multinational companies or NGOs for the avian influenza H5N1. WHO has easier and faster access to expertise through the networks that it has built of scientists and professionals active in the field concerned. For example, these networks have played a crucial role in the acquisition and dissemination of knowledge about SARS virology, epidemiology and clinical characteristics.

Finally, the capabilities that constitute the framework in which assets and skills can be exploited (2) reveal deficiencies and strengths in relationships, networks, and regimes. Relations and networks have contributed to the establishing of regimes, and thus expectations about certain types of behavior among its members. Playing within the rules has proved to be essential in addressing global risks. Reluctant cooperation can jeopardize both risk assessment and implementation of responses, as the SARS and avian influenza H5N1 cases showed respectively. Relationships and networks are said to be essential for forming and sustaining regimes. (2) In WHO's case, rules were established in the IHR 1969, but did not apply to SARS, resulting in an action-based rather than a rule-based legitimacy (WHO, during the avian influenza outbreak, benefited from both once the IHR 2005 came into force). Networks clearly constituted a central piece of the risk disposition, and relations included different actors, particularly in the avian influenza case, in which other organizations, states, nongovernmental actors, and private companies were represented. Power struggles among organizations, and in particular between WHO and OIE, to lead risk governance processes of avian influenza H5N1 (and obtain resources accordingly), as well as competing interests among scientific networks in handling SARS showed at the same time the ability of and difficulty for WHO in leading complex risk governance processes such as the SARS and avian influenza H5N1, complexity that will reveal even greater in the case of H1N1 influenza.

This analysis suggests that an institutional capacity essentially based on regimes, rule-based legitimacy, and resources may not be sufficient to drive risk governance processes. The importance of skills, in particular, flexibility, leadership and diversity, competencies and knowledge, and the mobilization of this knowledge, as well as the positive role of networks appear as critical factors in driving global risk governance processes in health. While the actor driving the risk governance process matters, and multilateral institutions are well positioned to play this role, their institutional capacity should combine an adequate level of assets, skills, and capabilities. WHO further developed networks and relations in order to palliate a lack of resources as well as obtain financial support and action commitments from different partners in the avian flu case, and later in the H1N1 pandemic.

4.2   Pandemic influenza A (H1N1): outlook on a contested management

Dr. Margaret Chan, Director-General of WHO, declared the world at the start of a pandemic on June 11, 2009, when about 30,000 cases of a novel

H1N1 virus were identified in 74 countries. (210) It was the first influenza pandemic of the twenty-first century, and its outbreak and rapid spread represented the first complete real-life test of the revised IHR. The outbreak was expected to cause a pandemic of moderate severity, but a serious threat to infected people between 30 and 50 years old, create a burden on the functioning of health systems, and present challenges for economies and international travel and trade.

The outbreak started in Mexico in April 2009, and lasted until August 2010, causing over 18,449 deaths in 214 countries and regions. The case fatality ratio was approximately 0.04% (211), and was relatively low compared to an earlier estimate of 0.4% (with a range from 0.3% to 1.8%) (212) and to historical standards. As countries were not required to test and report cases after July 2009, their last published estimates of cases detected early indicated 94,512 laboratory confirmed cases and 429 deaths. (213) When WHO alerted the world about this influenza outbreak on April 24, 2009, the facts that the virus was of animal origin and had not been previously detected in pigs or humans, that it affected young age groups, and that it spread quickly in multiple outbreaks in Mexico and the United States were of high concern. (214)

The pandemic influenza A(H1N1) occurred in an international context of growing concern about infectious diseases, and in particular about the avian influenza A(H5N1) pandemic that led governments to pledge about USD 4.3 billion, according to World Bank estimates. (215 pp. 90–98) An influenza pandemic H5N1 was portrayed as a potential economic and humanitarian disaster for which everyone should be prepared. (216) WHO had published pandemic preparedness guidelines in 1999 and 2005, but put a revised version on its website on April 25, 2009, simultaneously with the H1N1 outbreaks in Mexico and in the United States. WHO assessed that 68% of 119 reviewed national plans were built based on its plan, but few countries tested their plans (8%) with simulation exercises. (217 p. 66)

WHO brought the H1N1 issue to the international arena after cases were confirmed in Mexico and the United States and positioned itself as the leading and central actor to manage this pandemic. It issued recommendations and information about it, assessed the risk on a continuous basis, and coordinated the international response.

The implementation of the IHR and of these pandemic plans designed for a severe influenza pandemic (of type A[H5N1]) drew criticism, particularly about inefficiencies in the deployment of the IHR and pandemic plans, the independence of WHO's experts, (218) the adequacy of measures, and the costs of the pandemic response. For about one year, the world was on alert regarding the H1N1 pandemic, while its estimated case fatality ratio remained low compared to those of SARS or the Spanish flu. Europe particularly felt the H1N1 pandemic risk assessment resulted in a disproportionate, uncoordinated, overly costly response. However, Asian countries and the United States were for the most part satisfied by the way WHO handled the pandemic, while Africa was largely saved from it. This nevertheless caused a loss of confidence in WHO and a breach in its legitimacy, which led the WHO Director-General to mandate an independent investigation about its management and response to the H1N1 pandemic and the functioning of the IHR. (217)

The review committee set up to conduct this investigation found no malfeasance by WHO, but proposed areas of improvement, mainly in risk governance, the implementation of national and local capacities called for in the IHR, and the preparedness of the world for a long-lasting pandemic. (217) We will account for the results of this evaluation, while mainly reporting on WHO's risk analysis and formation of international response to the pandemic H1N1. To reiterate the limitations expressed in the introduction, the H1N1 case was essentially subject to documentation review and confrontation of information from different sources that are gathered into this outlook. The purpose is not to review any one study of the H1N1 pandemic. We believe, however, that this perspective on the risk governance process and the changes in procedures that occurred at WHO due to the H1N1 pandemic are of interest in understanding the evolution of the organization, its legitimacy, and its means of action after the management of these three diseases in fewer than ten years, as well as its position within the global risk governance of pandemics. Many studies have been published on the lessons learned at WHO's level and at the national and international levels, analyzing the successes and failures of the risk governance process, and dealing with specific aspects of the assessment, such as the effectiveness of the surveillance system, or the response, such as cost-effectiveness of measures. This discussion will not cover all these studies, but will analyze some key aspects of risk assessment and response from WHO's perspective, as well as show the main changes that WHO implemented to prepare for future pandemics (or international public health emergencies).

4.2.1   H1N1 risk analysis

WHO's authority was based on the revised IHR that came into force on June 15, 2007, and provided the framework for countries' notification, reporting of cases, and communication with WHO, as well as WHO's outbreak management procedures, including the setup of an emergency committee. The H1N1 pandemic was the first public health event to be assessed and reported under the revised IHR. The risk analysis and formation of an international response were based on the principles, processes, and instruments set up to deal with SARS and were further developed to counter a potential avian influenza A(H5N1) pandemic.

The IHR require countries to report significant public health events to WHO (based on Annex 2), and they are expected to exchange information and to cooperate, mostly through the National Focal Points (NFPs). WHO has formed an international response based on the scientific assessment of the risk to public health. Countries have to take WHO's advice into account and must justify any more restrictive measures to it, such as travel or trade restrictions. (217 p. 21) The IHR are meant to balance the protection of public health with the preservation of international exchanges.

The H1N1 story brings into focus several aspects of WHO's risk analysis. Its risk assessment activities were anchored on three pillars. First was the IHR, with, on one side, its Global Alert and Response (GAR) system, and on the other, the emergency committee that provided structures and instruments with which WHO could assess risk, report, disseminate information, and assist member states. During the H1N1 pandemic, WHO headquarters relied on regional offices that were in touch with the national focal points of member states, collecting information and communicating to assess risk. The emergency committee met nine times during the pandemic, mostly by teleconference, and its experts advised the Director-General on assessing the risk, declaring the pandemic on and over, and proposing risk mitigation strategies.

Second, the Global Influenza Surveillance and Response System (GISRS), known as the GISN prior to May 2011, serves as a global alert and monitoring mechanism for new viruses, including risk assessment, laboratory diagnostics, antiviral assessment, and vaccine recommendations. During the H1N1 pandemic, it monitored the evolution of the virus and analyzed antiviral susceptibility, concluding a high sensitivity to oseltamivir and zanamivir. (219) WHO CCs for influenza, Essential Regulatory Laboratories (ERLs), and other institutions developed candidate vaccine viruses under its coordination. (220)

Third, the Global Influenza Program and Mexico reported the outbreak under Annex 2 of the revised IHR. WHO verified it, activated an influenza surveillance network that could perform laboratory tests, led field investigations to learn about the cases detected in affected areas, and evaluated these results and the regional and then international spread of the disease to issue recommendations. It constituted the emergency committee under the revised IHR for the first time. The identities of this committee's members were confidential, and the committee met regularly to advise the WHO Director-General on risk evaluation and recommend measures. The Director-General declared pandemic phases according to the latest revision of the WHO pandemic preparedness plan published just before the H1N1 outbreak started. (221) The WHO influenza task force activated the influenza surveillance network, followed up on risk assessments, and proposed countermeasures to be applied in the different phases.

The Influenza Pandemic Plan issued in spring 2009 (221) guided WHO's actions during the H1N1 pandemic. It was the result of several consultations with a broad constituency from November 2007 to April 2009. (217 p. 16) It included guidelines for tracking risk and its possible sources, as well as for determining the causal chain of a pandemic risk and proposed actions in affected and unaffected countries. It had six phases, like the previous plan, but phases 1 to 4 were concerned with virus transmissibility and the possibility of rapid containment, while phases 5 and 6 concerned sustainable human-to-human transmission. (221 p. 27) The difference between phases 5 and 6 mainly relates to the spread of the disease: at least two countries in one WHO region declared phase 5, while another in another region declared phase 6, the pandemic-in-progress phase. When the WHO Director-General announced the pandemic was in progress on June 11, the criteria had technically been met for a few weeks already. This declaration triggered the deployment of pandemic measures as prescribed in most national plans (although some countries had already launched them) and generated post-pandemic criticism about their deployment despite the moderate severity and fatality of the disease. However, assessing severity at the beginning of a pandemic is difficult mainly due to the unavailability and unreliability of data about the cases, (222 p. 307) viral characteristics, and reproduction rate. The H1N1 pandemic's rapid spread and uncertain severity necessitated significant measures, such as vaccine orders (217 p. 116) and the purchase of antivirals. This uncertainty, and the Director-General's declaration, were not reflected in the interpretation of most pandemic plans, including that of WHO. As prescribed by its plan, WHO also coordinated laboratory research to determine the characteristics of the virus, the use of the antivirals stockpile, and the manufacture of vaccines. It enhanced surveillance and provided guidelines to national health authorities regarding surveillance, risk groups, and case management. In addition, WHO set up a task force that coordinated H1N1 risk assessment process and response. It could rely on GISN, which had grown over the past few years to prepare for a pandemic of H5N1 origin. It also gathered and exchanged information on FluNet, a web-based interactive platform.

WHO mobilized its influenza network and followed up on clinical management, virology, and epidemiology, using the structures, procedures, and processes tested on SARS and further developed against the avian influenza H5N1. These experts mainly exchanged their views during teleconferences. (223 p. 5) To better assess the pandemic's evolution, impact, and response to interventions, WHO set up a network of public health experts and mathematical modeling groups in academic institutions. (222 p. 306) Modeling requires sufficient and accurate data, so the use of these results raised issues about their adequacy for the needs of policymakers and of communication of the uncertainty surrounding the modeling exercise. (222 p. 307) Finally, surveillance systems appeared relatively efficient in gathering information on confirmed cases and deaths, but failed to report the number of infected people seeking health care, particularly in developing countries, rendering a comprehensive risk assessment more difficult. WHO reviewed its risk assessment periodically in light of new data from state members regarding the number of cases and case fatality ratio, adapting its procedures to the challenges of mass reporting and the duration of the pandemic. (223) It also seems that the disease could develop differently from one setting to another, for example, in terms of transmission, which was confirmed by studies (224) and the attack rate, as well as the case fatality rate.

A key actor in the pandemic risk assessment and the recommendation of measures was the emergency committee. Its constitution, composition, and frequency of meetings were not published during the pandemic. WHO's decision to keep the names of its members confidential in order to protect them from external pressures resulted in the perception that the organization wanted to hide its members' connections from the public, whether they were to institutions or to the private sector. (218) In addition, WHO was not equipped at the time with formal and transparent procedures for dealing with declared conflicts of interest, which increased mistrust of its committee and the whole organization. WHO published the names and declared the conflicts of interest (assessed as not material) at the end of the pandemic in August 2009. In addition to speculation about the composition of the committee and its links with industry, the fact that only a subset of the committee advised on the decision to move from phase 4 to 5 was contested. (217 p. 115)

In terms of cost analysis, there is no evidence that WHO proceeded to specific analyses other than those provided for in the preparedness activities regarding the avian influenza H5N1. While macroeconomic benchmarks are openly referred to, institutional analyses of funds needed to assess, plan, and run measures are unpublished or partially published, mainly ex post H1N1 and for specific measures such as vaccination. The World Bank expressed the cost of a pandemic in relation to the GDP, an indicator that remained a reference throughout the pandemic. The cost of the influenza A(H1N1) pandemic was estimated from 0.7% to 4.8% of GDP in 2009, a figure confirmed in a later report as up to 4.8% of GDP, with 71 million fatalities and an expected total cost of USD 3 trillion (225 p. ix).

4.2.2   H1N1 pandemic response

WHO relied on the structures, processes, and instruments developed to handle the SARS and avian influenza H5N1 cases. Its international response to H1N1 influenza was mainly based on the influenza pandemic plan of 2009 that maintained the concept of containment applied after 2002. This approach up to phase 4 aimed at containing the disease at its source, healing patients with antivirals, and applying quarantine measures to the affected zone, thus keeping the disease contained within national or even regional borders. However, the containment protocol developed during H5N1 pandemic preparedness activities appeared useless due to the speed with which the disease spread. In fact, this instrument was deemed to be efficient within a three weeks' time window to stop a virus at its source. (217 p. 18)

WHO's international response to influenza H1N1 in the form of recommendations and guidelines resulted in the publication of about 60 documents between the end of April and August 2009 relating to mass gatherings, travel, trade, school measures, behavioral interventions, and the use of antivirals and vaccines. (217 p. 97) WHO's measures mainly aimed at reducing the spread of the disease and the number of cases, while preserving travel and trade. The proliferation of guidelines in a short period of time as well as complements of information made it sometimes difficult for actors to sort information by importance and relevance. WHO's response also included applying the IHR to communicate with health authorities and extend support to member states, monitoring surveillance, expertise and research activities, and communicating to the public.

WHO conducted its actions by referring to a science-based assessment of the risk, the IHR provisions, and the guidelines elaborated to counter a pandemic, including the WHO Pandemic Influenza Preparedness and Response (2009) and the WHO Interim Protocol (October 2007). Both relied on the cooperation of WHO member states that had been significantly involved in preparedness activities (consultation, elaboration of documents, simulations, etc.). Within the IHR framework, the NFPs played a key role in reporting new cases of H1N1, particularly at the beginning of the pandemic. The Event Information Site (EIS) available to WHO officers, NFP personnel, and selected public health professionals was a privileged, secure means of communication between WHO and these partners (in addition to emails and phone calls/conferences). But both WHO and NFPs rapidly faced an overload of information and difficulty in reporting cases. WHO started to aggregate cases and countries as well, sometimes resulting in discrepancies between figures. Verifying and cross-checking information represented a large burden on WHO's personnel and showed some limits of the system when dealing in real time with an influenza virus spreading rapidly worldwide. (223 p. 5) In addition, data often came from different sources that used no standard format nor methodology of reporting. Reports on cases and deaths were incomplete, (217 p. 78) making severity assessments even more difficult. It seems that informal clinical and epidemiological networks that gathered in teleconferences with affected countries, partners, and the GISN provided useful information, particularly at the beginning of the pandemic. However, the reporting of cases and clinical management remained an issue during the pandemic and made the compilation of data and publication of information challenging for WHO.

Although WHO did not prescribe travel restrictions, some countries went beyond its recommendations and imposed them on Mexico, the United States, and Spain, which were all affected early. Flights coming from these countries were banned (Cuba was the first country to suspend flights to Mexico (226) on April 28, 2009). Countries such as the United Kingdom, Australia, France, and Switzerland prescribed postponing unessential travel for the public. (226) These practices go against the IHR that plans for WHO to communicate with these countries to make them reconsider their measures. Although FAO, OIE and the World Trade Organization issued a joint statement declaring that consumption of pork posed no sanitary risk, from April 29, 2009, to June 10, 2009, about 20 countries banned imports of pork meat from Mexico, Canada, and the United States. (226) These national initiatives challenge international organizations' authority (especially WHO's) in establishing and coordinating global governance. WHO does not have any means of legal enforcement other than an incentive-based system, including negotiations with concerned member states. The organization is submitted to conflicting pressures from states for more cooperation on the fight against diseases, yet maintenance of states' prerogatives in applying measures other than the ones prescribed.

Banned flights and screening policies have marginal benefit compared to its costs; the disease can cross borders by other means than flights. Such measures may delay the disease, but will definitely not prevent it. China imposed entry screening policies that later proved to delay local transmission of A(H1N1) influenza for an average of 7–12 days. (227 pp. 1–14) The cost-benefit relationship for societal measures (e.g., social distancing measures, wearing masks, quarantine, etc.) has been less studied than drug prescriptions, vaccine production, and hospital measures, which saw assessment and use during the H1N1 pandemic. The evolution of the public health measures proposed by WHO until the end of May 2009 progressed from advice on the use of masks, to behavioral interventions to reduce transmission, suspension of classes and restrictions on mass gatherings. Some documents responded to requests from countries, while other reviewed the different measures and their impact.

Antiviral stockpiling and vaccination, both mitigation measures presented as effective, were retained from the H5N1 pandemic preparedness and implemented in the H1N1 pandemic. An antiviral stockpile was released based on an agreement with Roche (global stockpile of 3 million doses and regional stockpile of 2 million doses) that raised few concerns in receiving countries. However, WHO reported that the virus was sensitive to both medicines (oseltamivir and zanamivir) in early stages of the pandemic, which was contested due to the lack of data on the effectiveness of these treatments for patients with H1N1 influenza in different parts of the world. Guidelines were established following a protocol including expertise, but were mostly based on evidence from seasonal influenza or H5N1 influenza in May 2009 and revised in February 2010 with H1N1 data. (217 p. 91) In the assessment of the effectiveness of antivirals, clinical networks such as the ones instituted for SARS, appeared to play a critical role. In parallel, WHO also gathered information about resistance to these medicines, but mostly through the GISN. The second measure was the advice on vaccines and vaccination that consisted one of the privileged responses to an influenza pandemic. While vaccination was already considered a cost-effective measure for the H5N1 influenza (228) and was confirmed for the H1N1 pandemic in the North American context, for example, (229, 230, 231) it has been carried out with variable results that range from perceived success in some Asian countries to perceived failure in European countries like France or Switzerland. WHO obtained from GlaxoSmithKline and

Sanofi Pasteur a conversion of their H5N1 vaccine donation pledge to the H1N1 pandemic with an increase to 150 million doses. (217 p. 95) Based on the plans, 200 million of doses of vaccine had to be distributed in about 100 countries: in total, 78 million doses were distributed to 77 countries. (217 p. 97) The sharing of viruses, access to vaccine, vaccine production, and distribution remain critical issues that have generated conflicting positions among organizations, countries, and the private sector. In 2007, WHO initiated negotiations on the virus and benefit sharing, following up on the refusal of Indonesia to share H5N1 viruses. These resulted in the Pandemic Influenza and Preparedness Framework that facilitates the sharing of viruses and benefits, and provides significant financing from the industry, but does not legally bind its signatories. (232)

The management of H1N1 was largely decentralized, with WHO regional and even national offices playing a significant role, even issuing specific regional guidance. In addition, member states and regional organizations such as the European Union or ASEAN deployed pandemic plans of their own and did not do so in accordance with WHO's phases and recommendations, complaining about their lack of flexibility (233 p. 292) and therefore their inapplicability to regional or national specificities, or the timing difference in the evolution of the disease within regional or national contexts. This interplay between the global, national, and local levels in some circumstances did not facilitate the coordination or monitoring of the response from WHO's viewpoint and underscored that it has no means of enforcement.

4.2.3 Perspective

WHO's management of the H1N1 pandemic was largely criticized and it brought to light several deficiencies debated both in the media and the scientific literature. Firstly, governance inefficiencies include (but are not limited to) the severity assessment issue, the overcomplexity of the pandemic phases structure, deficiencies in case reporting, work overload in surveillance and a profusion of guidelines that are sometimes inconsistent with each other. Secondly, WHO experts involved in the preparation of guidelines or in the emergency committee were accused of collusion with the private sector, especially the antiviral producers and the vaccine industry. (218) The lack of transparency regarding the management of conflicts of interest largely contributed to breaches or even a loss of confidence in the organization. Finally, both internal and external communication was perceived as suboptimal, and the overall management of the pandemic resulted in alleged disproportionate costs mostly generated by overestimating this mild pandemic. It was frequently pointed out that WHO's guidance was designed for a more severe disease, (234 p. 1) namely of type H5N1, which served as a reference up to 2009.

However, notwithstanding these limitations addressed by WHO and other actors after the pandemic, less attention was given to the aspects that went well. The management of the H1N1 pandemic is the result of more than ten years of work on pandemic preparedness, represents the first stress test of the IHR, and relied on the whole arsenal of systems largely based on the latest technologies and the mobilization of unprecedented expertise. The IHR and the 2009 pandemic guidance provided the frame within which WHO conducted its risk assessment and monitored the global response to the H1N1 virus. The IHR represented a considerable improvement in the governance of infectious diseases with a more robust frame for action. (235 p. 509) It was used by WHO and member states and facilitated their cooperation. (236) WHO used the NFPs to share information, and set up the emergency committee, while member states used the notification procedure and reported case information to WHO. Its role in global risk governance of influenza was mainly defined in terms of 2009 pandemic guidance: coordination under the IHR, designation of the global pandemic phase, recommendations on whether and when to switch from seasonal to pandemic vaccine production, rapid containment of the initial emergence of pandemic influenza, and early assessment of pandemic severity. (217 p. 69) WHO actually conducted these activities thanks to the teams, groups, and committees either operating on a routine basis for influenza or especially set up to handle H1N1. Despite criticism of its integrity, timeliness, and appropriateness of action, WHO had to cope with the immaturity of national capacities planned under the IHR (235 p. 506), as well as insufficient methodology and resources in national surveillance and a year-long pandemic (compared to SARS, which lasted a few months, and the H5N1 pandemic that has not yet arisen).

The H1N1 pandemic had an impact on the structures, procedures, and practices of risk governance at WHO. (237) As a learning organization, WHO reviewed the H1N1 pandemic, acknowledging some of the criticism it received and was willing to improve its practices. The Review Committee issued recommendations that can be grouped in three axes: reinforcement of core national and local capacities required to achieve the IHR, improvement of WHO's performance, and improvement of worldwide preparedness for a future pandemic or any global public health emergency. (217)

First, it seems that the H1N1 has been the engine to accelerate implementation of core national capacities subject to a yearly progress report and to improve the EIS, of which a new version was launched in fall 2013. Both member states and WHO ensured the NFPs' resources and authority: WHO ensured training for NFP representatives, which also enhances the constitution of networks in the sight of a future crisis. Second, the report highlighted areas of improvement for WHO in its structures, procedures, and practices. WHO reserved a team to manage a pandemic or any similar event of a long duration, simplified its pandemic preparedness guidance, and provided mechanisms to evaluate a pandemic's severity. While the severity is difficult to assess and mainly depends on two elements that are highly uncertain and sometimes not available, especially at the beginning of an outbreak – the seriousness of the disease (with the case fatality ratio) and the transmissibility (with the reproduction number) – WHO proposes severity assessment guidance, including representative parameters for core severity indicators. (238 pp. 22–24) Finally, the organization revised its guidance through consultations and issued, at member states' request, specific guidelines on risk assessment, (239) revised guidelines for influenza pandemic, and the PIP framework. However, the relationship between the IHR and the WHO pandemic alert system, as well as compliance enforcement mechanisms of the IHR do not seem to have been addressed yet. (235)

Transparency regarding the involvement of expertise has been one key area of change. WHO now publishes the names of members of the Emergency Committee and it instituted a procedure to manage conflicts of interest at two levels, for the inclusion in the IHR Roster of experts and in the emergency committee. This procedure was applied for the emergence of the MERS-CoV in 2013, which represented an opportunity for WHO to show the implementation of these revised practices. WHO also extended expert competences from 53 to 72 categories in the IHR Roster and added about 200 experts to the list. In addition, a Compliance, Risk Management and Ethics Office has been created under the Director-General.

Compared to other global crisis management cases, WHO's governance of the pandemic risk was quite appropriate. (240 p. 11) It gathered many stakeholders, increased surveillance, and improved disease detection mechanisms. Specific structures as the Strategic Health Operations Centre (SHOC) provided information to support WHO's decision-makers. WHO used the IHR, its networks, and its expertise to continuously reassess the situation and make decisions. Criticism addressed to WHO has often not taken into account the concrete difficulties of deploying a pandemic plan in a climate of emergency, uncertainty, and fear, and were often formulated based on later events. WHO had to cope with tight time constraints and intense pressures. It had to anticipate vaccine production quickly, while it had little information about the virus's characteristics and potential evolution. Plans that did not allow for flexibility were deployed and left the WHO managing team (and national decision-makers) unable to step back and adjust their plan. (240) While foundations for WHO's action in governing pandemic risk were in place with the IHR and the structures and processes run during the H1N1 pandemic, WHO mainly encountered issues in management techniques and communication.

WHO positioned itself as the central governor of the H1N1 pandemic. Building on the multistakeholders approach developed against the H5N1 potential pandemic and in the revision of the influenza pandemic plan, WHO acknowledged that other actors had to be involved in the management of the pandemic. While WHO had a global role, national centers for disease control such as the American CDC, the European CDC, and the Chinese CDC gained regional roles, and other actors from civil society played important parts as they were closer to affected communities. WHO built more effective cooperation and communication with these actors and has been looking into ways to incorporate their voices into the governance of international public health events of international concern, while respecting its accountability to its member states. It is a delicate balance as the involvement of actors from the private sector in preparing the response to an influenza pandemic emerging in France (241 pp. 292–303) and the relationships between WHO and the antiviral and vaccine producers have shown.

In addition, closer cooperation among international organizations and United Nations agencies has also been elicited. Interagency conflicts and tensions, particularly between WHO, OIE, and FAO, to secure funds, ensure their legitimacy, and conduct activities to reduce the risk of H5N1 have at the same time inspired unprecedented cooperation under the "One World, One Health" framework. (206 pp. 213–226) In 2008, with the support of the World Bank and the UNSIC, WHO, OIE, and FAO prepared a global strategy to reduce risks at the interface between animal and human health. (242) In the continuity, the three groups have expressed in a tripartite concept note, (243) the bases of their joint approach in assessing and managing emerging zoonotic diseases and collaboration in setting consistent standards at the human-animal health interface in 2010. The Global Early Warning System (GLEWS) combines the intelligence mechanisms of the three organizations. Cooperation among these institutions took place during the H1N1 pandemic, but appeared even more critical afterward, due to the still ongoing risk of an avian influenza pandemic H5N1, or H7N9, or the emergence of MERS-Cov cases. WHO also aims at building common approaches with other actors under the Emergency Management Framework for events including pandemics and also disasters and conflicts.

In the end, WHO aims at enlarging its action while remaining secure against attacks on its legitimacy and competencies. While assuming a leadership and support role for member states, WHO clearly identifies national responsibilities for risk assessment and flexible planning. The argument for integrating these plans in continuity planning and a whole-society approach therefore makes sense and releases the organization from the sole responsibility of risk assessment. However, WHO should not be disconnected from states, and the whole-society approach is still under design. Cooperation, improvement of practices, and the promotion of action under more comprehensive and integrative frameworks are strategies boosted by the results of the management of the H1N1 pandemic. These recent developments should give the organization an advantage should another public health emergency of international concern be declared.

4.3 Conclusions

The conclusions that can be drawn from the analysis of the SARS outbreak, the avian influenza H5N1, and the 2009 H1N1 influenza pandemic go beyond a comparison of their single histories to emphasize the importance of the role of WHO within global risk governance in health and the modalities of its action. This book has shown the importance of risk analysis under a multilateral institution in the formation of an appropriate international response to a global risk in health. It suggests that the combination of a science-based risk approach and a multilateral institution's capacity for action are essential elements – but not the sole elements – in global risk governance in health. The results of this study shed light on the importance of scientific expertise in addressing risk at the global level, which questions participative and discursive models as discussed by Callon, Lascoumes, and Barthes (244), and the development of inclusive models of governance as advocated by Renn (2). First, interdisciplinary, science-based risk approaches provide a frame for action by which multilateral institutions can address uncertainty, estimate risk, define research priorities, confront the latest findings and concerns, and cover a wider range of aspects to design responses that are characterized by cooperation and commitment, risk reduction, and monitoring, as in the cases of SARS, avian influenza, and influenza A H1N1. Risk analysis not only results in increased preparedness for coping with global risks but also provides a roadmap to address these risks in real time once they occur, as the SARS outbreak showed. Following the H1N1 crisis, WHO revised its approach for more flexibility and published new procedures, such as a manual to provide guidance on the rapid risk assessment of acute public health risks (239).

Second, global risks pose major challenges in governance, and multilateral institutions contribute to the establishment of innovative steering mechanisms to better cope with these risks. Our analysis suggests that multilateral institutions, by developing an effective combination of assets, skills, and capabilities that result in an increased legitimacy for action, can drive global risk governance processes, thereby achieving more optimal outcomes. This study spotlighted the essential leading role of WHO in the SARS and avian influenza (H5N1) cases, thereby highlighting this institution's innovation and learning capabilities in terms of risk governance. Empirical evidence was developed regarding WHO's increasing global role as a coordinator of risk assessment, in particular in the constitution, composition, and modalities of the work of expertise and of the completion of the response in the SARS and avian influenza cases. WHO's setup of virtual networks in the case of SARS, as well as its organization of multistakeholder technical meetings in the case of avian influenza played an essential role in ensuring a continuous iterative risk assessment process that included the latest research results available. WHO, through debriefing and development of best practices, as is done in the business world, improved and strengthened its processes, which was evident in how it managed the H1N1 pandemic as compared to the SARS pandemic. This learning process can be further illustrated by the lessons learned from the H1N1 pandemic that were detailed in the above outlook.

While the IHR Review Committee found no evidence of malfeasance (217 p. xvi), and its report highlighted several issues related to WHO's capacity to run the roadmap in the influenza H1N1 pandemic. It concluded that WHO's institutional capacity should be expanded. First, the completion of the IHR regime, which will not palliate its structural absence of enforceable sanctions, will provide member states and their NFPs with the required core capacities for handling a pandemic. Second, WHO strengthened its relationships with member states and other actors by reaching an agreement on the sharing of viruses and access to vaccine (245). WHO should also reinforce its capacity of inquiry and negotiation when states apply decisions that affect travel and trade, which are not recommended by the organization. In terms of networks, WHO should act with more transparency in order to assert its legitimacy and balance its accountability to the member states and the public, while integrating stakeholders from the private sector and NGOs. In terms of assets, in particular resources and organizational integration, the access to a reserve workforce and a special fund will facilitate the deployment of the response, as well as the enhancement of technological possibilities, such as the WHO Event Information Site for NFPs. The review of the pandemic preparedness guidance was completed, and it integrated a "new severity framework" in response to criticism regarding the insufficient account for the severity within the pandemic risk assessment.

Finally, multilateral institutions not only function as providers of information (246) but also as providers of global public goods. The appropriate international response ensures the provision of a global public good, that is, risk reduction, which is expected to benefit all countries and populations. To provide this global public good, institutional capacity matters – in particular, the ability to mobilize actors toward a common objective, take into account their strategies and perceptions, and find resources to carry out actions. Cooperation is essential to carrying out a risk analysis as well as to ensuring the coordination and completion of the risk response. Evidence was accumulated about the importance of cooperation as a central element in containing SARS or reducing the risk of a human influenza pandemic, in focusing on mutual benefits to all and the cost-effectiveness of risk analysis. This is particularly well illustrated by the evolution of WHO over the past ten years toward the Emergency Response Framework, which intends to be a holistic model that can be applied to events that impact public health, such as natural disasters, chemical accidents, armed conflicts, food insecurity, or the emergence of disease (247). WHO hereby confirms its strategic interest in occupying a leading role in the governance of public health risks.

After a period in which its action was challenged, and thanks to the emergence of SARS, WHO positioned itself as the leading actor in the governance of global public health risks – in particular, infectious diseases. In competition for its leading role with OIE in the management of the avian influenza H5N1, WHO further developed its practices and procedures, reinforcing a multistakeholders approach. WHO revised its pandemic preparedness plan from the perspective of an inevitable pandemic, be it of H5N1 origin or not. This context of uncertainty also provided favorable grounds on which to finalize the revision of the IHR, which provided WHO with a larger scope of intervention, and to complete a revision of the pandemic plan of 2005. Shaken by the H1N1 pandemic, the organization engaged in a review process in order to regain legitimacy and confidence from the various actors and reinforce its capacity. WHO developed new strategies, procedures, and more effective tools to be tested with the MERS-CoV, avian influenza A H7N9, or other emerging diseases. While WHO confirmed its strategy of positioning itself as the leading actor in the governance of a future influenza pandemic (or another global risk to health), the organization has insisted on the clarification of roles and responsibilities of member states in the process. Member states have to cope with the IHR and strengthen their national public health capacities, while adopting a whole-society approach to integrate the participation of stakeholders in the governance of future pandemics or other health events. Balancing this strategy of leaders with the competencies granted by member states is a delicate but necessary exercise. By leveraging the emergence of infectious diseases that can result in pandemics and therefore providing a global public good with the management of the responses to these risks, the organization also seeks to gain and maintain a strategic position vis-à-vis other actors in global risk governance in health (237). As a large organization subject to changes in economic conjuncture, power plays, and major societal changes, WHO has to ensure its own continuity, particularly in terms of positioning and financing (237). Facing a decline in the budget's organization since the global financial crisis of 2008 and the layoff of about 900 employees between December 2010 and July 2012 (248) has been more challenging to the organization than handling the effects of the H1N1 crisis. Interestingly, the budget allocated to outbreak and crisis response grew about four times between 2008–2009 and 2012–2013 (from USD 116 million to USD 469 million, which respectively represent about 2.7% and 11.8% of WHO's budget) to be set at USD 228 million for 2014–2015 or 5.7% of WHO's budget, which may be interpreted as a sign that the action of the organization in this field is still recognized.

Interdependence is a source of risks and, at the same time, provides opportunities to better cope with them. Risk governance mechanisms rely on the interplay between multiple actors, resources, and capacities that are rendered feasible through the increasing possibilities offered by modern technologies and means of exchange. Multilateral institutions, thanks to their recognized capacities, competencies, and legitimacy, can initiate and drive global risk governance processes that mobilize and coordinate the actions of the different actors involved in these activities.

Global risk governance appears, therefore, possible if a scientific assessment of the risk constitutes the basis for action of a multilateral institution that has gained the capacity and legitimacy to act globally within a given field and can integrate viewpoints and federate actors from different horizons toward a common objective, as WHO has done with regard to public health.

Notes

Introduction

1. "Risk" shall be understood as "an uncertain consequence of an event or an activity with respect to something that humans value", (1 p. 261 cited in: 2 p. 5).
2. Interdependence "refers to situations characterized by reciprocal effects among countries or among actors in different countries", (3 p. 105).
3. The Organization for Economic Cooperation and Development (OECD) clearly identifies and explains these phenomena in (4 pp. 29–63).
4. Multilateral institutions can be defined as "international organizations, regimes, and networks governed by formal international agreements", (20 pp. 1–2).

1 Thinking the International Response to a Global Health Risk

1. The risk literature refers to this actor as a "whistleblower." The whistleblower usually makes public information about risk-related issues or problems within an organization. This actor exposes itself to reactions from the organization or authorities, and its warning may not be taken into account systematically by the adequate institution and level of hierarchy for corrective action. We do recognize the importance of the whistleblower analysis in establishing the existence and framing the risk, but as the focus of our study is the risk analysis process, we consider that the warning was adequately relayed to the multilateral institution, recognized as risk, and generated action. As a reference for whistleblower literature, see (21).
2. WHO defines the mortality rate as "the number of deaths occurring in a given population at risk during a specified time period" (also known as the recall period). In emergencies, this is usually expressed as deaths per 10,000 persons per day; alternatively, as deaths per 1000 persons per month or per year (29).
3. WHO defines the case fatality ratio as "the proportion of cases of a given disease that result in death." Often abbreviated to CFR (29).
4. The reproduction number R^0 is defined as the average number of secondary cases generated by one primary case in a susceptible population.
5. In this approach, (25 pp. 75–96). the deliberation process includes scientists, public officials, and interested and affected parties, while our approach primarily focuses on interactions among experts, multilateral institutions' personnel, and states' representatives. This deliberation often already takes place in a blurred zone between risk assessment and risk management called risk characterization.

2 Severe Acute Respiratory Syndrome: Analysis of a Successful Containment

1. The case fatality ratio or rate is the proportion of cases of a given disease that results in death. It is often abbreviated CFR and expressed per 100 cases.
2. "The Global Public Health Intelligence Network (GPHIN) is a secure, Internet-based 'early warning' system that gathers preliminary reports of public health significance in seven languages on a real-time, 24/7 basis. This unique, multilingual system gathers and disseminates relevant information on disease outbreaks and other public health events by monitoring global media sources such as news wires and websites. The information is filtered for relevancy by an automated process, and then analyzed by Public Health Agency of Canada GPHIN officials. The output is categorized and made accessible to users. Notifications about public health events that may have serious public health consequences are immediately forwarded to users" (37).
3. The GOARN, set up in 2000, is a technical collaboration of existing institutions and networks that pool human and technical resources for the rapid identification, confirmation, and response to outbreaks of international importance. The GOARN provides an operational framework to link this expertise and skill in order to keep the international community constantly alert to the threat of outbreaks and ready to respond. The GOARN contributes to global health security by combating the international spread of outbreaks, ensuring that appropriate technical assistance reaches affected states rapidly, and contributing to long-term epidemic preparedness and capacity building. WHO coordinates international outbreak responses using resources from the GOARN (38).
4. The name of Epidemic Alert and Response was changed in 2005 to Epidemic and Pandemic Alert and Response in recognition of the emergence of the risk of a human influenza pandemic that could be caused by the H5N1 avian influenza.
5. Medical Officer, World Health Organization, Interview by author, WHO Headquarters, December 5, 2008.
6. International Heath Regulations Coordinator, World Health Organization, Interview by author, WHO Headquarters, November 20, 2008.
7. This published document (45) is used in this book as proxy for the unpublished revised IHR legal draft that was ready when the SARS outbreak occurred. It is referred to as "IHR revision project" in the text.
8. For further details about the full content of the SARS resolution, refer to: (32).
9. For further details about the full content of the resolution on the revision of IHR, refer to: (48).
10. National IHR Focal Point means the national center, designated by each State party, which shall be accessible at all times for communications with WHO IHR Contact Points under IHR.
11. Medical Officer, World Health Organization, Interview by author, WHO Headquarters, December 5, 2008.
12. The complete list of these institutions is available in: (50).
13. "Appendix 5: People Who Worked on SARS Response, February to July 2003," in: (34 pp. 269–280).

14. Consultants who were assigned to several missions may be counted more than once in this table, which aggregates all participants (e.g., WHO headquarters experts who traveled to affected areas may be registered as headquarters and field mission staff). However, the impact remains marginal and does not affect the pattern. In addition, information about field expertise is missing for 29 participants, of whom 22 were from the US Centers for Disease Control (CDC) who were involved in the Taiwan field mission, five from WHO, one from Médecins Sans Frontières, and one a freelance writer. The table also includes the 30 staff members of WHO Western Pacific Region for whom the field expertise was available. The field of expertise for WHO headquarters staff was not mentioned.

15. Figures computed from a database built based on "Appendix 5: People who worked on SARS response, February to July 2003," in: (34 pp. 269–280).

16. These figures were computed based on the records obtained by searching the names of the participants at that meeting in *The Lancet* and *The New England Journal of Medicine*'s databases (55).

17. Two Chinese institutions joined the SARS virology network on March 27, 2003. The complete list of institutions that were part of this network is available on: (56).

18. Koch's postulates are four criteria designed to establish a causal relationship between a microbe and a disease. First, the microorganism must be found in abundance in all organisms suffering from the disease, but not in healthy organisms. Second, the microorganism must be isolated from a diseased organism and grown in pure culture. Third, the cultured microorganism should cause disease when introduced into a healthy organism. Fourth, the microorganism must be reisolated from the inoculated, diseased experimental host and shown to be identical to the original specific causative agent.

19. The virology network counts 8 partners of the global influenza program out of 11 (then 13) institutions. The influenza network had already been activated at the beginning of the outbreak, when an avian influenza outbreak was suspected.

20. Several institutions, among which was the US CDC, have claimed to have discovered the virus. In fact, it seems that the causative agent was isolated in China beforehand, but that the information could not be released since it would contradict the analysis of the Chinese CDC specialist who confirmed chlamydia as a source of the disease. SARS coronavirus can coinfect with chlamydia, which results in a more severe disease.

21. The complete list of the institutions, including WHO, that were part of the SARS epidemiological network can be found at: (50).

22. The complete list of institutions of the SARS clinical network is available at: (50).

23. Ground rounds are virtual meetings held through videoconferences (and phone conferences) that gather experts, WHO personnel, and field missions to share information about the SARS outbreaks worldwide.

24. These items will be updated in the documents produced after the SARS crisis, e.g., the WHO Consensus document on the epidemiology of severe acute respiratory syndrome (SARS) published in November 2003.

25. Medical Officer, World Health Organization, Interview by author, WHO Headquarters, December 5, 2008.

26. Medical Officer, World Health Organization, Interview by author, WHO Headquarters, December 5, 2008.
27. From July 1998 to August 2001, WHO verified 578 outbreaks, of which 56% were initially picked up by GPHIN, in: (63).
28. The capacity was reinforced, (53) and in 2008, the networks counted 122 national centers in 94 countries.
29. The Chinese center joined the network later in the process.
30. All collaborating centers except the Australian center were part of the SARS dedicated network.
31. Based on the superspreading events in Hong Kong Hotel and Amoy Gardens Residence, transmission by air conditioning or the sewage system was suspected and investigated.
32. Twenty-five of twenty-six hospital staff in Hanoi, and 24 of 39 hospital staff in Hong Kong rapidly progressed to respiratory failure, requiring intensive care and causing the deaths of some previously healthy persons.
33. Starting in May 10, the pattern of local transmission is expressed in Patterns A, B, C, and Uncertain, instead of low (+), medium (++), high (+++), and Uncertain according to the same definitions, except for Pattern C.
34. Recent local transmission has occurred when, in the last 20 days, one or more reported probable cases of SARS have most likely acquired their infection locally regardless of the setting in which this may have occurred.
35. The final document released in November 2003 also incorporates published data and data presented at the SARS Clinical Management Workshop, June 13–14, 2003, Hong Kong, Special Administrative Region of China, the WHO Global Conference on Severe Acute Respiratory Syndrome, Kuala Lumpur, Malaysia, June 17–18, 2003, and during teleconferences of the WHO Ad Hoc Working Group on the Epidemiology of SARS.
36. On April 7, Stephan Roach, Morgan Stanley chief economist, estimated the global impact of SARS at about USD 30 billion, in: (62).
37. Costs by countries (62, 89) are China: $2.2 billion, Hong Kong: $1.7 billion, Indonesia: $400 million, South Korea: $2 billion, Malaysia: $660 million, the Philippines: $270 million, Singapore: $950 million, Taiwan: $820 million, Thailand: $490 million, Vietnam: $15 million, Japan: $1.1 billion.
38. This figure is computed based on data by country provided in: (91 p. 4).
39. Medical Officer, World Health Organization, Interview by author, WHO Headquarters, December 5, 2008.
40. This table is based on (104) and (105).
41. WHO considered this screening measure as an additional protective measure, while its effectiveness was contested by a Canadian study. (106)
42. The source for all epidemic curves (except if other source mentioned) is: (112).
43. The graphs tend to illustrate a trend. Scale is therefore adapted to each country.
44. Due to political reasons, the SARS outbreak in Taiwan was mostly handled by members of the US CDC sent to the field, although WHO was represented on the team.
45. Notwithstanding the attitude of mainland China, Hong Kong authorities cooperated with WHO starting from the beginning of the outbreak. Dr. Margaret Chan, who had worked at the Hong Kong Department of Health

since 1978, joined WHO as Director of the Department for Protection of the Human Environment in 2003.

46. The accuracy of the reporting of cases in Beijing was questioned by WHO team leader Dr. Bekedam in a press conference held on April 16, 2003.

47. Asian Development Bank, "Asian Development Outlook 2003 Update: Assessing the Impact and Cost of SARS in Developing Asia," 2003, study performed by the Oxford Economic Forecasting Group, pp. 88–89.

48. The involvement of the Director-General remains unclear at this stage, while she clearly and openly supported the global alert of March 15, 2003.

49. The Hong Kong report of the SARS Expert Committee has established a chronology of the evolution of scientific knowledge on SARS in which the WHO, the CDC and scientists' publications have been indicated by date of issuance. This chronology shows the constant update of guidelines and recommendations about SARS (77).

3   Avian Influenza H5N1: International Preparedness against a Future Influenza Pandemic

1. Computed based on the WHO cumulative number of confirmed cases as of December 31, 2008. Case fatality ratio (CFR): the number of deaths divided by the total number of cases.

2. Other estimates go up to USD 15 billion (130 p. 4).

3. From 1994 to 2003, Dr. Margaret Chan was Director of the Department of Health of Hong Kong Special Administrative Region of China, and was confronted with the avian influenza outbreak of 1997 and the SARS epidemic of 2003. She joined WHO in 2003, and occupied different high-level positions until her nomination as WHO Director-General in 2006.

4. A new influenza virus subtype is causing disease in humans, but is not yet spreading efficiently and sustainably among humans (133).

5. In June 2005, Dr. Margaret Chan was appointed Director, Communicable Diseases Surveillance and Response, as well as Representative of the Director-General for Pandemic Influenza. In September 2005, she was named Assistant Director-General for Communicable Diseases and became Director-General of WHO on November 9, 2006. She was reelected in 2012 for a second term that will run through June 2017.

6. The consultation led to debates about specificity and flexibility. Partisans of a list of diseases to be used in addition to the concept (PHEIC), such as representatives from the United States, wanted to make sure that in any cases and independently of the risk assessment, certain diseases known for their potential significant effects would be addressed. Representatives of other countries and WHO considered that PHEIC allowed more flexibility to address any event and that a list could reduce the importance of the performance of risk assessment to capture all events that might become a PHEIC.

7. We obtained a copy of this draft and the list of participants at that meeting, the opening session of which was open to the public and journalists. Our analysis of the composition of expertise and computations are based on this document.

8. This draft (150) was further updated up to October 2007 (152).

9. International Heath Regulations Revision Project Leader, World Health Organization, Interview by Author, WHO Headquarters, June 28, 2005.
10. International Heath Regulations Revision Project Leader, World Health Organization, Interview by Author, WHO Headquarters, June 28, 2005.
11. Dr. Fukuda replaced Dr. Stöhr, who was senior adviser, Influenza Pandemic Vaccine Development, at WHO from 2006–2007, and who joined Novartis in 2007.
12. The Epidemic Alert and Response unit changed its name to Epidemic and Pandemic Alert and Response (EPR) in 2005 during the H5N1 avian influenza outbreak.
13. Dr. Malik Peiris's team in Hong Kong announced on March 21, 2003, the isolation of a new virus that would be proven to be the causative agent of SARS.
14. This model (30) estimates 89,000 to 207,000 deaths resulting from a pandemic in the United States, for a total cost ranging from $71.3 billion to $166.5 billion (USD).
15. There seems to be no consensus on the figure of deaths worldwide; an estimate of 40 million is more often given, but that varies up to 100 million (174).
16. Hong Kong and the Palestinian Autonomous Territories have been considered as separate reporting entities by OIE and assimilated to countries. The same approach has been used in this book for comparability reasons.
17. Case fatality ratio (CFR) computed based on WHO data: the number of deaths divided by the total number of cases.
18. WHO reports only laboratory-confirmed cases; the total number of cases includes number of deaths, and all dates refer to onset of illness.
19. OIE data have been updated as of February 22, 2009.
20. WHO estimated the capacity to 1 to 2 billion doses a year in 2009.

4 Cases Comparison: Outlook on H1N1 Influenza Pandemic and Conclusions

1. WHO's budget is composed of about 25% of regular member states' contributions and 75% of voluntary contributions from member states and other donors, such as the Bill and Melinda Gates Foundation or the Rockefeller Foundation.

Bibliography

Abraham T. *Twenty-First Century Plague: The Story of SARS.* Baltimore: Johns Hopkins University Press. 2007.

Advisory Council on Food and Environmental Hygiene. *Comprehensive Plan of Action to deal with the Global Problem of Avian Influenza.* Honk Kong. 2005, ACFEH Paper 58.

Anderson R, Fraser C, Ghani A, Donnelly C, Riley S, Ferguson N, et al., editors. *Epidemiology, Transmission Dynamics and Control of SARS: The 2002–2003 Epidemic.* Oxford: Oxford University Press; 2005.

BBC News. China "sorry" for slow bug response 2003 [updated June 6, 2009]. Available from: http://news.bbc.co.uk/2/hi/health/2919967.stm.

BBC News. Killer bug traced to HK hotel 2009 [updated June 6, 2009]. Available from: http://news.bbc.co.uk/2/hi/health/2867055.stm.

Bell C, Lewis M. The economic implications of epidemics old and new. Center for Global Development – Working Paper 2005; 54.

Bell M, Warren A, Budd L. Scales of governance: The role of surveillance in facilitating new diplomacy during the 2009–2010 H1N1 pandemic. *Health & Place.* 2012;18(6):1404–1411.

Bernstein M, Jaspe J. Les tireurs d'alarme dans les conflits sur les risques technologiques. Entre intérêts particuliers et crédibilité. *Politix, Revue des sciences sociales du politique.* 1998;11(44):109–134.

Bloom E, de Wit V, Carangal-San Jose MJ. Potential Economic Impact of an Avian Flu Pandemic on Asia. *ERD Policy Brief Series.* 2005;42.

Brahmbhatt M. editor Avian and Human Pandemic Influenza – Economic and Social Impacts. Meeting on avian influenza and human pandemic influenza 2005 November 7–9; Geneva, Switzerland.

Brender N. Risk analysis under multilateral institutions: a determining factor in the formation of global risk responses in health: the cases of Bovine Spongiform Encephalopathy (BSE), Severe Acute Respiratory Syndrome (SARS), and avian influenza [Th Univ Genève, 2010 IHEID 837]. Geneva: Graduate Institute of International and Development Studies; 2010.

Brender N, Gilbert C. OMS : logique de l'OMS en matière de pandémie et gestion de H1N1. Project "Emergence et risques sanitaires" (ATP), CIRAD, 2010–2013, Note de synthèse des résultats des travaux de recherche de l'axe 2, Gouvernance des émergences zoosanitaires, 2013.

Briand S, Mounts A, Chamberland M. Challenges of global surveillance during an influenza pandemic. *Public Health.* 2011;125(5):247–256.

Brockman D, Hufnagel L, Geisel T, editors. *Dynamics of Modern Epidemics.* Oxford etc.: Oxford University Press; 2005.

Brown D. CDC Issues guidelines for battling flu pandemic school closings likely, but restricting travel not suggested. Washington Post, February 2, 2007:A03.

Burci GL, editor La gestion d'une crise sanitaire international: le cas du SRAS. Quatorzièmes rencontres internationales d'Aix-en-Provence – La société internationale et les grandes pandémies. December 8–9, 2006; Aix-en-Provence.

Callon M, Lascoumes P, Barthe Y, editors. *Agir dans un monde incertain : essai sur la démocratie technique.* Paris: Ed. du Seuil; 2001.

Carlson, M. A brief history of the 1987 stock market crash with a discussion of the Federal Reserve response. *Federal Reserve Board Finance and Economics Discussion Series,* 2007-13.

Cetron M, Maloney S, Koppaka R, Simone P Isolation and quarantine: containment strategies for SARS 2003. In: Knobler S, Mahmoud M, Lemon S, Mack A, Sivitz L, Oberholtzer K, editors. *Learning from SARS: Preparing for the Next Disease Outbreak. Forum on Microbial Threats, Board of Health.* Institute of Medicine of the National Academies. Washington: National Academies Press. 2004:71–83.

Checchi F, Roberts L. HPN Network Paper 52, *Interpreting and Using Mortality Data in Humanitarian Emergencies: A Primer for Non-Epidemiologists.* London: Overseas & Development Institute. 2005:1–38.

Check E. Is this our best shot? *Nature.* 2005;435(7041):404–406.

Chien YJ. How did international agencies perceive the avian influenza problem? The adoption and manufacture of the "One World, One Health" framework. *Sociology of Health & Illness.* 2013;35(2):213–226.

Cohen D, Carter P. Conflicts of interest. WHO and the pandemic flu "conspiracies". *BMJ* (Clinical research ed). 2010;340:c2912.

Commission of the European Communities. Communication from the Commission to the Council, The European Parliament, The European Economic and Social Committee and the Committee of the Regions on Pandemic Influenza Preparedness and Response Planning in the European Community. 2005 COM(2005) 607 final.

Cowling BJ, Lau LL, Wu P, Wong HW, Fang VJ, Riley S, et al. Entry screening to delay local transmission of 2009 pandemic influenza A (H1N1). *BMC Infectious Diseases.* 2010;10(1):82.

Davis M. *The Monster at Our Door : The Global Threat of Avian Flu.* New York: The New Press; 2005. VIII, 212 pp.

Dingwerth K, Pattberg P. Global governance as a perspective on world politics. *Global Governance: A Review of Multilateralism and International Organizations.* 2006;12(2):185–203.

Duffin J, Sweetman A, editors. *SARS in Context : Memory, History, Policy.* Montreal; Ithaca: School of Policy Studies Queen's University: McGill-Queen's University Press; 2006.

Durbin A, Corallo A, Wibisono T, Aleman D, Schwartz B, Coyte P. A cost effectiveness analysis of the H1N1 vaccine strategy for Ontario, Canada. *Journal of Infectious Diseases Immunity.* 2011;3(3):40–49.

Enserink M. Influenza. WHO adds more "1918" to pandemic predictions. *Science.* 2004;306(5704):2025.

Enserink M. SARS in China: China's missed chance. *Science.* 2003;301(5631):294–296.

Eysenbach G. SARS and population health technology. *Journal of Medical Internet Research.* 2003 Apr–Jun; 5(2):e14.

FAO-OIE-WHO Collaboration. Sharing responsibilities and coordinating global activities to address health risks at the animal-human-ecosystems interfaces: a tripartite concept note. April; 2010.

FAO, OIE, WHO, UN System Influenza Coordination, UNICEF, World Bank. Contributing to One World, One Health. A strategic framework for reducing

Federal Office of Public Health. Swiss influenza pandemic plan – strategies and measures in preparation for an influenza pandemic. Federal Office of Public Health in Bern. 2007.

Ferguson N, Cummings D, Cauchemez S, Fraser C, Riley S, Meeyai A, et al. Strategies for containing an emerging influenza pandemic in Southeast Asia. *Nature*. 2005;437(7056):209–214.

Fidler DP. SARS, *Governance and the Globalization of Disease*. Basingstoke: Palgrave Macmillan; 2004. XVII, 219 pp.

Fidler DP, Gostin LO. The WHO pandemic influenza preparedness framework: a milestone in global governance for health. *JAMA*. 2011;306(2):200–201.

Figuié M. Towards a global governance of risks: international health organisations and the surveillance of emerging infectious diseases. *Journal of Risk Research*. 2013; 17:469–483.

Food and Agriculture Organization of the United Nations. *Highly Pathogenic Avian Influenza and beyond*. The FAO response, Rome. 2008.

Fraser C. SARS: public health needs in the case of re-emergence 2004 [updated June 9, 2004]. Available from: www.who.int/entity/vaccine_research/about/gvrf_2004/en/gvrf_2004_fraser.pdf.

Fraser C, Donnelly CA, Cauchemez S, Hanage WP, Van Kerkhove MD, Hollingsworth TD, et al. Pandemic potential of a strain of influenza A (H1N1): early findings. *Science*. 2009;324(5934):1557–1561.

Fukuda K, editor, Pandemic influenza global considerations, approaches & strategy. 2005 General Conference of the International Risk Governance Council – Implementing a global approach to risk governance; 2005 September 20–21; Beijing.

Graham JD, International Risk Governance Council. *The Emergence of Risks : Contributing Factors*. Geneva: IRGC, International Risk Governance Council; 2010.

Greaves F. What are the most appropriate methods of surveillance for monitoring an emerging respiratory infection such as SARS? *Journal of Public Health*. 2004;26(3):288–292.

Hashim A, Jean-Gilles L, Hegermann-Lindencrone M, Shaw I, Brown C, Nguyen-Van-Tam J. Did pandemic preparedness aid the response to pandemic (H1N1) 2009? A qualitative analysis in seven countries within the WHO European Region. *Journal of Infection and Public Health*. 2012;5(4):286–96.

Heymann D, Rodier G. Hot spots in a wired world: WHO surveillance of emerging and re-emerging infectious diseases. *The Lancet Infectious Diseases*. 2001;1(5):345–353.

Heymann DL, editor. *The International Response to the Outbreak of SARS, 2003*. Oxford etc.: Oxford University Press; 2005.

Heymann, DL. *Severe Acute Respiratory Syndrome (SARS): Global Alert, Global Response* (PowerPoint Presentation). 2003.

Hien TT, Liem N, Dung N, San L, Mai P, Chau N, et al. Avian influenza A (H5N1) in 10 patients in Vietnam. *New England Journal of Medicine*. 2004;350(12):1179–1188.

Holbrooke R, Garrett L. *"Sovereignty" That Risks Global Health*. Washington Post, August 10, 2008:B07.

Hutubessy R, Chisholm D, Edejer Tan-Torres T. Generalized cost-effectiveness analysis for national-level priority-setting in the health sector. Cost Effectiveness

Intergovernmental Working Group on the Revision of International Health Regulations. International Health Regulations. Working Paper for Regional Consultations. 2004 IGWG/IHR/Working paper/12.2003.

Kamradt-Scott A. Changing perceptions: of pandemic influenza and public health responses. *American Journal of Public Health*. 2012;102(1):90–98.

Kates R, Hohenemser C, Kasperson J. *Perilous Progress: Managing the Hazards of Technology*: Westview Press, Boulder CO. 1985.

Katz R. Use of revised International Health Regulations during influenza A (H1N1) epidemic, 2009. *Emerging Infectious Diseases*. 2009;15(8):1165–1170.

Keogh-Brown MR, Smith RD. The economic impact of SARS: How does the reality match the predictions? *Health Policy*. 2008;88(1):110–120.

Keohane R, Martin L. The promise of institutionalist theory. *International Security*. 1995;20(1):39–51.

Keohane R, Nye J. Globalization: What's new? what's not? (and so what?). *Foreign Policy*. 2000 (118):104–119.

Keohane RO, Buchanan A. The legitimacy of global governance institutions. *Ethics & International Affairs*. 2006;20(4):405–437.

Keohane RO, Macedo S, Moravcsik A. Democracy-enhancing multilateralism. *International Organization*. 2009;63(01):1–31.

Khazeni N, Hutton DW, Garber AM, Owens DK. Effectiveness and cost-effectiveness of expanded antiviral prophylaxis and adjuvanted vaccination strategies for an influenza A (H5N1) pandemic. *Annals of Internal Medicine*. 2009;151(12):840–853.

Kickbusch I. SARS: Wake-up call for a strong global health policy: how to stop a virus that doesn't respect sovereignty. Yale Global Online; 2003.

Kilbourne ED. A virologist's perspective on the 1918–19 pandemic. In: Phillips H, Killingray D, editors. The Spanish influenza pandemic of 1918–19 : new perspectives – Routledge studies in the social history of medicine 12. London etc.: Routledge; 2003. p. XXI, 357.

Knobler, Stacey, Adel Mahmoud, Stanley Lemon, Alison Mack, Laura Sivitz and Katherine Oberholtzer (Eds) Learning from SARS: Preparing the Next Disease Outbreak – Workshop Summary. Washington (DC): National Academies Press (US). 2004.

Kuperman AJ. Mitigating the moral hazard of humanitarian intervention: lessons from economics. *Global Governance: A Review of Multilateralism and International Organizations*. 2008;14(2):219–240.

Lagadec P. "La drôle de grippe" – Pandémie grippale 2009 : essai de cadrage et de suivi. 2010.

The Lancet. TheLancet.com – Home Page 2009 [updated June 7, 2009]. Available from: http://www.thelancet.com/home.

Lee JW, McKibbin WJ. Globalization and disease: the case of SARS. *Asian Economic Papers*. 2004;3(1):113–131.

Lee K, editor. *Globalization and Health: An Introduction*. Basingstoke: Palgrave Macmillan; 2003.

Lee K, editor. *Health Impacts of Globalization : Towards Global Governance*. Basingstoke: Palgrave Macmillan; 2003.

Lipsitch M, Cohen T, Cooper B, Robins J, Ma S, James L, et al. Transmission dynamics and control of severe acute respiratory syndrome. *Science*. 2003;300(5627):1966–1970.

Longini IM, Nizam A, Xu S, Ungchusak K, Hanshaoworakul W, Cummings D, et al. Containing pandemic influenza at the source. *Science*. 2005;309(5737):1083–1087.

Low, DE. SARS: Lessons from Toronto. In Knobler, Stacey, Adel Mahmoud, Stanley Lemon, Alison Mack, Laura Sivitz and Katherine Oberholtzer (Eds.) Learning From SARS: Preparing the Next Disease Outbreak – Workshop Summary. Washington (DC): National Academies Press (US). 2004, 63–70.

MacLean AR, editor. *SARS: A Case Study in Emerging Infections*. Oxford etc.: Oxford University Press; 2005.

McKibbin WJ, Sidorenko A. *Global Macroeconomic Consequences of Pandemic Influenza*. Lowy Institute for International Policy; Sydney Australia. 2006.

Meltzer MI, Cox NJ, Fukuda K. The economic impact of pandemic influenza in the United States: priorities for intervention. *Emerging Infectious Diseases*. 1999;5(5):659–671.

Murphy C. The 2003 SARS outbreak: global challenges and innovative infection control measures. *Online Journal of Issues in Nursing*. 2006; 11:6.

Murray CJL, Evans DB, Acharya A, Baltussen RMPM. Development of WHO guidelines on generalized cost-effectiveness analysis. *Health Economics*. 2000;9:235–251.

National Research Council. *Risk Assessment in the Federal Government: Managing the Process*. Washington, DC: National Academy Press 1983.

National Research Council (U.S.) – Committee on Improving Risk Analysis Approaches. *Science and Decisions: Advancing Risk Assessment*: National Academies Press; Washington DC. 2009.

Official website of the G8 summit 2006 in Saint-Petersburg. Statement of G8 Health Ministers Meeting [updated April 28, 2006]. Available from: http://en.g8russia.ru/news/20060428/1148826.html.

Offlu. OIE/FAO Network of Expertise on Animal Influenza. Available from: http://www.offlu.net/.

Ong A, Kindhauser M, Smith I, Chan M. A global perspective on avian influenza. *Annals Academy of Medicine*. 2008;37(6):477–481.

Opatowski L, Fraser C, Griffin J, de Silva E, Van Kerkhove MD, Lyons EJ, et al. Transmission characteristics of the 2009 H1N1 influenza pandemic: comparison of 8 Southern hemisphere countries. *PLoS Pathogens*. 2011;7(9):e1002225.

Organisation de coopération et de développement économiques (Paris), editor. Les risques émergents au XXIe siècle : vers un programme d'action. Paris: OCDE. 2003.

Organization for Economic Cooperation and Development (OECD). Emerging systemic risks in the 21st century: an agenda for action. Paris: OCDE. 2003.

Osterholm M. Preparing for the next pandemic. *New England Journal of Medicine*. 2005;352(18):1839–1842.

Paquet G. The new governance, subsidiarity, and the strategic state in Governance in the 21st century. 2001:183–215.

Pearson H, Clarke T, Abbott A, Knight J, Cyranoski D. SARS: what have we learned? *Nature*. 2003;424(6945):121–126.

Peiris J, Lai S, Poon L, Guan Y, Yam L, Lim W, et al. SARS Study Group. 2003. Coronavirus as a possible cause of severe acute respiratory syndrome. *Lancet*. 2003;361(9366):1319–1325.

Plant AJ, editor. SARS and public health: lessons for future epidemics. River Edge N.J. etc.: World Scientific; 2003.

Prosser LA, Lavelle TA, Fiore AE, Bridges CB, Reed C, Jain S, et al. Cost-effectiveness of 2009 pandemic influenza A (H1N1) vaccination in the United States. *PLoS One.* 2011;6(7):e22308.

Public Health Agency of Canada. Global Public Health Intelligence Network (GPHIN) – Information 2004 [updated November 2004]. Available from: http://www.phac-aspc.gc.ca/media/nr-rp/2004/2004_gphin-rmispbk-eng.php.

Rao K, Wu X, Gu T. *China Health Information System: Review and Assessment.* Beijing: Center for Health Statistics Information, Ministry of Health, 2006.

Relman DA, Choffnes ER, Mack A. *Infectious Disease Movement in a Borderless World:* workshop summary: National Academies Press; Washington DC. 2010.

Renn O, editor. *Risk Governance : Coping with Uncertainty in a Complex World.* London: Earthscan; 2008.

Renn O, Walker KD, *International Risk Governance Council, Editors. Global Risk Governance: Concept and Practice Using the IRGC Framework.* Dordrecht: Springer; 2008.

Riley S, Fraser C, Donnelly CA, Ghani A, Abu-Raddad L, Hedley A, et al. Transmission dynamics of the etiological agent of SARS in Hong Kong: impact of public health interventions. *Science.* 2003;300(5627):1961–1966.

Rossi V, Walker J. *Assessing the Economic Impact and Costs of Flu Pandemics Originating in Asia.* Oxford: Oxford Economic Forecasting ; 2005.

Ryan M. Status of Human Preparedness and Response. *Meeting on Avian and Human Influenza;* November 7–9; World Health Organization Headquarters, Geneva; 2005.

Salehi R, Ali SH. The social and political context of disease outbreaks: the case of SARS in Toronto. *Canadian Public Policy.* 2006;32(4):373–385.

Sander B, Bauch CT, Fisman D, Fowler RA, Kwong JC, Maetzel A, et al. Is a mass immunization program for pandemic (H1N1) 2009 good value for money? Evidence from the Canadian experience. *Vaccine.* 2010;28(38):6210–6220.

SARS Expert Committee. SARS in Hong Kong: from experience to action, October 2003. Available at: www.sars-expertcom.gov.hk/english/reports/reports.html (accessed Nov. 2003).

Saywell T, Fowler GA, Crispin SW. The cost of SARS: $11 billion and rising. *Dow Jones Far Eastern Economic Review.* 2003.

Scoones I, Forster P. The international response to highly pathogenic avian influenza: science, policy and politics. STEPS Working Paper No. 10. Brighton: STEPS Centre, 2008.

Sjöberg L, Peterson M, Fromm J, Boholm A, Hanson SO. Neglected and overemphasized risks: the opinions of risk professionals. *Journal of Risk Research.* 2005;8(7):599–616.

Smith A, Young J, Gibson J. How now, mad-cow? Consumer confidence and source credibility during the 1996 BSE scare. *European Journal of Marketing.* 1999;33:1107–1122.

Smith RD. Responding to global infectious disease outbreaks: lessons from SARS on the role of risk perception, communication and management. *Social Science & Medicine.* 2006;63(12):3113–3123.

St John R, King A, Jong D, Bodie-Collins M, Squires S, Tam T. Border screening for SARS. *Emerging Infectious Diseases.* 2005;11(1):6–10.

Stern PC, Fineberg HV, National Research Council (USA) CoRC, editors. *Understanding Risk: Informing Decisions in a Democratic Society.* Washington,

Steyer V, Gilbert C. Exploring the ambiguous consensus on public-private partnerships in collective risk preparation. *Sociology of Health & Illness*. 2013;35(2):292–303.

Stöhr K. Avian influenza and pandemics – research needs and opportunities. *New England Journal of Medicine*. 2005;352(4):405–407.

Stöhr K. Global pandemic preparedness 2006 June 21, 2006. Available from: www.who.int/entity/csr/disease/influenza/stohr.pdf.

Stöhr K. A multicentre collaboration to investigate the cause of severe acute respiratory syndrome. *The Lancet*. 2003;361(9370):1730–1733.

Stöhr K, Esveld M. Will vaccines be available for the next influenza pandemic? *Science*. 2004;306(5705):2195–2196.

Taubenberger JK, editor. *Genetic Characterization of the 1918 "Spanish Influenza" Virus*. New York: Routledge; 2003.

Ungchusak K, Auewarakul P, Dowell S, Kitphati R, Auwanit W, Puthavathana P, et al. Probable person-to-person transmission of avian influenza A (H5N1). *New England Journal of Medicine*. 2005;352(4):333–340.

Unite for Sight. Unite For Sight's 4th Annual International Health Conference – Speakers 2007 [updated June 6, 2009]. Available from: http://www.uniteforsight.org/conference/2007/conf_speakers.php#davidheymann.

United Nations. A coordinated UN System Response to Avian and Human Influenza Draft Strategy Note [updated October 5, 2005]. Available from: http://www.fao.org/avianflu/en/strategydocs.html.

United Nations. A More Secure World Our Shared Responsibility: Report of the Secretary-General's High-level Panel on Threats, Challenges and Change. New York: United Nations, Dept. of Public Information; 2004.

United States Department of Health & Human Services. HHS Pandemic Influenza Plan. 2005.

United States Department of Health & Human Services. National Vaccine Program Office – Pandemics and Pandemic Scares in the 20th Century. Available from: http://www.hhs.gov/nvpo/pandemics/flu3.htm.

United States Department of State. U.S. Launches International Partnership on Avian and Pandemic Influenza Washington [updated September 22, 2005]. Available from: http://www.state.gov/r/pa/prs/ps/2005/53865.htm.

United States General Accounting Office. *Emerging Infectious Diseases: Asian SARS Outbreak Challenged International and National Responses*. Washington DC: 2004 GAO-04-564.

van Asselt M, Renn O. Risk governance. *Journal of Risk Research*. 2011;14(4):431–449.

van Asselt MB, van Bree L. Uncertainty, precaution and risk governance. *Journal of Risk Research*. 2011;14(4):401–408.

Van Kerkhove MD, Ferguson NM. Epidemic and intervention modelling: a scientific rationale for policy decisions? Lessons from the 2009 influenza pandemic. *Bulletin of the World Health Organization*. 2012;90(4):306–310.

van Kerkhove MD, Hirve S, Koukounari A, Mounts AW. Estimating age-specific cumulative incidence for the 2009 influenza pandemic: a meta-analysis of A (H1N1) pdm09 serological studies from 19 countries. *Influenza and Other Respiratory Viruses*. 2013;7(5):872–886.

van Zwanenberg P, Millstone E, editors. *BSE: Risk, Science, and Governance*. Oxford: Oxford University Press; 2005.

Wallinga J, Teunis P. Different epidemic curves for severe acute respiratory syndrome reveal similar impacts of control measures. *American Journal of*

Webster RG, editor. Pandemic Influenza Emergence and Control. 13ème Colloque Wright, Grandes Epidémies: le retour?; November 18, 2008; Geneva.

Wilson K, Brownstein JS, Fidler DP. Strengthening the International Health Regulations: lessons from the H1N1 pandemic. *Health Policy and Planning.* 2010;25(6):505–509.

The World Bank – East Asia and Pacific Region. Spread of avian flu could affect next year's economic outlook – Excerpted from the November 2005 East Asia Update – Countering Global Shocks. 2005.

The World Bank. Flu Outbreaks Reminder of Pandemic Threat, 2013 [updated March 5, 2013]. Available from: http://www.worldbank.org/en/news/feature/2013/03/05/flu-outbreaks-reminder-of-pandemic-threat.

The World Bank. International community pledges SU$1.9 billion to fight avian flu. Available from: web.worldbank.org.

The World Bank. People, Pathogens and our Planet – Volume 2 –The Economics of One Health. 2012 Doc No.: 69145-GLB.

The World Bank. Speak Out: Interview with Milan Brahmbhatt on Avian Flu 2009 [updated December 5, 2005]. Available from: http://discuss.worldbank.org/content/interview/detail/2739/.

World Health Assembly. Fifty-eighth World Health Assembly – Agenda item 13.1 – Revision of the International Health Regulations. Geneva: 2005 WHA58.3.

World Health Assembly. Fifty-sixth world Health Assembly – Agenda item 14.16 – Revision of the International Health Regulations. Geneva: 2003 May 28, 2003. WHA56.28.

World Health Assembly. Fifty-sixth World Health Assembly – Agenda item 14.16 – Severe acute respiratory syndrome (SARS). Geneva: 2003 WHA56.29 Doc No.: WHA56.29.

World Health Organization – Western Pacific Regional Office. SARS Multi-Country Outbreak (WPRO Presentation) 2003 [updated July 15, 2003]. Available from: http://www.wpro.who.int/sars/docs/presentation/multicoun-tryoutbreaks.asp.

World Health Organization – Communicable Diseases Cluster. Avian influenza: assessing the pandemic threat. Geneva: 2005 WHO/CDS/2005.20.

World Health Organization – Department of Communicable Disease. Consensus document on the epidemiology of severe acute respiratory syndrome (SARS). Geneva: 2003 WHO/CDS/CSR/GAR/2003.11.

World health Organization – Department of Communicable Disease. Consensus document on the epidemiology of severe acute respiratory syndrome (SARS) – Annex 2: Final List of Participants. Geneva: 2003 WHO/CDS/CSR/GAR/2003.11.

World Health Organization – Department of Communicable Disease. Influenza pandemic plan. The role of WHO and guidelines for national and regional planning. Geneva: 1999. Report No.: WHO/CDS/CSR/EDC/99.1.

World Health Organization – Department of Communicable Disease. Severe acute respiratory syndrome (SARS): Status of the outbreak and lessons for the immediate future. 2003.

World Health Organization – Department of Communicable Disease. WHO global influenza preparedness plan – The role of WHO and recommendations for national measures before and during pandemics. Geneva: 2005 WHO/CDS/CSR/GIP/2005.5.

World Health Organization – Department of Communicable Disease. WHO SARS Risk Assessment and Preparedness Framework. Geneva: 2004 WHO/CDS/CSR/ARO/2004.2.

World Health Organization – Director-General. Pandemics: working together for an effective and equitable response – Address to the Pacific Health Summit – Seattle, Washington, United States of America –13 June 2007 [updated June 17, 2007]. Available from: http://www.who.int/dg/speeches/2007/20070613_seattle/en/.

World Health Organization – Epidemic and Pandemic Alert and Response. Advice to international travellers 2004 [updated February 6, 2004]. Available from: http://www.who.int/csr/disease/avian_influenza/travel_2004_02_06/en/index.html.

World Health Organization – Epidemic and Pandemic Alert and Response. Affected Areas – Severe Acute Respiratory Syndrome (SARS) 2003 [updated June 6, 2009]. Available from: http://www.who.int/csr/sars/areas/2003_03_16/en/index.html.

World Health Organization – Epidemic and Pandemic Alert and Response. Areas with recent local transmission of Severe Acute Respiratory Syndrome (SARS) 2003 [updated May 2, 2003]. Available from: http://www.who.int/csr/sars/areas/2003_05_02/en/index.html.

World Health Organization – Epidemic and Pandemic Alert and Response. Avian influenza. Available from: http://www.who.int/csr/disease/avian_influenza/en/.

World Health Organization – Epidemic and Pandemic Alert and Response. Avian influenza A(H5N1) in humans and poultry in Viet Nam 2004 [updated January 13, 2004]. Available from: http://www.who.int/csr/don/2004_01_13/en/index.html.

World Health Organization – Epidemic and Pandemic Alert and Response. Avian influenza A(H5N1) in humans in Viet Nam and in poultry in Asian countries – update 2 [updated January 16, 2004]. Available from: http://www.who.int/csr/don/2004_01_16/en/index.html.

World Health Organization – Epidemic and Pandemic Alert and Response. Avian influenza frequently asked questions 2005 [updated December 5, 2005]. Available from: http://www.who.int/csr/disease/avian_influenza/avian_faqs/en/index.html.

World Health Organization – Epidemic and Pandemic Alert and Response. Avian influenza: guidelines. recommendations, descriptions [updated June 7, 2009]. Available from: http://www.who.int/csr/disease/avian_influenza/guidelinestopics/en/index.html.

World Health Organization – Epidemic and Pandemic Alert and Response. Cumulative number of confirmed human cases of avian influenza A(H5N1) reported to WHO 2009 [updated February 5, 2009]. Available from: http://www.who.int/csr/disease/avian_influenza/country/cases_table_2009_02_05/en/index.html.

World Health Organization – Epidemic and Pandemic Alert and Response. Cumulative Number of Confirmed Human Cases of Avian Influenza A/(H5N1) Reported to WHO 2009 [updated June 7, 2009]. Available from: http://www.who.int/csr/disease/avian_influenza/country/cases_table_2009_01_07/en/index.html.

World Health Organization – Epidemic and Pandemic Alert and Response. Current WHO phase of pandemic alert [updated June 7, 2009]. Available from: http://www.who.int/csr/disease/avian_influenza/phase/en/index.html.

World Health Organization – Epidemic and Pandemic Alert and Response. Disease Outbreak News, Update 72 – Situation in China 2003 [updated June 3, 2003]. Available from: http://www.who.int/csr/don/2003_06_03/en/index.html.

World Health Organization – Epidemic and Pandemic Alert and Response. Epidemic curves – Severe Acute Respiratory Syndrome (SARS). Available from: http://www.who.int/csr/sars/epicurve/epiindex/en/.

World Health Organization – Epidemic and Pandemic Alert and Response. Geographical spread of H5N1 avian influenza in birds – update 28, Situation assessment and implications for human health 2005 [updated August 18, 2005]. Available from: http://www.who.int/csr/don/2005_08_18/en/index. html.

World Health Organization – Epidemic and Pandemic Alert and Response. Global Outbreak Alert & Response Network [updated June 6, 2009]. Available from: http://www.who.int/csr/outbreaknetwork/en/.

World Health Organization – Epidemic and Pandemic Alert and Response. Guiding principles for international outbreak alert and response. Available from: http:// www.who.int/csr/outbreaknetwork/guidingprinciples/en/index.html.

World Health Organization – Epidemic and Pandemic Alert and Response. Influenza A(H5N1) in Hong Kong Special Administrative Region of China, Disease Outbreak Report 2003 [updated February 19, 2003]. Available from: http://www.who.int/csr/don/2003_2_19/en/index.html.

World Health Organization – Epidemic and Pandemic Alert and Response. Meeting on SARS virus detection and survival in food and water, Madrid, 2003 May 8–9 [updated May 22, 2003]. Available from: http://www.who.int/csr/sars/ guidelines/madridmeeting/en/.

World Health Organization – Epidemic and Pandemic Alert and Response. The operational response to SARS 2003 [updated June 6, 2009]. Available from: http://www.who.int/csr/sars/goarn2003_4_16/en/.

World Health Organization – Epidemic and Pandemic Alert and Response. Prise en charge des cas de Syndrome respiratoire aigu sévère (SRAS). Available from: http://www.who.int/csr/sars/managmentf/en/.

World Health Organization – Epidemic and Pandemic Alert and Response. Responding to the avian influenza pandemic threat. Recommended strategic actions. Geneva: 2005 WHO/CDS/CSR/GIP/2005.8.

World Health Organization – Epidemic and Pandemic Alert and Response. Severe Acute Respiratory Syndrome – Press briefing – April 11, 2003, Geneva 2003. Available from: http://www.who.int/csr/sars/Press_2003_04_11/en/.

World Health Organization – Epidemic and Pandemic Alert and Response. Severe Acute Respiratory Syndrome – Press conference, Hanoi, Viet Nam Hanoi 2003 [updated March 26, 2003]. Available from: http://www.who.int/csr/ sars/2003_03_27h/en/.

World Health Organization – Epidemic and Pandemic Alert and Response. Severe Acute Respiratory Syndrome (SARS)-multi-country outbreak – Update 58, 2003 [updated May 17, 2003]. Available from: http://www.who.int/csr/ don/2003_05_17/en/index.html.

World Health Organization – Epidemic and Pandemic Alert and Response. Severe Acute Respiratory Syndrome (SARS) – multi-country outbreak – Update 27, 2003 [updated April 11, 2003]. Available from: http://www.who.int/csr/ don/2003_04_11/en/index.html.

World Health Organization – Epidemic and Pandemic Alert and Response. Severe Acute Respiratory Syndrome (SARS) – multi-country outbreak – Update 33, 2003 [updated June 6, 2009]. Available from: http://www.who.int/csr/don/2003_04_18/en/index.html.

World Health Organization – Epidemic and Pandemic Alert and Response. Summary of WHO measures related to international travel 2003 [updated June 6, 2009]. Available from: http://www.who.int/csr/sars/travelupdate/en/.

World Health Organization – Epidemic and Pandemic Alert and Response. Summary table of areas that experienced local transmission of SARS during the outbreak period from 1 November 2002 to 31 July 2003, 2003 [updated November 21, 2003]. Available from: http://www.who.int/csr/sars/areas/areas2003_11_21/en/index.html.

World Health Organization – Epidemic and Pandemic Alert and Response. Terms of reference for WHO H5 Reference Laboratories 2006 [updated October 12, 2006]. Available from: http://www.who.int/csr/disease/influenza/torh5labs/en/index.html.

World Health Organization – Epidemic and Pandemic Alert and Response. Update 11 – WHO recommends new measures to prevent travel-related spread of SARS 2003 [updated 27 March 2003]. Available from: http://www.who.int/csr/sarsarchive/2003_03_27/en/.

World Health Organization – Epidemic and Pandemic Alert and Response. Update 17 – Travel advice – Hong Kong Special Administrative Region of China, and Guangdong Province, China 2003 [updated 2 April 2003]. Available from: http://www.who.int/csr/sarsarchive/2003_04_02/en/.

World Health Organization – Epidemic and Pandemic Alert and Response. Update 49, Disease outbreak reported, SARS case fatality ratio, incubation period 2003 [updated May 7, 2003]. Available from: http://www.who.int/csr/don/2003_05_07a/en/index.html.

World Health Organization – Epidemic and Pandemic Alert and Response. Update 54 Outbreaks in the initial "hot zones" indicate that SARS can be contained 2003 [updated May 13, 2003]. Available from: http://www.who.int/csr/don/2003_05_13b/en/index.html.

World Health Organization – Epidemic and Pandemic Alert and Response. Update 95 – SARS: Chronology of a serial killer 2003 [updated April 7, 2003]. Available from: http://www.who.int/csr/don/2003_07_04/en/.

World Health Organization – Epidemic and Pandemic Alert and Response. Vaccines for the new influenza A (H1N1) 2009 [updated June 7, 2009]. Available from: http://www.who.int/csr/disease/swineflu/frequently_asked_questions/vaccine_preparedness/en/index.html.

World Health Organization – Epidemic and Pandemic Alert and Response. WHO collaborative multi-centre research project on Severe Acute Respiratory Syndrome (SARS) diagnosis [updated June 6, 2009]. Available from: http://www.who.int/csr/sars/project/en/.

World Health Organization – Epidemic and Pandemic Alert and Response. WHO collaborative network of clinicians for SARS diagnosis and treatment. Available from: http://www.who.int/csr/sars/network/en/.

World Health Organization – Epidemic and Pandemic Alert and Response. WHO event management for international public health security – Operational Procedures, World Health Organization, 2008 WHO/HSE/EPR/ARO/2008.1.

World Health Organization – Epidemic and Pandemic Alert and Response. World Health Organization issues emergency travel advisory 2003 [updated March 15, 2003]. Available from: http://www.who.int/csr/don/2003_03_15/en/.

World Health Organization – Epidemic and Pandemic Alert and Response (EPR). Estimating the impact of the next influenza pandemic: enhancing preparedness Geneva 2004 [updated December 8, 2004]. Available from: http://www. who.int/csr/disease/influenza/preparedness2004_12_08/en/.

World Health Organization – Executive Board. Avian and pandemic influenza: developments, response and follow-up, and application of the International Health Regulations (2005) – Best practice for sharing influenza viruses and sequence data – Report by the Secretariat. Geneva: 2007 EB120/INF.DOC./3.

World Health Organization – Global Influenza Programme. Pandemic influenza preparedness and response: a WHO guidance document: World Health Organization; 2009.

World Health Organization – International Health Regulations. IHR News – Facts and figures 2008 [updated December 12, 2008]. Available from: http://www. who.int/ihr/ihrnewsissue5/en/index4.html.

World Health Organization – Media Centre. Donation of three million treatments of oseltamivir to WHO will help early response to an emerging influenza pandemic, Geneva 2005 [updated August 24, 2005]. Available from: http:// www.who.int/mediacentre/news/releases/2005/pr36/en/.

World Health Organization – Media Centre. Fact sheet n° 211 – Influenza (Seasonal) [updated April 2009]. Available from: http://www.who.int/ mediacentre/factsheets/fs211/en/.

World Health Organization – Media Centre. Global influenza meeting sets key action steps, agrees on urgent need for financing (Joint News Release WHO/ FAO/OIE/WORLD BANK) Geneva 2005 [updated November 9, 2005]. Available from: http://www.who.int/mediacentre/news/releases/2005/pr58/en/index. html.

World Health Organization – Media Centre. Global meeting to develop common approach on avian influenza and human pandemic influenza (Joint News Release WHO/FAO/OIE/World Bank – November 4, 2005) Geneva 2005 [updated November 4, 2005]. Available from: http://www.who.int/mediacentre/news/ releases/2005/pr56/en/.

World Health Organization – Media Centre. Meeting on avian influenza and human pandemic influenza, Geneva 2005. Available from: http://www.who. int/mediacentre/events/2005/avian_influenza/en/index.html.

World Health Organization – Media Centre. WHO extends its SARS-related travel advice to Beijing and Shanxi province in China and to Toronto, Canada 2003 [updated June 6, 2009]. Available from: http://www.who.int/mediacentre/ news/notes/2003/np7/en/.

World Health Organization – Media Centre. WHO issues a global alert about cases of atypical pneumonia 2003 [updated March 12, 2003]. Available from: http:// www.who.int/mediacentre/news/releases/2003/pr22/en/.

World Health Organization – Media Centre. World Health Organization issues emergency travel advisory 2003 [updated March 15, 2003]. Available from: http://www.who.int/mediacentre/news/releases/2003/pr23/en/.

World Health Organization – Regional Office for Europe. Making preparation count: lessons from the avian influenza outbreak in Turkey. Geneva: WHO; 2006.

World Health Organization – Regional Office for the Western Pacific. SARS: How a global epidemic was stopped. Manilla 2006.

World Health Organization – Working Group on Influenza Research at the Human and Animal Interface. Influenza research at the human and animal interface : report of a WHO working group, Geneva, Switzerland, September 21–22, 2006 WHO/CDS/EPR/GIP/2006.3.

World Health Organization. Annex Table 2, Deaths by cause, sex and mortality stratum in WHO regions, estimates for 2002. The world health report 2003: shaping the future. Geneva: WHO; 2003. p. xv.

World Health Organization. Change at WHO, Newsletter on WHO Reform. 2012.

World Health Organization. Constitution of World Health Organization. Basic Documents, Forty-fifth edition, Supplement,. Geneva 1948 (2006).

World Health Organization. Cumulative number of confirmed human cases for avian influenza A(H5N1) reported to WHO, 2003–2014, 2013. Available from: http://www.who.int/influenza/human_animal_interface/EN_GIP_20140124C umulativeNumberH5N1cases.pdf?ua=1.

World Health Organization. Current WHO global phase of pandemic alert: Avian Influenza A(H5N1). Available from: http://www.who.int/influenza/ preparedness/pandemic/h5n1phase/en/.

World Health Organization, editor Documentation provided at the meeting, including agenda and list of participants. Global Technical Meeting on Early Containment Protocol for Pandemic Influenza; 2006 March 6–8; Geneva.

World Health Organization. Dr. Margaret Chan, Director-General of the World Health Organization, Statement to the press by WHO Director-General Dr. Margaret Chan, World now at the start of 2009 influenza pandemic [updated June 11, 2009]. Available from: http://www.who.int/mediacentre/ news/statements/2009/h1n1_pandemic_phase6_20090611/en/index.html.

World Health Organization. Draft Medium-Term Strategic Plan 2008–2013. 2008 MTSP/2008–2013 – PPB/2008–2009.

World Health Organization. Emergency response framework Geneva 2013. Available from: http://www.who.int/hac/about/erf/en/.

World Health Organization. Fifty-ninth World Health Assembly – Agenda item 11.1 – Application of the International Health Regulations (2005). 2006 May 26. Report No.: WHA59.2.

World Health Organization. Global Alert and Response (GAR), Influenza-like illness in the United States and Mexico 2009 [updated April 24, 2009]. Available from: http://www.who.int/csr/don/2009_04_24/en/index.html.

World Health Organization. Global Alert and Response (GAR), Status of candidate vaccine virus development for the current Influenza A(H1N1) virus 2009 [updated May 8, 2009]. Available from: http://www.who.int/csr/resources/ publications/swineflu/vaccine_virus_development/en/.

World Health Organization. Global Crises – Global Solutions. Managing public health emergencies of international concern through the revised International Health Regulations. Geneva: 2002 WHO/CDS/CSR/GAR/2002.4.

World Health Organization. Global tuberculosis control : surveillance, planning, financing : WHO report 2008. Geneva: 2008 WHO/HTM/TB/2008.393.

World Health Organization. International health regulations (2005) 2nd ed. Geneva: World Health Organization; 2006.

World Health Organization. Number of deaths divided by the Cumulative Number of Reported Probable Cases of Severe Acute Respiratory Syndrome (SARS). Available from: http://www.who.int/csr/sars/country/en/index.html.

World Health Organization. Openness is key in fight against disease outbreaks. *Bulletin of the World Health Organization (BLT)*, 2006;84(10):765–840.

World Health Organization. Pandemic (H1N1) 2009 – update 58, Laboratory-confirmed cases of pandemic (H1N1) 2009 as officially reported to WHO by States Parties to the International Health Regulations [updated July 6, 2009]. Available from: http://www.who.int/csr/don/2009_07_06/en/index.html.

World Health Organization. Pandemic influenza preparedness Framework for the sharing of influenza viruses and access to vaccines and other benefits. WHO, Geneva. 2011.

World Health Organization. Pandemic Influenza Risk Management – WHO Interim Guidance. Geneva: 2013.

World Health Organization. Programme Budget 2012–2013 Geneva 2011. Available from: http://whqlibdoc.who.int/pb/2012–2013/PB_2012%E2%80%932013_eng.pdf.

World Health Organization, editor, Public Health measures during the influenza A(H1N1) 2009 pandemic. WHO Technical consultation October 26–28, 2010; Gammarth, Tunisia.

World Health Organization. Rapid risk assessment of acute public health events. 2012.

World Health Organization. Strengthening response to pandemics and other public-health emergencies: report of the Review Committee on the Functioning of the International Health Regulations (2005) and on Pandemic Influenza (H1N1) 2009. Geneva: 2011.

World Health Organization. Summary of influenza antiviral susceptibility surveillance findings, September 2010–March 2011, 2011. Available from: http://www.who.int/influenza/gisrs_laboratory/updates/antiviral_susceptibility/en/.

World Health Organization. Summary of probable SARS cases with onset of illness from 1 November 2002 to 31 July 2003 (Based on data as of 31 December 2003.) Geneva 2003. Available from: http://www.who.int/csr/sars/country/table2004_04_21/en/index.html.

World Health Organization. A summary of tracking avian influenza A(H5N1) specimens and viruses shared with WHO from 2003 to 2007. 2008.

World Health Organization, editor, Summary report. Meeting on avian influenza and human pandemic influenza 2005 7–9 November; Geneva, Switzerland.

World Health Organization. WHO Interim Protocol: Rapid operations to contain the initial emergence of pandemic influenza – October 2007. Geneva. 2007.

World Health Organization. WHO Pandemic influenza draft protocol for rapid response and containment – Updated draft March 17, 2006. Geneva. 2006.

World Health Organization. WHO strategic action plan for pandemic influenza (rev. 2a). Geneva. 2007 WHO/CDS/EPR/GIP/2006.2a.

World Health Organization. WHO strategic action plan for pandemic influenza (rev. 2c). Geneva. 2007 WHO/CDS/EPR/GIP/2006.2c.

World Health Organization. The world health report 2002 : reducing risks, promoting healthy life Geneva. 2002.

World Health Organization. The World Health Report 2003, Shaping the Future. Geneva. 2003.

World Health Organization. The World Health Report 2007, A Safer Future. Global Public Health Security in the 21st Century. WHO, Geneva. 2007.

World Health Organization, Food and Agriculture Organization of the United Nations. Understanding the Codex Alimentarius. 3rd ed. Rome: WHO/FAO. 2006.

World Health Organization. WHO Influenza Pandemic Task Force – Report of the first meeting. 2006 WHO/CDS/EPR/GIP/2006.5.

World Organization for Animal Health. Avian influenza, facts and figures 2009 [updated 20-Jan-2009]. Available from: http://www.oie.int/eng/info_ev/en_AI_factoids_2.htm.

World Organization for Animal Health. Facts & Figures: Avian Influenza [updated 7 June 2009]. Available from: http://www.oie.int/Eng/info_ev/en_AI_factoids_4.htm.

World Organization for Animal Health. HANDISTATUS II. Available from: http://www.oie.int/hs2/report.asp.

World Organization for Animal Health. WAHID Interface – OIE World Animal Health Information Database. Available from: http://www.oie.int/wahis/public.php?page=home.

Wuethrich B. Infectious disease: an avian flu jumps to people. *Science*. 2003;299(5612):1504.

Xiaoqin Fan E. SARS: economic impacts and implications. *ERD Policy Brief Series*. 2003;15.

Zhong N. Management and prevention of SARS in China. Philosophical transactions – *Royal Society of London Biological Sciences*. 2004;359(1447):1115–1116.

References

1. Kates R, Hohenemser C, Kasperson J, Perilous progress: managing the hazards of technology: Westview Press; Boulder CO; 1985.
2. Renn O, Walker KD, International Risk Governance Council, editors. Global risk governance: concept and practice using the IRGC framework. Dordrecht: Springer; 2008.
3. Keohane R, Nye J. Globalization: What's new? What's not? (And so what?). *Foreign Policy*. 2000; (118):104–19.
4. Organization for Economic Cooperation and Development (OECD). Emerging Systemic Risks in the 21st Century: An Agenda for Action. Paris 2003.
5. Carlson M. A Brief History of the 1987 Stock Market Crash with a Discussion of the Federal Reserve Response. 2007.
6. Renn O, editor. *Risk Governance: Coping with Uncertainty in a Complex World*. London: Earthscan; 2008.
7. van Asselt M, Renn O. Risk governance. *Journal of Risk Research*. 2011;14(4):431–449.
8. National Research Council (U. S.) – National Research Council. *Science and Decisions: Advancing Risk Assessment*: National Academies Press; 2009.
9. National Research Council. *Risk Assessment in the Federal Government: Managing the Process*. Washington, DC: National Academy Press; 1983.
10. Graham JD, International Risk Governance Council. *The Emergence of Risks: Contributing Factors*. Geneva: IRGC, International Risk Governance Council; 2010.
11. van Asselt MB, van Bree L. Uncertainty, precaution and risk governance. *Journal of Risk Research*. 2011;14(4):401–408.
12. van Zwanenberg P, Millstone E, editors. *BSE: Risk, Science, and Governance*. Oxford: Oxford University Press; 2005.
13. Smith A, Young J, Gibson J. How now, mad-cow? Consumer confidence and source credibility during the 1996 BSE scare. *European Journal of Marketing*. 1999;33; 110–1122 (11/12).
14. Lee K, editor. *Globalization and Health: An Introduction*. Basingstoke: Palgrave Macmillan; 2003.
15. Brender N. Risk analysis under multilateral institutions: a determining factor in the formation of global risk responses in health: the cases of Bovine Spongiform Encephalopathy (BSE), Severe Acute Respiratory Syndrome (SARS), and avian influenza [Th Univ Genève, 2010 IHEID 837]. Geneva: Graduate Institute of International and Development Studies; 2010.
16. World Health Organization, Food and Agriculture Organization of the United Nations. Understanding the Codex Alimentarius. 3rd ed. Rome: WHO/FAO; 2006.
17. World Health Organization. International health regulations (2005) 2nd ed. Geneva: World Health Organization; 2006.
18. Dingwerth K, Pattberg P. Global governance as a perspective on world politics. *Global Governance: A Review of Multilateralism and International Organizations*.

19. Lee K, editor. *Health Impacts of Globalization: Towards Global Governance.* Basingstoke: Palgrave Macmillan; 2003.
20. Keohane RO, Macedo S, Moravcsik A. Democracy-enhancing multilateralism. *International Organization.* 2009;63(01):1–31.
21. Bernstein M, Jaspe J. Les tireurs d'alarme dans les conflits sur les risques technologiques. Entre intérêts particuliers et crédibilité. *Politix, Revue des sciences sociales du politique.* 1998;11(44):109–134.
22. Keohane RO, Buchanan A. The legitimacy of global governance institutions. *Ethics & International Affairs.* 2006;20(4):405–437.
23. Sjöberg L, Peterson M, Fromm J, Boholm A, Hanson SO. Neglected and overemphasized risks: the opinions of risk professionals. *Journal of Risk Research.* 2005;8(7):599–616.
24. World Health Organization – Epidemic and Pandemic Alert and Response. WHO event management for international public health security – Operational Procedures. World Health Organization, 2008 WHO/HSE/EPR/ARO/2008.1.
25. Stern PC, Fineberg HV, National Research Council (USA) CoRC, editors. *Understanding Risk: Informing Decisions in a Democratic Society.* Washington, D.C.: National Academy Press; 1996.
26. World Health Organization. The world health report 2002: reducing risks, promoting healthy life Geneva: 2002.
27. Hutubessy R, Chisholm D, Edejer Tan-Torres T. Generalized cost-effectiveness analysis for national-level priority-setting in the health sector. *Cost Effectiveness and Resource Allocation.* 2003;1(1):8.
28. Murray CJL, Evans DB, Acharya A, Baltussen RMPM. Development of WHO guidelines on generalized cost-effectiveness analysis. *Health Economics.* 2000;9:235–251.
29. Checchi F, Roberts L.HPN Network Paper 52: Interpreting and using mortality data in humanitarian emergencies: a primer for non-epidemiologists. London: Overseas & Development Institute, 2005:1–38.
30. Meltzer MI, Cox NJ, Fukuda K. The economic impact of pandemic influenza in the United States: priorities for intervention. *Emerging Infectious Diseases.* 1999;5(5): 659–671.
31. Kuperman AJ. Mitigating the moral hazard of humanitarian intervention: lessons from Eeconomics. *Global Governance: A Review of Multilateralism and International Organizations.* 2008;14(2):219–240.
32. World Health Assembly. Fifty-Sixth World Health Assembly – Agenda item 14.16 – Severe acute respiratory syndrome (SARS). Geneva: 2003 WHA56.29 Doc No.: WHA56.29.
33. World Health Organization. Summary of probable SARS cases with onset of illness from 1 November 2002 to 31 July 2003 (Based on data as of December 31, 2003.) Geneva 2003 [May 12, 2008]. Available from: http://www.who.int/csr/sars/country/table2004_04_21/en/index.html.
34. World Health Organization – Regional Office for the Western Pacific. SARS: How a global epidemic was stopped. Manilla 2006.
35. MacLean AR, editor. *SARS: A Case Study in Emerging Infections.* Oxford etc.: Oxford University Press; 2005.
36. World Health Organization. Openness is key in fight against disease outbreaks. *Bulletin of the World Health Organization (BLT).* 2006;84(10):765–840.

37. Public Health Agency of Canada. Global Public Health Intelligence Network (GPHIN) – Information 2004 [updated November 2004]. Available from: http://www.phac-aspc.gc.ca/media/nr-rp/2004/2004_gphin-rmispbk-eng.php.
38. World Health Organization – Epidemic and Pandemic Alert and Response. Global Outbreak Alert & Response Network [updated June 6, 2009]. Available from: http://www.who.int/csr/outbreaknetwork/en/.
39. World Health Organization. Annex Table 2, Deaths by cause, sex and mortality stratum in WHO regions, estimates for 2002. The world health report 2003: shaping the future. Geneva: WHO; 2003. p. xv, 193 pp.
40. Smith RD. Responding to global infectious disease outbreaks: lessons from SARS on the role of risk perception, communication and management. *Social Science & Medicine*. 2006;63(12):3113–3123.
41. Fidler DP. *SARS, Governance and the Globalization of Disease*. Basingstoke etc.: Palgrave Macmillan; 2004. XVII, 219 pp.
42. World Health Organization – Epidemic and Pandemic Alert and Response. Guiding principles for international outbreak alert and response. Available from: http://www.who.int/csr/outbreaknetwork/guidingprinciples/en/index.html.
43. World Health Organization – Department of Communicable Disease. WHO SARS Risk Assessment and Preparedness Framework. Geneva: 2004 WHO/CDS/CSR/ARO/2004.2.
44. World Health Organization – Department of Communicable Disease. Influenza pandemic plan. The role of WHO and guidelines for national and regional planning. Geneva: 1999. Report No.: WHO/CDS/CSR/EDC/99.1.
45. World Health Organization. Global Crises – Global Solutions. Managing public health emergencies of international concern through the revised International Health Regulations. Geneva: 2002 WHO/CDS/CSR/GAR/2002.4.
46. World Health Assembly. Fifty-eighth World Health Assembly – Agenda item 13.1 – Revision of the International Health Regulations. Geneva: 2005 WHA58.3.
47. Heymann DL, editor. The international response to the outbreak of SARS, 2003. Oxford etc.: Oxford University Press; 2005.
48. World Health Assembly. Fifty-sixth world Health Assembly – Agenda item 14.16 – Revision of the International Health Regulations. Geneva: 2003 May 28, 2003. WHA56.28.
49. Relman DA, Choffnes ER, Mack A. Infectious disease movement in a borderless world: workshop summary: National Academies Press; Washington DC; 2010.
50. World Health Organization – Epidemic and Pandemic Alert and Response. The operational response to SARS 2003 [updated June 6, 2009]. Available from: http://www.who.int/csr/sars/goarn2003_4_16/en/.
51. Unite for Sight. Unite for Sight's 4th Annual International Health Conference – Speakers 2007 [updated June 6, 2009]. Available from: http://www.uniteforsight.org/conference/2007/conf_speakers.php#davidheymann.
52. World Health Organization – Epidemic and Pandemic Alert and Response. Severe Acute Respiratory Syndrome (SARS)-multi-country outbreak – Update 58 2003 [updated May 17, 2003; cited July 23, 2008]. Available from: http://www.who.int/csr/don/2003_05_17/en/index.html.

53. Stöhr K. A multicentre collaboration to investigate the cause of severe acute respiratory syndrome. *The Lancet.* 2003;361(9370):1730–1733.
54. Abraham T. *Twenty-First Century Plague: The Story of SARS.* Baltimore: Johns Hopkins University Press; 2007.
55. World health Organization – Department of Communicable Disease. Consensus document on the epidemiology of severe acute respiratory syndrome (SARS) – Annex 2: Final List of Participants. Geneva: 2003 WHO/CDS/CSR/GAR/2003.11.
56. World Health Organization – Epidemic and Pandemic Alert and Response. WHO collaborative multi-centre research project on Severe Acute Respiratory Syndrome (SARS) diagnosis [updated June 6, 2009]. Available from: http://www.who.int/csr/sars/project/en/.
57. Peiris J, Lai S, Poon L, Guan Y, Yam L, Lim W, et al. SARS Study Group. 2003. Coronavirus as a possible cause of severe acute respiratory syndrome. *The Lancet.* 2003;361(9366):1319–1325.
58. World Health Organization – Epidemic and Pandemic Alert and Response. Severe Acute Respiratory Syndrome – Press briefing – April 11, 2003 Geneva 2003. Available from: http://www.who.int/csr/sars/Press_2003_04_11/en/.
59. BBC News. Killer bug traced to HK hotel 2009 [updated June 6, 2009]. Available from: http://news.bbc.co.uk/2/hi/health/2867055.stm.
60. United States General Accounting Office. Emerging Infectious Diseases: Asian SARS Outbreak Challenged International and National Responses. Washington DC: 2004 GAO-04–564.
61. World Health Organization – Epidemic and Pandemic Alert and Response. WHO collaborative network of clinicians for SARS diagnosis and treatment [August 4, 2008]. Available from: http://www.who.int/csr/sars/network/en/.
62. World Health Organization – Epidemic and Pandemic Alert and Response. Update 95 – SARS: Chronology of a serial killer 2003 [updated April 7, 2003; cited July 15, 2008]. Available from: http://www.who.int/csr/don/2003_07_04/en/.
63. Heymann D, Rodier G. Hot spots in a wired world: WHO surveillance of emerging and re-emerging infectious diseases. *The Lancet Infectious Diseases.* 2001;1(5):345–353.
64. Eysenbach G. SARS and population health technology. *Journal of Medical Internet Research.* 2003 Apr–Jun;5(2):e14.
65. Enserink M. SARS in China: China's missed chance. *Science.* 2003;301(5631):294–296.
66. Rao K, Wu X, Gu T. China Health Information System: review and assessment. Beijing: Center for Health Statistics Information, Ministry of Health, 2006.
67. Plant AJ, editor. *SARS and Public Health: Lessons for Future Epidemics.* River Edge N.J. etc.: World Scientific; 2003.
68. World Health Organization – Epidemic and Pandemic Alert and Response. Update 49, Disease Outbreak Reported, SARS case fatality ratio, incubation period 2003 [updated May 7, 2003; cited August 23, 2008]. Available from: http://www.who.int/csr/don/2003_05_07a/en/index.html.
69. Pearson H, Clarke T, Abbott A, Knight J, Cyranoski D. SARS: what have we learned? *Nature.* 2003;424(6945):121–126.

70. Lipsitch M, Cohen T, Cooper B, Robins J, Ma S, James L, et al. Transmission dynamics and control of severe acute respiratory syndrome. *Science* (New York, NY). 2003;300(5627):1966–1970.

71. Murphy C. The 2003 SARS outbreak: global challenges and innovative infection control measures. *Online Journal of Issues in Nursing.* 2006;11(1):6.

72. Anderson R, Fraser C, Ghani A, Donnelly C, Riley S, Ferguson N, et al., editors. *Epidemiology, Transmission Dynamics and Control of SARS: The 2002–2003 Epidemic.* Oxford etc.: Oxford University Press; 2005.

73. Riley S, Fraser C, Donnelly CA, Ghani A, Abu-Raddad L, Hedley A, et al. Transmission dynamics of the etiological agent of SARS in Hong Kong: impact of public health interventions. *Science*; 2003;300(5627):1961–1966.

74. Wallinga J, Teunis P. Different epidemic curves for severe acute respiratory syndrome reveal similar impacts of control measures. *American Journal of Epidemiology.* 2004;160(6):509–516.

75. Brockman D, Hufnagel L, Geisel T, editors. *Dynamics of Modern Epidemics.* Oxford etc.: Oxford University Press; 2005.

76. World Health Organization – Department of Communicable Disease. Consensus document on the epidemiology of severe acute respiratory syndrome (SARS). Geneva: 2003 WHO/CDS/CSR/GAR/2003.11.

77. SARS Expert Committee. SARS in Hong Kong: from experience to action, October 2003. Available at: www.sars-expertcom.gov.hk/english/reports/reports.html (accessed Nov 2003)

78. Zhong N. Management and prevention of SARS in China. *Philosophical Transactions–Royal Society of London Biological Sciences.* 2004;359(1447):1115–1116.

79. World Health Organization – Media Centre. WHO issues a global alert about cases of atypical pneumonia 2003 [updated March 12, 2003]. Available from: http://www.who.int/mediacentre/news/releases/2003/pr22/en/.

80. World Health Organization – Epidemic and Pandemic Alert and Response. World Health Organization issues emergency travel advisory 2003 [updated March 15, 2003; cited July 20, 2003]. Available from: http://www.who.int/csr/don/2003_03_15/en/.

81. World Health Organization – Epidemic and Pandemic Alert and Response. Severe Acute Respiratory Syndrome (SARS) – multi-country outbreak – update 27. [updated on April 11, 2003]. Available from: http://www.who.int/csr/don/2003_04_11/en/index.html.

82. World Health Organization – Epidemic and Pandemic Alert and Response. Affected Areas – Severe Acute Respiratory Syndrome (SARS) 2003 [updated June 6, 2009]. Available from: http://www.who.int/csr/sars/areas/2003_03_16/en/index.html.

83. World Health Organization – Media Centre. WHO extends its SARS-related travel advice to Beijing and Shanxi province in China and to Toronto, Canada 2003 [updated June 6, 2009]. Available from: http://www.who.int/mediacentre/news/notes/2003/np7/en/.

84. Salehi R, Ali SH. The social and political context of disease outbreaks: the case of SARS in Toronto. *Canadian Public Policy.* 2006;32(4):373–385.

85. Low, D.E. SARS: Lessons from Toronto.In Knobler, Stacey, Adel Mahmoud, Stanley Lemon, Alison Mack, Laura Sivitz and Katherine Oberholtzer (Eds.)

Learning From SARS: Preparing the Next Disease Outbreak – Workshop Summary. Washington (DC): National Academies Press (US); 2004, 63–70.

86. World Health Organization – Epidemic and Pandemic Alert and Response. Severe Acute Respiratory Syndrome – Press conference, Hanoi, Viet Nam Hanoi 2003 [updated March 26, 2003; cited July 23, 2008]. Available from: http://www.who.int/csr/sars/2003_03_27h/en/.

87. World Health Organization – Epidemic and Pandemic Alert and Response. Meeting on SARS virus detection and survival in food and water, Madrid, May 8–9 2003 2003 [updated May 22, 2003; cited August 4, 2008]. Available from: http://www.who.int/csr/sars/guidelines/madridmeeting/en/.

88. World Health Organization – Epidemic and Pandemic Alert and Response. Prise en charge des cas de Syndrome respiratoire aigu sévère (SRAS). Available from: http://www.who.int/csr/sars/managmentf/en/.

89. Saywell T, Fowler GA, Crispin SW. The cost of SARS: $11 billion and rising. *Dow Jones Far Eastern Economic Review*. 2003.

90. Kickbusch I. SARS: wake-up call for a strong global health policy: how to stop a virus that doesn't respect sovereignty. *Yale Global Online*. 2003.

91. Xiaoqin Fan E. SARS: economic impacts and implications. *ERD Policy Brief Series*. 2003;15.

92. Lee JW, McKibbin WJ. Globalization and disease: the case of SARS. *Asian Economic Papers*. 2004;3(1):113–131.

93. World Health Organization. Global tuberculosis control: surveillance, planning, financing: WHO report 2008. Geneva: 2008 WHO/HTM/TB/2008.393.

94. Rossi V, Walker J. *Assessing the Economic Impact and Costs of Flu Pandemics Originating in Asia*. Oxford: Oxford Economic Forecasting; 2005.

95. Fraser C. SARS: public health needs in the case of re-emergence 2004 [updated June 9, 2004; cited September 3, 2008]. Available from: www.who.int/entity/vaccine_research/about/gvrf_2004/en/gvrf_2004_fraser.pdf.

96. Brown D. CDC issues guidelines for battling flu pandemic. school closings likely, but restricting travel not suggested. Washington Post, February 2, 2007:A03.

97. World Health Organization. The World Health Report 2003, Shaping the future. Geneva: 2003.

98. World Health Organization – Epidemic and Pandemic Alert and Response. Update 54 Outbreaks in the initial "hot zones" indicate that SARS can be contained 2003 [updated May 13, 2003; cited August 20, 2008]. Available from: http://www.who.int/csr/don/2003_05_13b/en/index.html.

99. World Health Organization – Epidemic and Pandemic Alert and Response. Disease Outbreak News, Update 72 – Situation in China 2003 [updated June 3, 2003; cited August 20, 2008]. Available from: http://www.who.int/csr/don/2003_06_03/en/index.html.

100. SARS Multi-Country Outbreak (WPRO Presentation) 2003 [updated July 15, 2003]. Available from: http://www.wpro.who.int/sars/docs/presentation/multicountryoutbreaks.asp.

101. World Health Organization – Media Centre. World Health Organization issues emergency travel advisory 2003 [updated March 15, 2003]. Available from: http://www.who.int/mediacentre/news/releases/2003/pr23/en/.

102. World Health Organization – Epidemic and Pandemic Alert and Response. Update 11 – WHO recommends new measures to prevent travel-related spread of SARS 2003 [updated March 27, 2003]. Available from: http://www.who.int/csr/sarsarchive/2003_03_27/en/.

103. World Health Organization – Epidemic and Pandemic Alert and Response. Update 17 – Travel advice – Hong Kong Special Administrative Region of China, and Guangdong Province, China 2003 [updated April 2, 2003]. Available from: http://www.who.int/csr/sarsarchive/2003_04_02/en/.

104. World Health Organization. Number of deaths divided by the cumulative number of reported probable cases of Severe Acute Respiratory Syndrome (SARS) [August 20, 2008]. Available from: http://www.who.int/csr/sars/country/en/index.html.

105. World Health Organization – Epidemic and Pandemic Alert and Response. Summary table of areas that experienced local transmission of SARS during the outbreak period from 1 November 2002 to 31 July 2003 2003 [updated November 21, 2003; cited August 20, 2008]. Available from: http://www.who.int/csr/sars/areas/areas2003_11_21/en/index.html.

106. St John R, King A, Jong D, Bodie-Collins M, Squires S, Tam T. Border screening for SARS. *Emerging Infectious Diseases*. 2005;11(1):6–10.

107. World Health Organization – Epidemic and Pandemic Alert and Response. Summary of WHO measures related to international travel 2003 [updated June 6, 2009]. Available from: http://www.who.int/csr/sars/travelupdate/en/.

108. World Health Organization – Epidemic and Pandemic Alert and Response. Areas with recent local transmission of Severe Acute Respiratory Syndrome (SARS) 2003 [updated May 2, 2003; cited September 1, 2008]. Available from: http://www.who.int/csr/sars/areas/2003_05_02/en/index.html.

109. Duffin J, Sweetman A, editors. SARS in context: memory, history, policy. Montreal; Ithaca: School of Policy Studies Queen's University: McGill-Queen's University Press; 2006.

110. Heymann, DL. Severe Acute Respiratory Syndrome (SARS): global alert, global response (PowerPoint Presentation). 2003.

111. Knobler, Stacey, Adel Mahmoud, Stanley Lemon, Alison Mack, Laura Sivitz and Katherine Oberholtzer (Eds.) Learning from SARS: preparing the next disease outbreak – workshop summary. Washington (DC): National Academies Press (US); 2004.

112. World Health Organization – Epidemic and Pandemic Alert and Response. Epidemic curves – Severe Acute Respiratory Syndrome (SARS) [July 19, 2008]. Available from: http://www.who.int/csr/sars/epicurve/epiindex/en/.

113. World Health Organization – Department of Communicable Disease. Severe Acute Respiratory Syndrome (SARS): Status of the Outbreak and Lessons for the Immediate Future. 2003.

114. BBC News. China "sorry" for slow bug response 2003 [updated June 6, 2009]. Available from: http://news.bbc.co.uk/2/hi/health/2919967.stm.

115. World Health Organization. The World Health Report 2007, A safer future. global public health security in the 21st century. WHO; Geneva: 2007.

116. Keogh-Brown MR, Smith RD. The economic impact of SARS: How does the reality match the predictions? *Health Policy*. 2008;88(1):110–120.

117. Greaves F. What are the most appropriate methods of surveillance for monitoring an emerging respiratory infection such as SARS? *Journal of Public Health*. 2004;26(3):288–292.

118. World Health Organization – Epidemic and Pandemic Alert and Response. Severe Acute Respiratory Syndrome (SARS) – multi-country outbreak – Update 33 2003 [updated June 6, 2009]. Available from: http://www.who.int/csr/don/2003_04_18/en/index.html.

119. Burci GL, editor La gestion d'une crise sanitaire international: le cas du SRAS. Quatorzièmes rencontres internationales d'Aix-en-Provence – La société internationale et les grandes pandémies; 2006 December 8–9; Aix-en-Provence. Paris: Editions A.Pedone; 2007.

120. United Nations. *A More Secure World Our Shared Responsibility: Report of the Secretary-General's High-level Panel on Threats, Challenges and Change*. New York: United Nations, Dept. of Public Information; 2004.

121. Bell C, Lewis M. *The Economic Implications of Epidemics Old and New*. Center for Global Development – Working Paper 2005;54.

122. Cetron M, Maloney S, Koppaka R, Simone P Isolation and quarantine: containment strategies for SARS 2003. In: Knobler S, Mahmoud M, Lemon S, Mack A, Sivitz L, Oberholtzer K, editors. *Learning from SARS: Preparing for the Next Disease Outbreak*. Forum on microbial threats, board of health. Institute of Medicine of the National Academies. Washington: National Academies Press; 2004. p. 71–83.

123. Check E. Is this our best shot? *Nature*. 2005;435(7041):404–406.

124. Taubenberger JK, editor. *Genetic Characterization of the 1918 "Spanish Influenza" Virus*. New York: Routledge; 2003.

125. World Health Organization – Epidemic and Pandemic Alert and Response. Cumulative number of confirmed human cases of avian influenza A/(H5N1) Reported to WHO 2009 [updated June 7, 2009]. Available from: http://www.who.int/csr/disease/avian_influenza/country/cases_table_2009_01_07/en/index.html.

126. World Health Organization. Cumulative number of confirmed human cases for avian influenza A(H5N1) reported to WHO, 2003–2014 2013. Available from: http://www.who.int/influenza/human_animal_interface/EN_GIP_20140124CumulativeNumberH5N1cases.pdf?ua=1.

127. World Organization for Animal Health. Avian influenza, facts and figures 2009 [updated January 20, 2009; cited February 10, 2009]. Available from: http://www.oie.int/eng/info_ev/en_AI_factoids_2.htm.

128. Stöhr K. Avian influenza and pandemics – research needs and opportunities. *New England Journal of Medicine*. 2005;352(4):405–407.

129. United Nations. A coordinated UN System Response to Avian and Human Influenza Draft Strategy Note [updated October 5, 2005; cited February 10, 2009]. Available from: http://www.fao.org/avianflu/en/strategydocs.html.

130. World Health Organization – Epidemic and Pandemic Alert and Response. Responding to the avian influenza pandemic threat. Recommended strategic actions. Geneva: 2005 WHO/CDS/CSR/GIP/2005.8.

131. World Health Organization – Epidemic and Pandemic Alert and Response. Avian influenza A(H5N1) in humans in Viet Nam and in poultry in Asian countries – update 2 2004 [updated January 16, 2004; cited February 8, 2009]. Available from: http://www.who.int/csr/don/2004_01_16/en/index.html.

132. World Health Organization – Epidemic and Pandemic Alert and Response. Geographical spread of H5N1 avian influenza in birds – update 28, Situation assessment and implications for human health 2005 [updated August 18, 2005; cited August 20, 2007]. Available from: http://www.who.int/csr/don/2005_08_18/en/index.html.

133. World Health Organization – Epidemic and Pandemic Alert and Response. Current WHO phase of pandemic alert [updated June 7, 2009]. Available from: http://www.who.int/csr/disease/avian_influenza/phase/en/index.html.

134. World Health Organization – Media Centre. Global meeting to develop common approach on avian influenza and human pandemic influenza (Joint News Release WHO/FAO/OIE/World Bank – November 4, 2005) Geneva 2005 [updated November 4, 2005; cited July 20, 2007]. Available from: http://www.who.int/mediacentre/news/releases/2005/pr56/en/.

135. World Bank. Flu Outbreaks Reminder of Pandemic Threat, 2013 [updated March 5, 2013]. Available from: http://www.worldbank.org/en/news/feature/2013/03/05/flu-outbreaks-reminder-of-pandemic-threat.

136. United States Department of State. U.S. Launches International Partnership on Avian and Pandemic Influenza Washington [updated September 22, 2005; cited June 8, 2006]. Available from: http://www.state.gov/r/pa/prs/ps/2005/53865.htm.

137. Official website of the G8 summit 2006 in Saint-Petersburg. Statement of G8 Health Ministers Meeting [updated April 28, 2006; cited June 8, 2006]. Available from: http://en.g8russia.ru/news/20060428/1148826.html.

138. Wuethrich B. Infectious disease: an avian flu jumps to people. *Science.* 2003;299(5612):1504.

139. World Health Organization – Epidemic and Pandemic Alert and Response. Influenza A(H5N1) in Hong Kong Special Administrative Region of China, Disease Outbreak Report 2003 [updated 19 February 2003; cited February 8, 2009]. Available from: http://www.who.int/csr/don/2003_2_19/en/index.html.

140. World Health Organization – Epidemic and Pandemic Alert and Response. Advice to international travellers 2004 [updated February 6, 2004]. Available from: http://www.who.int/csr/disease/avian_influenza/travel_2004_02_06/en/index.html.

141. Advisory Council on Food and Environmental Hygiene. Comprehensive plan of action to deal with the global problem of avian influenza. Honk Kong: 2005 ACFEH Paper 58.

142. Intergovernmental Working Group on the Revision of International Health Regulations. International Health Regulations. Working Paper for Regional Consultations. 2004 IGWG/IHR/Working paper/12.2003.

143. World Health Organization – Epidemic and Pandemic Alert and Response. Avian influenza A(H5N1) in humans and poultry in Viet Nam 2004 [updated January 13, 2004; cited February 8, 2009]. Available from: http://www.who.int/csr/don/2004_01_13/en/index.html.

144. World Health Organization. Fifty-Ninth World Health Assembly – Agenda item 11.1 – Application of the International Health Regulations (2005). 2006 May 26, 2006. Report No.: WHA59.2.

145. World Health Organization – Department of Communicable Disease. WHO global influenza preparedness plan – The role of WHO and recommendations

for national measures before and during pandemics. Geneva: 2005 WHO/CDS/CSR/GIP/2005.5.

146. World Health Organization. Constitution of World Health Organization. Basic Documents, Forty-fifth edition, Supplement, Geneva 1948 (2006).

147. World Health Organization, editor. Summary report. Meeting on avian influenza and human pandemic influenza 2005 November 7–9; Geneva, Switzerland.

148. World Health Organization – Media Centre. Global influenza meeting sets key action steps, agrees on urgent need for financing (Joint News Release WHO/FAO/OIE/WORLD BANK) Geneva 2005 [updated 9 November 2005]. Available from: http://www.who.int/mediacentre/news/releases/2005/pr58/en/index.html.

149. World Health Organization. WHO strategic action plan for pandemic influenza (rev. 2a). Geneva: 2007 WHO/CDS/EPR/GIP/2006.2a.

150. World Health Organization. WHO Pandemic influenza draft protocol for rapid response and containment – Updated draft March 17, 2006. Geneva: 2006.

151. World Health Organization, editor Documentation provided at the meeting, including agenda and list of participants. Global Technical Meeting on Early Containment Protocol for Pandemic Influenza; 2006 March 6–8; Geneva.

152. World Health Organization. WHO Interim Protocol: Rapid operations to contain the initial emergence of pandemic influenza – October 2007. Geneva: 2007.

153. World Health Organization. WHO Influenza Pandemic Task Force – Report of the first meeting. 2006 WHO/CDS/EPR/GIP/2006.5.

154. World Health Organization – Executive Board. Avian and pandemic influenza: developments, response and follow-up, and application of the International Health Regulations (2005) – Best practice for sharing influenza viruses and sequence data – Report by the Secretariat. Geneva: 2007 EB120/INF.DOC./3.

155. World Health Organization – Regional Office for Europe. Making preparation count: lessons from the avian influenza outbreak in Turkey. Geneva 2006.

156. The Lancet. TheLancet.com – Home Page 2009 [updated 7 June 2009]. Available from: http://www.thelancet.com/home.

157. World Health Organization. WHO strategic action plan for pandemic influenza (rev. 2c). Geneva: 2007 WHO/CDS/EPR/GIP/2006.2c.

158. World Health Organization – International Health Regulations. IHR News – Facts and figures 2008 [updated December 12, 2008]. Available from: http://www.who.int/ihr/ihrnewsissue5/en/index4.html.

159. Hien TT, Liem N, Dung N, San L, Mai P, Chau N, et al. Avian influenza A (H5N1) in 10 patients in Vietnam. *New England Journal of Medicine.* 2004;350(12):1179–1188.

160. Ungchusak K, Auewarakul P, Dowell S, Kitphati R, Auwanit W, Puthavathana P, et al. Probable person-to-person transmission of avian influenza A (H5N1). *New England Journal of Medicine.* 2005;352(4):333–340.

161. World Health Organization – Communicable Diseases Cluster. Avian influenza: assessing the pandemic threat. Geneva: 2005 WHO/CDS/2005.20.

162. World Health Organization – Working Group on Influenza Research at the Human and Animal Interface. Influenza research at the human and animal

interface: report of a WHO working group, Geneva, Switzerland September 21–22 2006 WHO/CDS/EPR/GIP/2006.3.

163. Ferguson N, Cummings D, Cauchemez S, Fraser C, Riley S, Meeyai A, et al. Strategies for containing an emerging influenza pandemic in Southeast Asia. *Nature.* 2005;437(7056):209–214.

164. Longini IM, Nizam A, Xu S, Ungchusak K, Hanshaoworakul W, Cummings D, et al. Containing pandemic influenza at the source. *Science.* 2005;309(5737):1083–1087.

165. World Health Organization – Media Centre. Donation of three million treatments of oseltamivir to WHO will help early response to an emerging influenza pandemic Geneva 2005 [updated August 24, 2005]. Available from: http://www.who.int/mediacentre/news/releases/2005/pr36/en/.

166. Holbrooke R, Garrett L. *"Sovereignty" That Risks Global Health.* Washington Post, August 10, 2008:B07.

167. World Health Organization – Epidemic and Pandemic Alert and Response. Terms of Reference for WHO H5 Reference Laboratories 2006 [updated October 12, 2006]. Available from: http://www.who.int/csr/disease/influenza/torh5labs/en/index.html.

168. World Health Organization. Current WHO global phase of pandemic alert: Avian Influenza A(H5N1). Available from: http://www.who.int/influenza/preparedness/pandemic/h5n1phase/en/.

169. World Health Organization – Epidemic and Pandemic Alert and Response. Avian influenza frequently asked questions 2005 [updated December 5, 2005]. Available from: http://www.who.int/csr/disease/avian_influenza/avian_faqs/en/index.html.

170. Kilbourne ED. A virologist's perspective on the 1918–19 pandemic. In: Phillips H, Killingray D, editors. *The Spanish Influenza Pandemic of 1918–19: New Perspectives – Routledge Studies in the Social History of Medicine 12.* London etc.: Routledge; 2003. pp. xxi, 357.

171. Webster RG, editor. Pandemic Influenza Emergence and Control. 13ème Colloque Wright, Grandes Epidémies: le retour?; November 18, 2008; Geneva.

172. Enserink M. Influenza. WHO adds more "1918" to pandemic predictions. *Science.* 2004;306(5704):2025.

173. Stöhr K, Esveld M. Will vaccines be available for the next influenza pandemic? *Science.* 2004;306(5705):2195–2196.

174. United States Department of Health & Human Services. National Vaccine Program Office – Pandemics and Pandemic Scares in the 20th Century. Available from: http://www.hhs.gov/nvpo/pandemics/flu3.htm.

175. World Health Organization – Epidemic and Pandemic Alert and Response (EPR). Estimating the impact of the next influenza pandemic: enhancing preparedness Geneva 2004 [updated December 8, 2004]. Available from: http://www.who.int/csr/disease/influenza/preparedness2004_12_08/en/.

176. Davis M. *The Monster at Our Door: The Global Threat of Avian Flu.* New York: The New Press; 2005. VIII, 212 pp.

177. Osterholm M. Preparing for the next pandemic. *New England Journal of Medicine.* 2005;352(18):1839–1842.

178. Ong A, Kindhauser M, Smith I, Chan M. A global perspective on avian influenza. *Annals Academy of Medicine.* 2008;37(6):477–475.

228 *References*

179. United States Department of Health & Human Services. HHS Pandemic Influenza Plan. 2005.
180. World Health Organization – Media Centre. Fact sheet n° 211 – Influenza (Seasonal) [updated April 2009]. Available from: http://www.who.int/mediacentre/factsheets/fs211/en/.
181. Commission of the European Communities. Communication from the Commission to the Council, The European Parliament, The European Economic and Social Committee and the Committee of the Regions on Pandemic Influenza Preparedness and Response Planning in the European Community. 2005 COM(2005) 607 final.
182. Federal Office of Public Health. Swiss Influenza Pandemic Plan – Strategies and measures in preparation for an influenza pandemic. 2007.
183. Organisation de coopération et de développement économiques (Paris), editor. Les risques émergents au XXIe siècle: vers un programme d'action. Paris: OCDE; 2003.
184. McKibbin WJ, Sidorenko A. *Global Macroeconomic Consequences of Pandemic Influenza*. Lowy Institute for International Policy; 2006.
185. The World Bank – East Asia and Pacific Region. Spread of avian flu could affect next year's economic outlook – Excerpted from the November 2005 East Asia Update – Countering Global Shocks. Washington DC; 2005.
186. The World Bank. Speak Out: Interview with Milan Brahmbhatt on Avian Flu 2009 [updated December 5, 2005]. Available from: http://discuss.worldbank.org/content/interview/detail/2739/.
187. Bloom E, de Wit V, Carangal-San Jose MJ. Potential economic impact of an avian flu pandemic on Asia. ERD Policy Brief Series. 2005;42.
188. World Health Organization – Media Centre. Meeting on avian influenza and human pandemic influenza Geneva 2005. Available from: http://www.who.int/mediacentre/events/2005/avian_influenza/en/index.html.
189. Brahmbhatt M, editor. Avian and Human Pandemic Influenza – Economic and Social Impacts. Meeting on avian influenza and human pandemic influenza 2005 November 7–9; Geneva, Switzerland.
190. World Health Organization – Director-General. Pandemics: working together for an effective and equitable response – Address to the Pacific Health Summit – Seattle, Washington, United States –June 13, 2007 [updated June 17, 2007]. Available from: http://www.who.int/dg/speeches/2007/20070613_seattle/en/.
191. World Health Organization – Epidemic and Pandemic Alert and Response. Avian influenza: guidelines. recommendations, descriptions [updated June 7, 2009]. Available from: http://www.who.int/csr/disease/avian_influenza/guidelinestopics/en/index.html.
192. World Health Organization – Epidemic and Pandemic Alert and Response. Cumulative Number of Confirmed Human Cases of Avian Influenza A(H5N1) Reported to WHO 2009 [updated February 5, 2009; cited February 6, 2009]. Available from: http://www.who.int/csr/disease/avian_influenza/country/cases_table_2009_02_05/en/index.html.
193. World Organization for Animal Health. Facts & Figures: Avian Influenza [updated 7 June 2009]. Available from: http://www.oie.int/Eng/info_ev/en_AI_factoids_4.htm.

194. World Organization for Animal Health. WAHID Interface – OIE World Animal Health Information Database. Available from: http://www.oie.int/wahis/public.php?page=home.
195. World Organization for Animal Health. HANDISTATUS II. Available from: http://www.oie.int/hs2/report.asp.
196. Food and Agriculture Organization of the United Nations. Highly pathogenic avian influenza and beyond. The FAO response. 2008.
197. Offlu. OIE/FAO Network of Expertise on Animal Influenza. Available from: http://www.offlu.net/.
198. The World Bank. International community pledges SU$1.9 billion to fight avian flu. Available from: web.worldbank.org.
199. Ryan M. Status of human preparedness and response. Meeting on Avian and Human Influenza; November 7–9; World Health Organization Headquarters, Geneva 2005.
200. World Health Organization – Epidemic and Pandemic Alert and Response. Avian influenza. Available from: http://www.who.int/csr/disease/avian_influenza/en/.
201. Stöhr K. Global Pandemic Preparedness 2006 June 21, 2006. Available from: www.who.int/entity/csr/disease/influenza/stohr.pdf.
202. Fukuda K, editor. Pandemic Influenza Global Considerations, Approaches & Strategy. 2005 General Conference of the International Risk Governance Council – Implementing a global approach to risk governance; 2005 September 20–21; Beijing.
203. World Health Organization. Draft Medium-Term Strategic Plan 2008–2013. 2008 MTSP/2008–2013 – PPB/2008–2009.
204. World Health Organization. A summary of tracking avian influenza A(H5N1) specimens and viruses shared with WHO from 2003 to 2007. 2008.
205. World Health Organization – Epidemic and Pandemic Alert and Response. Vaccines for the new influenza A (H1N1) 2009 [updated June 7, 2009]. Available from: http://www.who.int/csr/disease/swineflu/frequently_asked_questions/vaccine_preparedness/en/index.html.
206. Chien YJ. How did international agencies perceive the avian influenza problem? The adoption and manufacture of the "One World, One Health" framework. *Sociology of Health & Illness.* 2013;35(2):213–226.
207. Figuié M. Towards a global governance of risks: international health organisations and the surveillance of emerging infectious diseases. *Journal of Risk Research.* 2013(ahead-of-print):1–15.
208. Paquet G. The new governance, subsidiarity, and the strategic state. Governance in the 21st Century. 2001:183–215.
209. World Health Organization. Programme Budget 2012–2013 Geneva 2011. Available from: http://whqlibdoc.who.int/pb/2012–2013/PB_2012%E2%80%932013_eng.pdf.
210. World Health Organization. Dr. Margaret Chan, Director-General of the World Health Organization, Statement to the press by WHO Director-General Dr. Margaret Chan, World now at the start of 2009 influenza pandemic [updated June 11, 2009]. Available from: http://www.who.int/mediacentre/news/statements/2009/h1n1_pandemic_phase6_20090611/en/index.html.

211. van Kerkhove MD, Hirve S, Koukounari A, Mounts AW. Estimating age-specific cumulative incidence for the 2009 influenza pandemic: a meta-analysis of A (H1N1) pdm09 serological studies from 19 countries. *Influenza and Other Respiratory Viruses.* 2013;7(5):872–886.

212. Fraser C, Donnelly CA, Cauchemez S, Hanage WP, Van Kerkhove MD, Hollingsworth TD, et al. Pandemic potential of a strain of influenza A (H1N1): early findings. *Science.* 2009;324(5934):1557–1561.

213. World Health Organization. Pandemic (H1N1) 2009 – update 58, Laboratory-confirmed cases of pandemic (H1N1) 2009 as officially reported to WHO by States Parties to the International Health Regulations [updated July 6, 2009]. Available from: http://www.who.int/csr/don/2009_07_06/en/index.html.

214. World Health Organization. Global Alert and Response (GAR), Influenza-like illness in the United States and Mexico 2009 [updated April 24, 2009]. Available from: http://www.who.int/csr/don/2009_04_24/en/index.html.

215. Kamradt-Scott A. Changing perceptions: of pandemic influenza and public health responses. *American Journal of Public Health.* 2012;102(1):90–98.

216. Scoones I, Forster P. The international response to highly pathogenic avian influenza: science, policy and politics. STEPS Working Paper No. 10. Brighton: STEPS Centre, 2008

217. World Health Organization. Strengthening response to pandemics and other public-health emergencies: report of the Review Committee on the Functioning of the International Health Regulations (2005) and on Pandemic Influenza (H1N1) 2009. Geneva: 2011.

218. Cohen D, Carter P. Conflicts of interest. WHO and the pandemic flu "conspiracies". *BMJ* (Clinical research ed). 2010;340:c2912.

219. World Health Organization. Summary of influenza antiviral susceptibility surveillance findings, September 2010–March 2011 2011. Available from: http://www.who.int/influenza/gisrs_laboratory/updates/antiviral_susceptibility/en/.

220. World Health Organization. Global Alert and Response (GAR), Status of candidate vaccine virus development for the current Influenza A(H1N1) virus 2009 [updated May 8, 2009]. Available from: http://www.who.int/csr/resources/publications/swineflu/vaccine_virus_development/en/.

221. World Health Organization – Global Influenza Programme. Pandemic influenza preparedness and response: a WHO guidance document: World Health Organization; 2009.

222. Van Kerkhove MD, Ferguson NM. Epidemic and intervention modelling: a scientific rationale for policy decisions? Lessons from the 2009 influenza pandemic. *Bulletin of the World Health Organization.* 2012;90(4):306–310.

223. Briand S, Mounts A, Chamberland M. Challenges of global surveillance during an influenza pandemic. *Public Health.* 2011;125(5):247–256.

224. Opatowski L, Fraser C, Griffin J, de Silva E, Van Kerkhove MD, Lyons EJ, et al. Transmission characteristics of the 2009 H1N1 influenza pandemic: comparison of 8 Southern hemisphere countries. *PLoS Pathogens.* 2011;7(9):e1002225.

225. World Bank. People, Pathogens and Our Planet – Volume 2 –The Economics of One Health. 2012 Doc No.: 69145-GLB.

226. Bell M, Warren A, Budd L. Scales of governance: The role of surveillance in facilitating new diplomacy during the 2009–2010 H1N1 pandemic. *Health & Place.* 2012;18(6):1404–1411.

227. Cowling BJ, Lau LL, Wu P, Wong HW, Fang VJ, Riley S, et al. Entry screening to delay local transmission of 2009 pandemic influenza A (H1N1). *BMC Infectious Diseases.* 2010;10:82.

228. Khazeni N, Hutton DW, Garber AM, Owens DK. Effectiveness and cost-effectiveness of expanded antiviral prophylaxis and adjuvanted vaccination strategies for an influenza A (H5N1) pandemic. *Annals of Internal Medicine.* 2009;151(12):840–853.

229. Prosser LA, Lavelle TA, Fiore AE, Bridges CB, Reed C, Jain S, et al. Cost-effectiveness of 2009 pandemic influenza A (H1N1) vaccination in the United States. *PLoS One.* 2011;6(7):e22308.

230. Durbin A, Corallo A, Wibisono T, Aleman D, Schwartz B, Coyte P. A cost effectiveness analysis of the H1N1 vaccine strategy for Ontario, Canada. *Journal of Infectious Diseases Immunity.* 2011;3(3):40–49.

231. Sander B, Bauch CT, Fisman D, Fowler RA, Kwong JC, Maetzel A, et al. Is a mass immunization program for pandemic (H1N1) 2009 good value for money? Evidence from the Canadian Experience. *Vaccine.* 2010;28(38):6210–6220.

232. Fidler DP, Gostin LO. The WHO pandemic influenza preparedness framework: a milestone in global governance for health. *JAMA.* 2011;306(2):200–201.

233. Hashim A, Jean-Gilles L, Hegermann-Lindencrone M, Shaw I, Brown C, Nguyen-Van-Tam J. Did pandemic preparedness aid the response to pandemic (H1N1) 2009? A qualitative analysis in seven countries within the WHO European Region. *Journal of Infection and Public Health.* 2012;5(4):286–296.

234. World Health Organization, editor Public Health measures during the influenza A(H1N1) 2009 pandemic. WHO Technical consultation October 26–28, 2010; 2010; Gammarth, Tunisia.

235. Wilson K, Brownstein JS, Fidler DP. Strengthening the International Health Regulations: lessons from the H1N1 pandemic. *Health Policy and Planning.* 2010;25(6):505–509.

236. Katz R. Use of revised International Health Regulations during influenza A (H1N1) epidemic, 2009. *Emerging Infectious Diseases.* 2009;15(8):1165–1170.

237. Brender N, Gilbert C. OMS: logique de l'OMS en matière de pandémie et gestion de H1N1. Project « Emergence et risques sanitaires » (ATP), CIRAD, 2010–2013, Note de synthèse des résultats des travaux de recherche de l'axe 2, Gouvernance des émergences zoosanitaires, 2013.

238. World Health Organization. Pandemic influenza risk management – WHO Interim Guidance. Geneva: 2013.

239. World Health Organization. Rapid risk assessment of acute public health events. 2012.

240. Lagadec P. 'La drôle de grippe' – Pandémie grippale 2009: essai de cadrage et de suivi. 2010.

241. Steyer V, Gilbert C. Exploring the ambiguous consensus on public-private partnerships in collective risk preparation. *Sociology of Health & Illness.* 2013;35(2):292–303.

242. FAO, OIE, WHO, UN System Influenza Coordination, UNICEF, World Bank. Contributing to One World, One Health. A Strategic Framework for

Reducing Risks of Infectious Diseases at the Animal-Human-Ecosystems Interface. 2008.

243. FAO-OIE-WHO Collaboration. Sharing Responsibilities and Coordinating global activities to address health risks at the animal-human-ecosystems interfaces: A Tripartite Concept Note. April; 2010.

244. Callon M, Lascoumes P, Barthe Y, editors. Agir dans un monde incertain: essai sur la démocratie technique. Paris: Ed. du Seuil; 2001.

245. World Health Organization. Pandemic influenza preparedness Framework for the sharing of influenza viruses and access to vaccines and other benefits. Geneva: 2011.

246. Keohane R, Martin L. The promise of institutionalist theory. *International Security.* 1995;20(1):39–51.

247. World Health Organization. Emergency response framework Geneva 2013. Available from: http://www.who.int/hac/about/erf/en/.

248. World Health Organization. Change at WHO, Newsletter on WHO Reform. 2012.

Index